A B

C000136716

A Blood Betrayal

*The Inside Story of
the Jersey Murders*

Barry Wood

HarperCollins*Publishers*

HarperCollins*Publishers*
77–85 Fulham Palace Road,
Hammersmith, London W6 8JB

A Paperback Original 1994

1 3 5 7 9 8 6 4 2

A catalogue record for this book
is available from the British Library

ISBN 0 00 638375 0

Photoset in Linotron Times by
Rowland Phototypesetting Ltd
Bury St Edmunds, Suffolk

Printed in Great Britain by
HarperCollinsManufacturing Glasgow

PROLOGUE

It had been intended as a surprise birthday celebration, a display of filial love to bring the whole family together. But there was no love lost between the four people sitting at table seventeen. The father was a tall, good-looking, bespectacled, middle-aged man wearing a suit; his wife, a handsome red-haired woman, was expensively dressed and animated. The sons mirrored the parents: the dark one, soberly dressed in a suit, wore glasses; the red-haired, good-looking one was animated like his mother and had the same blue eyes and cheekbones. They had been drinking before they arrived at the restaurant and the mood was sour even then. The backbiting increased as the evening wore on but it wasn't until after the third bottle of champagne was finished and a bottle of Chardonnay uncorked that hostilities broke out in earnest.

It was the father who said something in a low voice and caused the table to erupt. Suddenly everyone was shouting at once:

'Sorry! What in Christ's name do you mean you're sorry? Sorry is just not bloody good enough.' The father glowered at the two young men. Twenty years previously that same look could have brought silence instantly to a classroom of terrified Scottish schoolboys, but now his own grown sons snarled back defiantly. The older man's eyes blazed, his mouth twisted with rage, and as he shouted he looked at his sons with fierce hatred.

The red-haired son was also shouting, red-faced. Only the younger boy spoke in low controlled tones. He pointed an accusing finger at his father which seemed to enrage the older man further. Mortified, the mother pleaded for calm.

A fist was brought down hard on the table. A glass was knocked over. The mother screamed at everyone to stop, then fled tearfully from the table into the ladies' with her hands clamped over her ears. Like a lightning shower, the argument faded as quickly as it had started and when she emerged, red-eyed and trembling, twenty minutes later a sullen silence hung over the table.

Shortly after, the younger, dark-haired boy called for the bill, paid and at midnight the group marched silently out of the restaurant, the father hesitating only to nod a strained 'thank you' to the manager.

The waiters shrugged. Every family has its ups and downs.

CHAPTER 1

Determination and a capacity for hard work he had in abundance, but it was his eye for the main chance that made him. As a boy, Archibald Park Newall often said that he was going to be a rich man some day; by the time he reached his thirties, he was. He was the embodiment of the Scottish 'man o'pairts' and came from humble beginnings: he was the son of a shoe-maker. Newall trained as an engineer in Glasgow and displayed an entrepreneurial flair from a very young age: he founded the firm of A. P. Newall and Company in 1901 when he was only twenty-one. The company grew steadily and, by the time the First World War broke out, had won a lucrative contract manufacturing aeroplane parts. By October 1917 it was capitalized at £10,000. Newall, a brilliant engineer and an astute businessman, was visiting America when he made the discovery that would transform his fortunes – a cheap process for making super steel bolts: a simple invention, but one in which he saw the potential instantly. Can-nily, he took out the British patent for the process and shipped the necessary bolt-making machinery over to his premises at the Woodside Engineering Works in Possilpark on Glasgow's south side. Stamped 'Newall Hi-tensile', A.P. Newall's heat-treated precision nuts and bolts were soon rattling off the production line in their millions. They were used across the world – in

London's red double-decker buses and Royal Navy battleships; in the Forth railway bridge and in the vast railway networks of India. Archibald Newall got paid a royalty on every one.

The company expanded rapidly in the 1930s and by 1937 the nominal capital was all but doubled to make a total of £190,000. Of that, A.P. Newall himself held 40,000 £1 preference shares and 49,000 ordinary shares. His business success earned him a reputation in West of Scotland society; he was appointed Grand Master of the Scottish Freemasons Lodge and a Justice of the Peace. He was an enlightened employer in the spirit of Robert Owen, and introduced welfare and pension schemes for his workers. In 1945 he was presented with an illuminated clock and a silver tray from the Nut and Bolt Manufacturers Association of Great Britain in recognition of his role as a 'world pioneer' and for his 'many contributions' to industry.

In his later years, A.P. Newall gradually handed over the running of the firm to one of his two sons, and his son-in-law. But even in retirement there was no easing of his inventive flair. Always the visionary, he bought a farm, Perrystone, on a hillside on the Ayrshire coast overlooking the Heads of Ayr, and experimented with different methods of sterilizing milk from his own model dairy herd. Archibald Park Newall died from a stroke at his farm on 18 February 1950 at the age of seventy, having achieved all his life's ambitions.

Under the guidance of his eldest son, also called Archibald, A.P. Newall and Co. Ltd continued to flourish. On 12 April 1931 at Rowallan, the family's rambling grey stone mansion in the leafy, middle-class Glasgow suburb of Bearsden, young Archie's wife, Sheila, gave birth to twin baby boys who were named Stephen and Nicholas. The boys were identical in appearance; their characters, as they emerged during their teens, proved to be completely at odds. Stephen had inherited the Newall drive and ambition, while Nicholas was much more academically inclined. After National Service the twins' paths diverged. Stephen, always the more practical, became a sales manager with the family firm until, in the sixties, he sold out to the giant GKN conglomerate. Following in the family tradition, he moved to London and started up his own business in shipping and engineering.

Nick went to St Andrews University to read history and trained as a teacher. His first post was at New Park, a small middle-ranking prep school in St Andrews. Founded in 1933, New Park Preparatory School aimed to give middle-class boys a leg up in life with a rounded academic and sporting education. It had about 130 pupils, and Nick Newall was one of nine or ten teachers. School hours were unusually long: 8.30 a.m. to 5.45 p.m. For many of the pupils at New Park, Mr Newall's history lessons were a terrifying experience; they lived in sick, abject terror of the man. It has been said of Scottish schoolmastering that there is no better training in the art of verbally disembowelling another human being. Nick Newall was the most feared teacher at New Park and the most hated. In theory only the headmaster was allowed to cane the boys but Nick Newall was never reluctant to punish them. He ran his classes with iron discipline. Even by the standards of Scotland in the sixties, his methods were firmly of the old school. Reams of dates and names had to be committed to memory and faultlessly recited in front of his desk. The penalty for the slightest error was a scathing put-down in front of the rest of the class and a firm instruction to repeat the exercise the next day. He was a terror in the classroom, but he got results – especially on the sports field where, under him, the school rugby and cricket teams did well. And he liked to cut a dash; Nick Newall was good-looking – nearly six feet tall, with thick dark hair. He was a keen outdoors man and excelled at most sports, but his yacht was the centre of his life. Colleagues remember him in his glasses and tweed sports jacket with leather-patched elbows, pipe clenched between his teeth as he roared off down the quiet Fife lanes in his nippy little TR2.

He had been at New Park for six years when Elizabeth Nelson arrived to teach the juniors. She was a graduate of St Andrews and Edinburgh and, like Nicholas, she came from a prosperous West of Scotland middle-class industrial background. The family paint firm was based in Glasgow, and her father had built up the business in the twenties. The Nelsons were amongst the most prominent families in the town of Motherwell, fifteen miles south-east of Glasgow where her father had been chairman of the local football club. Aged only twenty-four, Elizabeth was much younger than most of the staff at New Park. She was a tall, good-looking young woman with blue eyes, a head of bright-red hair and an outgoing and exuberant manner.

She was already engaged to a medical student when she arrived at New Park, but the relationship did not survive her meeting with the striking Nick Newall. Even the pupils noticed that there was an electrical charge between them. Nick Newall made his play instantly. The attraction was mutual and the couple were often seen whizzing through the school gates in Nick's sports car. They had much in common but, from the pupils' point of view, they shared unfortunate characteristics. In Miss Nelson's case, her red hair proved to be an indication of a headstrong and inflammable temper. In the classroom she was prone to frequent and noisy explosions and, like Newall, she was not above raising her hands to the boys. Once she snatched a ruler off one boy's desk and shattered it over the head of another. The unfortunate victim was ordered to go and buy a replacement.

Initially both the Newall and Nelson parents were opposed to the marriage: Elizabeth's preferred the medical student to the aloof schoolteacher; but Nick and Elizabeth were determined. In late 1963, after they announced their engagement, an elegant private dinner took place in a club in Glasgow's Blytheswood Square specifically for the purpose of letting the Newalls and the Nelsons get to know each other.

Nick Newall and Elizabeth Nelson were married at Dalziel North Church in Elizabeth's home town of Motherwell on Wednesday 18 December 1963 – a wintry day when sleet and snowstorms blanketed Scotland. Their first home was a large house called North Dron in the Fife village of Dairsie near St Andrews. Sixteen months later, on 11 April 1965, Elizabeth was admitted to Redlands Hospital near Glasgow for the birth of her first child. The baby was hours overdue and Elizabeth had whiled away the time embroidering her name on a handkerchief. Finally, at 10.20 p.m. she gave birth to a boy. The next morning, just before prep, the New Park headmaster, Mr Roderick McLeod, announced the arrival of the Newalls' baby, adding immodestly that the boy had been named after him: Roderick Innes Nelson Newall, taking one middle name from each parent's side. A second son, Mark Stephen Innes Nelson Newall, was born just over a year later, on 22 June 1966, at the couple's home in Fife. That summer Nick decided to celebrate the arrival of his sons by naming the yacht he was having built after both of them. The boat, *Rodmark*, was launched in 1969. Life had ostensibly been good to Nick Newall: he had been born into money, was blessed with a healthy family and steady if unexciting job prospects, and things could hardly have looked better. But underneath there was a growing frustration. After more than ten years at New Park he yearned for a bit of adventure: he wanted to see something of the world, to just take off in the yacht and go. His opportunity came when the couple had a financial windfall which was to change their lives for ever. Using money her father had given her, Elizabeth had, on a whim, invested heavily in the Lesney toy company and in 1968 the shares began to soar. To the Newalls it meant financial independence and the chance to leave the drudgery of the classroom behind. Early in 1969 at the family house in North Dron Nick could be found poring over large sea charts. He had decided that he needed a challenge, and he made up his mind to cross the Atlantic. So the Newalls suddenly decided to give up their jobs as teachers and sell up. Despite the considerable misgivings of their respective families, the couple, together with their two young sons, bade farewell to their old lives and set sail from Scotland in the *Rodmark*. It was an impressive yacht – a six-berth forty-foot-long salmo salar ketch custom built for them in Burnham-on-Crouch in Essex for about £12,000. The voyage to the West Indies was to take a couple of months, but only 300 miles out of port the brave expedition was cut short by an emergency. Elizabeth suffered dreadfully from sea sickness and the nanny they had hired for the trip from epileptic fits. *Rodmark* was forced to pull into St Helier on Jersey.

As the casualties recovered, Nick's appetite for his epic voyage waned. Perhaps an Atlantic crossing with two small boys had been a little bit ambitious after all. And as he looked around him the attractions of Jersey grew. Situated twelve miles from the French coast, the largest of the Channel Islands was a place of unspoilt, spectacular coasts and lush hinterland with a year-round temperate climate far removed from the wind-swept east coast of Fife. Like thousands before and since, Nick and Elizabeth fell under the spell of Jersey, but the attractions did not end with the climate. The island's tax system made it a place where the comfort-ably off could look after their money. And there were family connections: Nick's father and mother had spent many happy family holidays on the nearby island of Sark and Nick's uncle still lived there. Kenneth Newall was a curious little figure – a midget, only four feet four inches tall. He had stopped growing when he was very small, and got around his estate, La Petite Ron-dellerie, in a specially adapted invalid car. Having no family of his own, he had been left the bulk of his father's estate on the understanding that it would be passed on to his brother's children – Nicholas and Stephen. He was worth well over a million pounds. Jersey was a good place from which to keep in with rich Uncle Kenneth, so Nick and Elizabeth decided to stay.

In 1969 they bought Martello Lodge, a large Queen Anne house overlooking St Brelade Bay on the island's northern coast. Surrounded by temperate waters and close to the challenge of the Bay of Biscay, Jersey was the perfect place for Nick to indulge his love of sailing. He soon sold the *Rodmark* for a bigger boat called *Rodmark II*, which was in turn traded in for the *September Tide*, a lumbering sixty-foot wooden yacht built in Scotland in the thirties. Though financially draining, the boat was to become the great love of Nick's life and he took it around the Bay of Biscay and along the French and Belgian coasts. He was an accomplished and fearless sailor who would venture out into rough waters which other sailors would not contemplate.

In 1972 the Newalls bought the 'Crow's Nest', a large house which overlooked one of the most beautiful bays on the island – the Grève de Lecq. It was to be the scene of the Newalls' happiest years on Jersey. The Grève de Lecq is a tiny secluded inlet on Jersey's northern coast, protected on three sides by steep bracken- and heather-covered hillside. A deep wooded valley, the Moulin de Lecq, rises from the bay, cutting deep into the headland. On the bay itself there is a tiny cluster of buildings: an open air café and a water mill converted into a restaurant. In days gone by the Grève de Lecq was the haunt of smugglers but today visitors flock there to enjoy the walks along the coastal paths, the spectacular views from the headland and the opportunities for swimming and surfing provided by the huge rollers that sweep in off the sea. It is often uncomfortably crowded in summer. High above the bay, to the west, the Crow's Nest sits in several acres of bushes and trees overlooking what many believe to be the best view on the island. From its huge picture windows, it is possible to take in the sweep of the bay and hillside opposite and on a clear day the nearby island of Sark and the French coast a few miles away. To the right is clearly visible the wooded glen that is formed by the Moulin de Lecq. The raw and rugged countryside is in stark contrast to the well-manicured hedgerows and lanes of the rest of Jersey; and, if anything, it looks more like the West Highlands of Scotland. The colours of the Grève de Lecq are the russets, greens and browns of the leaves and bracken, the yellow of the gorse and the purple of the heather, the blues of the sea and the slate grey of the fog that regularly rolls in. The sounds of the Grève de Lecq are the cries of the gulls and crows, the rush of the rollers breaking on the rocks two hundred feet below, and the whistle of the wind through the trees.

The Grève de Lecq is a children's paradise and Roderick and Mark explored every inch in their early years, building dens, playing in the caves, and climbing the rocks. Elizabeth Newall was often worried about the boys' safety: what if one of their tunnels were to cave in? So she took to ringing a school bell and the strange sound – an echo from a long-forgotten Scottish playground – would resound through the valley. Eventually there would be a flash of movement through the trees, the sound of childish giggling, then two little boys would dart from the bushes behind the house and into the garden. The one in front had a cheeky smile and close-cropped red hair; the other one, darker, slower, smaller and more ungainly, had large thick spectacles. The Grève de Lecq was an environment that offered the perfect escape and, even as young children, Roderick and Mark would often want to escape.

In those early days the Newalls were so devoted that they barely had room in their lives for anyone else. Nick would bring his wife breakfast in bed and leave small 'I luv you' notes scattered around the kitchen. But the couple had a talent for enjoying themselves – that much was obvious from the outset of their arrival on Jersey. They dived into the island's social scene with relish and soon their house was echoing to the sounds of loud dinner parties and barbecues. They were an attractive, outgoing young couple – a pair of intelligent, charming, bon viveurs who lived for the moment and cared not a hoot about tomorrow. Elizabeth was larger than life, an animated, noisy sort of woman. The phrase that was often to be used to describe her was 'jolly hockey sticks'. She was also an excellent cook. Nick

11

was wry and sardonic, with a bitter-sweet wit; he was a great raconteur, but many people found him arrogant and overbearing. There was a thoughtless, opinionated streak about him that was off-putting: he would sit puffing his pipe at a dinner party and make some thoughtless remark, deeply offending the sensibilities of his guests. Elizabeth was always having to smooth the waters after him. She built her whole life around her husband, who could be a demanding and self-centred man.

Within months of arriving on Jersey the Newalls had a large circle of friends: there was Angela Barnes, whose father was their bank manager, and who was always giving superb dinner parties in the large, rambling house, Clos de Hugh, in the village of St John; there was Michael and Ann Munx-Jones, and the Blayneys, in whose vineyard the Newall family's happiest summers would be spent toiling. Like the Newalls, the Blayneys had fallen under the spell of the island and had thrown up steady jobs on the mainland to start a new life. But that was where the resemblance ended, for Bob and Anne Blayney had a vision: they dreamed of owning and running their own commercial vineyard. They bought a dilapidated fifteenth-century French farmhouse with five and a half acres of field. In 1968 they had sewed their first seeds. The two couples had met at a buffet at Angela Barnes's house and had immediately hit it off. The Newalls shared the Blayneys' appreciation of good wine. Nick was keen to learn, and many a happy bottle would be consumed at the La Mare or at the Crow's Nest. And, while usually averse to any physical exertion that resembled work, Nick and Elizabeth did not hesitate to help out with the grape-picking. Every year at vintage time the vineyard was the scene of frantic activity. While Bob looked after the winery, Nick, Elizabeth, their sons and the

Blayneys' sons would be busy bringing in the grapes and weighing them before crushing. It was back-breaking work and had to take place round the clock, but every year the Newalls would pitch in. One year Bob's back went and Nick managed to do the bottling himself. In those crucial early years Bob and Anne found the Newalls' unpaid efforts invaluable. Occasionally at the Newalls' raucous dinner parties a couple of small, forlorn figures could be glimpsed – little Roderick and Mark. The boys seemed to be almost on the periphery of their parents' existence. Nick never seemed very interested in his sons; to tell the truth he would have been happy without any children at all. It was Elizabeth who had insisted on a baby and when Roderick was born she had then wanted a sister for him. As the boys grew older Nick's relationship with his boys was to become complicated. Like the good teacher he was, Nick was diligent in promoting their physical education and the boys were taught how to ski, sail, waterski and play tennis. But there was no real intimacy with his sons. Later, when Mark was in his teens, he severely injured his leg in a rugby accident. Nick refused to go and see his son in hospital on the mainland and even questioned the cost of the private medical treatment.

The boys were not completely starved of affection, however. Each summer they would spend time with their relatives. They would stay with Uncle Stephen and Aunt Gay and their five children or with Elizabeth's sister Nancy Clark and her husband, Alaster, and their two sons, who were about the same age as the boys. Indeed, Roderick and Mark both virtually grew up in the cast-off clothes of friends' and relatives' children. A highlight of most years was the annual visit to nearby Sark to see Uncle Kenneth. It was a relationship that Nick and Elizabeth, with an eye to the future, kept up, and they always made sure the boys were there to see their Uncle Ken. Although all the Channel Islands are traditional and set in their ways, the tiny island of Sark is positively feudal. Uncle Kenneth was an intelligent and kindly man who was popular with both Nick and Stephen Newall's children. Dressed in children's clothing, a beret on his head, he was a peculiar sight. The tiny magical island of Sark was connected with golden memories in the minds of all the Newall clan.

But for as long as anyone in the family could remember Roderick and Mark had fought. Their battles often exasperated their Auntie Nan. When they were quite little and were staying with her in Scotland time and again she would be forced to stop the car on lonely roads near her home in Gartcosh and threaten to dump the boys by the wayside unless they stopped their fighting. The boys were very different. As they grew into infancy it was clear that Roderick, with his reddish complexion and blue eyes, took after his mother physically – while Mark was more like his dad. Their temperaments were also drawn directly from their parents'. Like his mother, Roderick was outgoing, gregarious and naughty, while Mark was buttoned up and withdrawn and from his earliest years there was a streak of arrogance that reminded some of his father.

The boys' upbringing was a bone of contention between Nan and her sister Elizabeth. For though she could see they were well enough looked after, Nan felt that the parents were instilling in them an unnatural competitiveness. One day, when Mark was about five, his brother and Nan's two boys refused to let him join in a game. His aunt took him into the garden to play but warned him to avoid the large vicious dog next

14

door. Some time later she went back out but there was no sign of Mark anywhere. Eventually she found him inside the kennel, gently patting the dog. Light glinted off a pair of spectacles peeking out from the darkness. 'He's not at all vicious, Auntie Nan,' came the small voice. 'He's just lonely. Just like me.'

Nick Newall was finding that Jersey offered surprisingly little in the way of intellectual stimulation, and it was out of boredom as much as anything else that, in 1971, he decided to take up teaching again. Housed in an imposing mansion once owned and built by a local businessman, St Michael's Preparatory School ranks as one of Jersey's foremost schools. The island's élite send their offspring there to be prepared for common entrance and public school scholarships. It opened in the 1950s but by the mid sixties was on the verge of closure and down to fifty pupils. A change of ownership and staff transformed the school's fortunes and by the early seventies the roll had grown to 300.

At St Michael's Nick used the methods that he had used so effectively at New Park – a combination of fear and endless tests to drill history into his seven-to-thirteen-year-old charges. He liked to spice up his history lessons with horror stories of the 'babes in the tower' variety which frightened some children. And, as at New Park, he soon gained a reputation as the most feared master in the school. But it was not only in the classroom that he was unpopular: his uncompromising and single-minded manner led to frequent clashes in the staffroom. The school's owners came to regard him as one of the most difficult employees they had ever had. He was stubborn; he was awkward; he would argue about the smallest point and would never give an inch. Despite being a man of independent means who did not need to work, he was always complaining and worrying about his money. However, his drawbacks were counterbalanced by the fact that he got results in the classroom and was very good with parents.

At the age of five Roderick Newall came to St Michael's. More than twenty years later he is remembered as an angelic-looking, smiling boy, with a flop of reddish fair hair falling over his face. He appeared happy enough, but one teacher still remembers a faint but distinct undertow of uneasiness or anxiousness behind the blue eyes and easy smile. Several of the teachers wondered about the boy's home life with a father who was a holy terror in the classroom. Certainly, their fears were borne out when Mark started school. He was cold and unapproachable and completely lacked the warm affectionate nature of his brother. A hint of the home environment endured by the Newall brothers emerged one day when Mark loudly and continually complained to a teacher that his father had beaten him with a spiked golf shoe.

In 1971, when Roderick was six, his parents decided to send him to a prep school on the mainland – Lockers Park near Hemel Hempstead. St Michael's took this move as a snub. The school prided itself on its record in preparing pupils for public schools. Eventually Nick's relations with the other teachers at St Michael's deteriorated so bady that he left the school for good. It was not only the pupils who were delighted.

Why the Newalls chose to send their boys away was never explained. Lockers Park was a good school, but so was St Michael's; indeed, the only difference seemed to be that the boys would be boarding full-time. And with their boys off their hands the Newalls were free to enjoy an endless succession of long holidays – skiing in Switzerland, safariing in Africa, sailing in the

Mediterranean; spending the summer in Jersey and the winter in Spain in a small villa they had bought in Javea on the Costa Brava, which they had fallen in love with during a long sailing trip.

Founded in 1874, Lockers Park Preparatory School, like St Michael's, is an exclusive school whose past pupils have included Guy Burgess and Lord Mountbatten. From the day they arrived Roderick, and then Mark, were badly behaved, rebellious and just would not do what they were told. They both had tempers and there could be spectacular flare-ups. What disturbed some teachers about Roderick especially was his dishonesty. Twenty years on he is still remembered with exasperation by former Lockers Park teacher Mrs Rosemary Huband. He was 'the most efficient liar I ever met in more than thirty years of teaching. No matter how barefaced or blatantly he was caught out he would just look you in the eyes and tell a lie.' Some of her fellow-teachers wondered why he did it. Was it because he was so scared of what would happen to him if he owned up? There was no corporal punishment at Lockers Park, so what form of discipline was the boy used to at home? One teacher thought that compulsive dishonesty was a sign of fear of severe punishment.

With their parents so far away, there would be no weekends or half-terms at home. Instead the boys spent the time with Stephen and Gay Newall and their five children in Hampstead or with the Clarks and their two sons in Liberty Mews, Clapham. Towards the end of their time at Lockers Park both boys settled down considerably. They were both obviously bright and they left on a high note, sailing through their common entrance examinations on their way to Radley College – one of the most prestigious public schools in the country.

*   *   *

17

In the prime of life, the Newalls were living the good life – a life in the sun devoted to pleasure. The blue skies seemed to stretch on and on over the horizon. But appearances are deceptive, and even in those days there were dark clouds forming in the shape of financial reality. For Nick and Elizabeth's new-found wealth was an illusion that began to crumble soon after their arrival on Jersey, when Elizabeth's toy company stock took a sharp dive. She dithered about selling because she thought a quick sale would attract Capital Gains Tax. In the event it didn't matter, because the slide in value wiped more than three-quarters of the value off the shares. When it hit rock bottom, against everyone's advice she sold her stock, thus losing out again when the value began to rise. A sudden bout of belt-tightening was called for. It was the beginning of a pattern that was to repeat itself over and over again during the years ahead. The check on their lifestyle only seemed to be temporary and did not cramp the Newalls' enthusiasm for the good life one bit. Elizabeth had an income from her family firm and Nick had his father's legacy. In those early days Nick and Elizabeth spent freely on the good life, oblivious to the cost of it all. Foreign skiing holidays were an annual event and Nick never thought twice about buying a new boat.

There are many myths about money and for many years one of the most enduring concerned membership of Lloyd's. As far as many well-off people were concerned, there were few safer bets. To be elected a Lloyd's name was a badge of status and wealth that also carried considerable social cachet. In the seventies underwriters would sit back and wait for the cheques to come in at ten per cent a year on a total investment, and hardly anyone stopped to think that 'unlimited liability' might actually mean exactly what it said – and that names, as well as taking a share in the profits, would also have to stump up if there were losses. So when, in 1978, Nick Newall's bank manager asked him if he had ever thought of joining, his eyebrows rose with interest. A year later Nick and Elizabeth Newall were among a dozen couples invited to a special dinner by the Lloyd's managing agent, D. N. Green, at the island's Hôtel l'Horizon. The guests were the Jersey 'names' whose syndicates he managed.

The fact that Nick was a Lloyd's name may have been good to drop at dinner parties – like the fact that both the boys were down for Radley College – but sinking a quarter of a million pounds away just as Roderick was beginning his first term there was to stretch their resources to the limit.

One day Nick and Elizabeth's friend Angela Barnes was invited to the Crow's Nest for lunch. She soon discovered the ulterior motive: they wanted her to witness the signing of insurance policies they wanted to cash in. 'That's a relief, a bit more money in now,' said Nick. 'I've no need to go back to teaching next term.'

Within weeks the money had been blown on a new boat and a new kitchen in the house in Spain. But that was one of the charming and endearing things about the Newalls. Though greedy, selfish and financially irresponsible, they never for a moment tried to hide it. They were always going on about how a 'new pot of money' meant they could head off to Spain for a few months, or how all their money worries would be over 'when Uncle Kenneth on Sark' finally popped off. Money was to them something to be spent on maintaining the lifestyle they had become accustomed to. The idea of earning some or even saving for a rainy day was competely alien to them. They would retreat into fantasy. Nick had pretentions of being a writer: at dinner parties he would boast about the thriller he was writing; books and plays were sent off but, although Elizabeth would boast about his writing being 'our bread and butter', nothing was ever published. One idea that preoccupied Nick Newall was 'the perfect murder'. It was a theme he would return to time and again in his quest to become a thriller writer. Every time he met his brother-in-law Dr Clark he would quiz him on the mechanics of death. What was the most efficient poison? How much would do the trick? What was the average rate of decomposition and the best method of disposal of the bodies? 'Tell me, Alaster, how would you do it if you had to?' Nick would ask over dinner.

'Nick!' came the indignant voice of his wife. 'Do you really have to be so distasteful?'

'It's just research, darling,' he would say, puffing at his pipe. His stories, like the ones with which he had regaled his pupils, were always particularly gory. He eventually wrote a short story about a prep school master who killed his wife and stored her body in the deep freeze, which caused much hilarity but annoyed Elizabeth considerably. 'I do wish you'd find something else to write about, Nick,' she said in front of friends during dinner.

By the early eighties the first serious cracks had begun to appear in the Newalls' life. Ten years of nothing but a frenetic social life in the sun and little money coming in had bitten deep into their once-sizeable investments. The cost of the boys' school fees had eventually forced them to do some supply teaching, but Nick hated it. He could not get on with his colleagues and his arrogant, overbearing manner inevitably led to staffroom clashes. There had been tensions with relatives in Scotland as well. Elizabeth's father had given her £50,000 to invest and the couple were living off the interest. When he died her mother promptly demanded the return of the money. It was a valuable source of income and its loss left Nick and Elizabeth speechless with rage.

There was friction on the other side of the family between Nick and his brother Stephen – by now a successful businessman. Stephen had married well into the Craig Scottish steel dynasty. By this time he was living in turreted, baronial splendour in a large house overlooking the Firth of Clyde in the village of Rhu near Helensburgh.

The Newalls' spiralling money problems were exacerbated by several inept financial investments. Nick put some money in a property development in Lanzarote which turned belly up, and later Nick was conned into handing over £15,000 for a development in New Mexico which, on investigation, turned out to be a dustbowl. Elizabeth's fascination for money was only equalled by her incompetence with it. She was a dabbler – the worst kind of investor – and a complete soft touch when it came to money. All it took was for some investment 'hot tip' to be dropped into her ear at a dinner party and she would be on the phone to her broker. Gilts, bonds, securities – the whole language of money fascinated Elizabeth Newall, but she had no understanding of any of it and, together with her taste for a gamble, this proved to be a disastrous combination.

And behind all the financial chaos the shadow of Nick's Lloyds' syndicates cast into the future, ticking away like a financial time bomb.

CHAPTER 2

The motto of Radley College is 'Sicut Serpentes, Sicut Columbae' (just like a serpent, just like a dove); it hints at the twin values of resourcefulness and consideration that the school tries to inculcate in its pupils. New boys traditionally arrive to the strains of 'Jerusalem', sung by the school choir, rising high into the air of the stained-glass-windowed college chapel.

In 1978, the same year that Roderick Newall arrived, the general public were for the first time to get a glimpse inside this temple of learning and privilege, courtesy of a BBC fly-on-the-wall documentary. It was a tantalizing glimpse into a world few others could have known still existed, where the boys were dressed in dark, flowing gowns and the teachers frequently wore mortar boards. Set in rolling grounds a mile from the River Thames in Oxfordshire, Radley is traditionally bracketed only with Eton and Harrow and for generations the great and good of the land have sent their offspring there for a sound, upper-middle-class education.

A delicately carved miniature Chinese pagoda sits on a cabinet in the headmaster's study amongst numerous ornaments and trinkets, gifts from various boys over the years. When Tony Hudson looks at it, he is reminded of his days as a housemaster and of the boy who gave it to him. And he thinks back to a day in 1978 when the bloodied combatants of one of the nastiest fights anyone could remember at Radley were pulled apart. One was a young French boy, the other a thirteen-year-old whose violent ways were to give his housemaster many a headache in the years to come. His name was Roderick Newall.

Radley is divided up into eight houses known as 'socials' (from the Latin *socu*, meaning 'ally'), each comprising about sixty boys and each presided over by its own housemaster. His job involved not only the fostering of team spirit and discipline but also helping the boys deal with any personal problems. It was a demanding job with immensely long hours – 7.30 a.m. until midnight – but one which Tony Hudson, the housemaster of F Social, found immensely rewarding. Under his leadership F Social had become one of the most successful houses, both academically and on the sports field. In his time he had come across all sorts of different 'problem' boys, but nothing had prepared him for Roderick Newall. He had never come across a boy so headstrong, so quick-tempered or so willing to raise his fists. Young Newall's anger could explode in a second and his rage seemed to know no bounds. He would fight anyone – older and bigger boys, prefects, even housemasters. And there was a viciousness to his clashes that set them apart from the usual schoolboy brawls.

Tony Hudson had never swallowed the myth that schooldays are the best days of a child's life. He knew that for many of his charges schooldays were a period of struggle through what he called the 'long dark tunnel of teenage adolescence'. An enthusiastic, happy boy might enter the tunnel at thirteen but, with a bit of luck and guidance, should hopefully emerge four or five years later as a bright, confident, fully-formed eighteen-year-old ready for all that life could throw at him.

With Roderick he believed that the problem lay in a deep-seated lack of self-esteem: to solve it, the boy's confidence needed building up, not knocking down. With some boys this process was not an easy one; with Roderick Newall it was to prove to be virtually impossible. Despite hours of discussion and pleading, Mr Hudson never discovered the reason for the fury that seemed to rage within the boy. In his study he would talk with him long into the night to try and get him to come to terms with his anger. 'Roderick, you've got such a quick-fire temper,' Hudson would tell him after another vicious scrap. 'You really must try and keep it under control. Try counting to ten before responding to any provocation.'

There was another disturbing feature about young Newall: he never made any secret of the fact that he loathed and detested his parents. He often casually expressed this hatred in passing conversation with other boys, yet it was apparently heartfelt and went much deeper than the usual teenage rebelliousness. Again, despite many lengthy attempts to get to the bottom of the matter, Tony Hudson was never able to discover why the boy held his parents in such contempt.

Roderick was a tangle of contradictions – one minute temper tantrums, the next warmth and playfulness. But there was no doubting his academic potential. He was an exceptionally bright lad and had soon been jumped up a year, in accordance with the Radley practice of 'fast-tracking' its brightest and best.

Hudson's suspicions about Roderick's family background were confirmed when his brother Mark arrived the following year. It was traditional for brothers to be members of the same house but, to Tony Hudson's surprise, the boys' mother requested that Mark be put in a different 'social': the brothers hated each other so much they would be better apart. And so it proved. A vicious feud erupted between Roderick and his brother as soon as Mark arrived. Frequently the boys would have to be pulled apart. Invariably Mark would come off worse. On one occasion Roderick gave his little brother such a fierce hammering Mark was taken to hospital to have the face wounds treated. Undeterred, Mark retaliated by breaking into Roderick's study and emptying all his possessions out of the window into the quad – books, clothes, music centre, the lot. Tony Hudson and Chris Hirst, his opposite number at Mark's house, D Social, spent hours on the telephone trying to come up with an explanation for an animosity that seemed to go far beyond normal sibling rivalry. The Newall feud became the subject of frenzied debate between the other boys and when it was learnt that Roderick and Mark were pitted against each other in a inter-house water polo match virtually the whole school turned up, expecting the water to turn red, although it didn't come to that. As they got older, however, an uneasy truce of sorts was reached between Roderick and Mark. They even began to look out for each other. One day a boy called Mark a 'poof' and later Roderick gave the offending lad a thorough battering.

Every Wednesday evening between nine and eleven o'clock F Social members would gather for cocoa and a chat with Mr Hudson and his wife. The discussions were free-ranging and Tony Hudson encouraged vigorous debate about any and every subject. Roderick Newall was always a keen participant. Roderick also revelled in a 'macho' image and threw himself into sport. He rowed in the third eight and played rugby in the first fifteen, where his keen, fearless and competitive nature ensured that he shone – though his lack of height meant that he never quite got to the top of the school sporting ladder. He also enjoyed going on camps; expeditions with the Combined Cadet Force kindled an interest in the army. Both boys were keen on weight training, and Mark was particularly fond of martial arts, an interest which continued long after he left school.

Once every term in Mr Hudson's rooms a solemn Sunday-morning ritual was enacted. He would return from chapel to find Roderick's parents waiting for him to discuss their son's progress. It was an occasion Mr Hudson did not look forward to. The reason was Nicholas Newall. He was not an easy man: he was arrogant, selfish and condescending, and seemed more interested in point-scoring and sniping about the school fees than in the progress of his son. There was a kind of studied casualness about their visits and they always seemed to coincide with their return from one holiday or embarking on another. Whatever the source of the problem within the Newall family, Mr Hudson suspected the blame was not all on one side.

In the cliquey atmosphere of Radley Roderick was noticeable for being a bit of a loner but he made one special friendship that was to endure throughout his schooldays and far beyond. Charlie Shaw was the son of the Irish actor Robert Shaw and he shared the same taste for adventure and derring-do. From the age of thirteen the two were firm friends. Roderick frequently joined the large Shaw family of ten children at the family home in the West of Ireland. Roderick clearly relished being the centre of family life and soon grew close to all the other members of the family including Charlie's mother, to whom he would often confide.

That all was not well with Roderick's own home life was clear to Charlie. It was something Rod never spoke about but the trips to Ireland were never reciprocated and it was obvious that Roderick himself did not look forward to his few stays at home with his parents on Jersey. Exactly why this was Charlie never discovered and he never saw enough of Rod's parents to hint at an idea. The Newalls, unlike other parents, were infrequent visitors to normal parental days such as sports days.

Charlie was a bright boy and, like Rod, had been jumped up a year. But although both boys were expected to do the same amount of work as boys a year older, they were not allotted the same privileges. The older boys were allowed to go to discos or even allowed into the junior common room, while the younger boys were not. Always independent-minded, it was a system the boys hated and Charlie in particular began to rail against authority. Although both boys took a keen interest in the illicit side of public school life with its smoking, drinking and clandestine night-time excursions to Oxford, it was Charlie who first began to experiment with soft drugs. Charlie's brushes with the school authorities increased until one day at the age of sixteen he sat in his room and told Roderick he'd had enough, that was it: he was leaving. Sitting on the bed, Roderick pleaded with Charlie for two hours to change his mind but it was no use – Charlie had decided.

By the time the school found out about Charlie's departure Roderick had already spent hours trying to get a call through to his friend's mother in the West of Ireland, no mean feat in those days before STD. She was almost out of her mind with worry, but on the phone the seventeen-year-old Roderick calmed her down, assured her there was nothing to worry about and said that he was going to fetch Charlie back.

With the blessing of his masters Roderick set off on the train to London, caught up with Charlie and almost dragged his friend back physically. Charlie was later to be expelled from the school for being caught with drugs. Although shunned by many Old Radlians there was always one former pupil he could turn to and always one who remained loyal to him – Roderick Newall.

Roderick chose to leave school when he was seventeen, after only four years. Tony Hudson did not think this a very good idea. He did not agree with the school's 'fast-tracking' policy. No matter how good the boy's academic qualifications, the college could be sending out an 'unfinished product', someone who was not fully formed emotionally.

As part of Roderick's application to become an officer in the Royal Green Jackets, Tony Hudson was asked to submit his own report on the boy to the regiment. Affectionately, but not entirely playfully, he wrote that Roderick would either win the Victoria Cross or be cashiered. One year after leaving school Roderick returned to Radley and shyly presented his former housemaster with a small gift – the model Chinese pagoda. It was a gesture that touched Tony Hudson and seemed to heal the breach that had grown between them in four years of constant ups and downs, but at the same time it puzzled him. Most boys gave presents when they left. That Roderick should return to present his a year later was curious and he was not sure what it was the boy was trying to say. Years later, after long sessions with the detectives from Jersey, he was to reflect ruefully, 'Of all the families I met, if I had to predict one where this would happen, I'd have picked that one.'

After he had got his three A-levels, Roderick's parents had assumed he was heading for Oxbridge. But he told them that, after taking a year out, he intended going straight to Sandhurst as a junior officer. There were furious rows. 'All that money,' moaned Nick to Angela Barnes. 'What a complete waste.'

For a few weeks in 1982 Rod hurtled around the London streets as a motorcycle courier and then, after spending some time bumming around Australia on a motorbike, he returned to Scotland and got a job as an outdoor sports instructor with the John Ridgway Adventure School near Lairg in Sutherland.

From his isolated centre located at the end of a sea loch on one of the remotest parts of the Ardmore peninsula, former SAS man John Ridgway, with his wife Marie Christine, runs a unique outdoor school which offers gruelling courses in sailing, hillwalking and climbing. Over the years it has proved especially popular amongst companies seeking to teach their executives the values of self-reliance. With his natural sporting abilities it should have been an ideal job for Rod Newall.

Rod got off to a good start. With his natural physical prowess, he was a good instructor. But it was not to last. Although dormant for some time, Newall's uncontrollable temper combined with a surly inability to handle authority led to his untimely departure from Sutherland. And it all began with a badly cooked meal.

One evening Roderick, unhappy about the quality of the fare in the Adventure School dining room, went through into the kitchen to make himself something to eat. The newly hired cook was inexperienced and struggling. Roderick, offered to lend a hand.

That his motives were not altogether altruistic was obvious to everyone who saw Rod hanging around the attractive 17-year-old blonde. Deeply smitten, Roderick, whose culinary skills had been keenly

29

instilled by his mother, was soon spending more time in the kitchen than adventure training.

Before long they were a couple, but the romance led to an angry showdown with the boss. Ridgway felt Rod was paying more attention to Bridget than his work and one day he confronted him about it. Although a tough man, John Ridgway had only meant to administer a mild ticking off, but Newall's reaction was astonishing. Only a minute into his dressing-down, Newall's face suddenly reddened and he exploded. Lunging at the 45-year-old ex-SAS man, he struck him several times in the face. A fierce fight ensued and ended with Newall being fired on the spot. Distraught Rod, taking Bridget O'Connor with him, fled south to London and his Auntie Nan in Fulham.

'We were very worried,' said Ridgway's wife Marie Christine. 'He had the most ferocious temper and he just could not control it.'

Bridget O'Connor became Roderick's first serious girlfriend and during the two years they were together he took her to his parents' home in both Spain and Jersey. Bridget so enchanted Elizabeth that she would eject Mark from the chalet and let the young couple stay there together.

When he arrived at the regimental depot in Winchester to start his training, Roderick was worried that falling out with his previous employer and running off with his cook might have damaged his career prospects. Not a bit of it. 'Shows just the spirit we need,' said the recruiting officer proudly. After coasting through his regular commission board, Roderick Newall gained a commission to the Royal Green Jackets and entered Sandhurst in 1983.

Nine months later the lines of officer cadets, splendid in the standard uniform of midnight blue tunic, white belt, forage cap and George boots, marched in half-step across the Sandhurst parade ground to the sound of a brass band playing 'Auld Lang Syne', then slowly wheeled round and passed through the gates of Sandhurst College for the last time followed by the adjutant on a white horse. Amongst them was Second Lieutenant Roderick Newall and on the stand opposite amongst the dozens of other proud parents relishing the occasion stood Nick and Elizabeth Newall. It was a sweltering hot August day in 1984. Elizabeth was wearing a red and white dress she'd borrowed off her friend Angela Barnes especially for the passing out.

That night Roderick and his parents attended the Commissioning Ball and at midnight, the moment that an officer cadet is deemed to have become an officer, a firework display lit up the night sky illuminating the faces of the proud parents and their smiling sons.

From Sandhurst Second Lieutenant Newall was commissioned into the Royal Green Jackets. The regiment's nickname, 'the black mafia', is derived partly from the standard very dark bottle-green uniform and partly from its reputation for sticking together. It is fiercely proud of its renown as an élite regiment rivalled only by the Guards. That their son should have joined such a fashionable regiment mollified his socially conscious parents.

After basic training Roderick underwent a baptism of fire when he joined the Third Battalion Royal Green Jackets in January 1985 on patrol on the streets of West Belfast. Then, on 11 March, he was transferred to a base at Celle, West Germany, fifty miles from the East German border. The Third Battalion was based at Trenchard Barracks, an ugly grey building built in 1943, with a ceiling inlaid with swastikas and stained-glass windows depicting leaves, daggers and other icons of the Third Reich. Lieutenant Newall was placed in charge of Six Platoon, part of R Company, consisting of four 432 Forward Reconnaissance Vehicles manned by six or seven riflemen each. The FRVs look like biscuit tins on tracks but can hurtle across the countryside at great speed.

There can be fewer more daunting experiences for a twenty-year-old ex-public schoolboy than to be suddenly put in charge of a thirty- to thirty-five-strong platoon of inner-city youngsters from Newcastle, Oxford, Liverpool and London. Initially, every young lieutenant relies heavily on his platoon sergeant or sergeant-major. This man, a career soldier eight or ten years his elder, is charged with guiding the young officer through the vagaries of army life; the relationship between the two is crucial. Though nominally the lieutenant is in charge, his sergeant may from time to time 'gently suggest' a course of action. If he is wise the lieutenant will act on the advice; if not he may have problems. Respect is a hard-won commodity. Initially a young lieutenant will be called 'sir'; eventually this becomes 'boss' if it is felt he is up to scratch; if the officer falls flat on his face it's 'sir' again until he has redeemed himself.

It was Rod's misfortune that not long after he arrived in West Germany he began having serious communication problems with his platoon sergeant. John Needham had been in the army for eleven years and he had seen a few arrogant young officers who thought they knew it all come and go. If there was one thing he didn't like it was arrogance. If there was another, it was deviousness. Unfortunately he thought he detected both in young Lieutenant Newall. The dislike between the two men was mutual and instant. As well as finding him arrogant, Needham thought the boy condescending and duplicitous, quick to attribute blame and slow to face up to his responsibilities. They clashed from the outset when Newall questioned Needham's procedures. The company commander was called in to adjudicate and when he came down on the sergeant's side the relationship between the two men soured further. Newall's obvious lack of appetite for the boring but necessary administrative work involved in running the platoon became another bone of contention. He unashamedly took his duties as an officer rather less than seriously, and the carelessness of his appearance bordered on scruffiness; Sergeant Needham found himself forced to 'gently suggest' Newall get his clothes pressed or have his hair cut. One sweltering hot summer's day after an exercise on the German plain the sergeant advised Newall to get out of his NCB (Nuclear, Chemical and Biological) warfare protection suit. Out of pique at being told what to do, Roderick refused and eventually Needham, with the help of a couple of laughing riflemen, had physically to lift him out of it himself. Lieutenant Newall was red-faced and speechless with rage at the humiliation. About an hour later he returned wearing another suit: it was an act of childishness that further reduced the boy's standing in his sergeant's eyes.

Another problem faced the dashing young lieutenant: money. In a well-heeled regiment such as the Green Jackets it was unusual for a young officer not to have a private income with which to supplement his salary, especially if he was to play his full part in the social round of débutante parties and jaunts abroad. But Newall just could not keep up. He caused sniggers with his battered and rusty Allegro which looked incongruous outside the mess, parked beside the Golf GTIs, MGB GTs and BMWs, and he was deeply self-conscious about it. In a regiment where appearances

33

mattered it was something that was noticed and served to set him apart from his fellow officers. More than once his financial problems embarrassed him and once his battalion colonel, Mike Dewar, reprimanded him for not paying his mess bills on time. It was never a large sum – not more than £300 – but it was a point of honour amongst officers that bills were paid on the dot, and Newall had dragged his feet once too often.

Being short of money never curbed Roderick's expensive tastes, however. When compact discs were introduced he was the first in the regiment to get a player. Soon he had a massive pop music collection, ranging from Chris Rea to Andreas Volmar.

An old demon came back to haunt Rod from his Radley days: his temper. He chafed at discipline and had several huge rows with superior officers. One colonel remembered him slamming his fist down on a table so hard he thought his hand was broken. In twenty years with the army he'd never lost his temper so badly before. Nor was the battalion commander impressed with Newall. Although he was helpful to the point of smarminess, the colonel detected in him a basic lack of dedication. His confidential report on Newall's performance was not flattering: a question mark was raised over his reliability.

The highlight of the Third Battalion's year in West Germany were the field tactical exercises which lasted two to three weeks and turned vast acres of the West German countryside to mud. The premise was always that Soviet forces had broken through, and the last two or three days of the exercise would be particularly tough, with the carrier crews having to travel many miles without sleep. It was an environment in which Lieutenant Newall shone. He was tough, enterprising and daring and it struck other officers that, whatever his deficiencies on the parade ground, he was excellent in the field.

At the beginning of 1986 the Third Battalion went to Canada on a mobile exercise sweeping across the prairies in Alberta. Afterwards the men were given a few days' Rest and Recreation. Roderick flew to Los Angeles to see his old school friend Charlie Shaw. Since school Charlie had not managed to find a niche in life. He was trying to make it in the rock business, but for the moment the reality was more mundane: Charlie was a record-plugger, going from record shop to record shop.

As at Radley, Roderick had many acquaintances but few friends; Patrick Sanders was the closest that Rod Newall had. They met as green twenty-year-old subalterns. Rod had already been in Germany for six months and Patrick looked up to him for guidance and advice. Rod was different from the other officers: he was keen on New Age philosophies and religions, but he was also a voracious reader with eclectic tastes and Patrick was introduced to the works of Hunter S. Thompson, Norman Mailer and John Irving. Typically, with the ever-faddish Rod, a book would spark off a passionate but short-lived enthusiasm. Once he read of a man who decided to base every decision in his life on the throw of a dice. Excitedly Rod announced to Patrick that he planned to do exactly the same thing, but this soon went the way of his other cranky ideas: it was just another phase.

Rod could often be found lying on his bed, earphones on, book in hand, kit scattered about the floor. On the wall was a poster of a girl tennis player scratching her naked bottom. Most weekends would be spent clubbing or seeing rock bands with his latest girlfriend, Kathy, the nanny to a senior officer's family.

But there was another side to Rod: he loved taking risks. Patrick shivered when he remembered being in a sports car and bombing down the M3 with Rod at the wheel. White-faced, Patrick could only watch in terror as the needle edged up to 140 m.p.h. Rod loved taking things right to the very edge.

One evening in 1985 the two drove off to a gaming night at a nearby castle. Schloss Brederback was an old hunting lodge converted by the Queen's Own Hussars into the classiest mess in West Germany, and the scene of regular blackjack and backgammon nights. Roderick had written off his old Allegro only a few weeks before and bought himself a Mazda 626 with the insurance money. Both men were dressed in regulation dinner jackets and bow ties and, with Rod at the wheel and Patrick hanging on tightly, the car hurtled along the twisting mountain roads. On a tight bend the car hit a patch of ice and went into a spin. Tyres screamed as Rod frantically worked the steering wheel and the handbrake. Finally it rolled to a halt. Patrick collapsed against the dashboard, but Rod jumped out of the car and began leaping around the road, whooping triumphantly. Not for the first time, Patrick thought, It's almost as if he gets off on taking stupid risks.

In August 1986 Rod invited Patrick to come on a sailing holiday in Spain on his father's yacht, the *Chanson du Lecq*. At the villa in Javea Patrick met Rod's parents – the mother jolly and noisy, the father polite and slightly aloof. He remembered noticing a strange atmosphere, almost a stiffness between father and son, but the two boys soon set off into the Mediterranean together.

Out at sea Rod's thirst for danger resurfaced. In the middle of the night, in seas illuminated only by moon-light, the boys would play 'shark', chasing each other in diving gear under the boat – pissed out of their minds. They would leave a line of rope trailing in the water behind the *Chanson du Lecq*, and dive off the edge. Then, as the swell took the yacht away, they would count to a hundred and then race off after it. It was mad, it was dangerous, it was typical of Rod Newall.

Unlike his wild brother, Mark Newall had conformed during his later years at Radley. He became a prefect and was so well thought of by his housemaster that he was made Head of House in his final year. He left in 1984 with three A-levels and, like his brother, turned his back on Oxbridge – to the despair of his parents. Mark had always known what he wanted. Even when he was little he was preoccupied with money. 'It's all he thinks about,' his mother told friends when he was eight or nine. Now Mark intended earning a lot of money as fast as he could. The early eighties were the right time to make it and Jersey was the right place to keep it.

He returned to live with his parents, and at the age of seventeen got a job with Barclay Trust in St Helier. Given the enmity between parents and son, Mark's decision to come home and live in his parents' house was tempting fate, but he had little choice. Even older residents have trouble finding rented accommodation on Jersey and a teenager stood no chance. And Mark was determined enough in his pursuit of money to realize that the chance of a Jersey residence qualification should not be given up lightly. If the price of that was living in the same house as people he detested, he was willing to pay it. Nevertheless, from the moment Mark returned home there was an unmistakable atmosphere of contempt between parents and son. Even in front of strangers the back-biting and sniping was continual and an atmosphere of pure detestation seemed to permeate every corner of the Crow's Nest.

Despite the mutual antagonism the parents found that Mark had his uses. At the Crow's Nest he was treated as a caretaker, gardener and handyman and was even expected to wash the dishes after his parents' dinner parties. While Nick and Elizabeth were in the Spanish villa he was instructed to remain in Jersey to look after the house and tend the garden.

Whatever the problems at home, as far as Mark's career was concerned he couldn't have been in a better place. The financial industry in Jersey was booming. At the beginning of the eighties the Conservative government had relaxed exchange controls, making it easier for British citizens to move their money to the Channel Islands. The result was a financial bonanza. Billions of pounds poured into the islands as hundreds of non-resident companies sought to take advantage. It transformed the career prospects of young people on Jersey, who were snapped up by the staff-hungry financial services industry. With many of the brightest leaving to make careers on the mainland and residential restrictions preventing companies from bringing in new people, it was not long before the staff shortage became acute and poaching was a common problem. The middle-ranking St Helier syndicate bank, Sheppards, received a considerable blow in mid-1985, when virtually its entire broking team was poached by the London-based James Capel for its own newly opened office on the island.

Sheppards was desperate, and turned to an old City hand. James Colbeck Welch had worked in the Square mile for more than ten years; fed up, he had returned to his birthplace, Jersey, where his parents lived. The challenge appealed to him. His first task was to recruit new talent. One day a friend of his father's, Elizabeth Newall, told him her young son Mark was doing well in Barclay Trust, where he'd started as a lowly trainee.

Mark came along to Colbeck Welch's office and gave an impressive interview. The young man seemed steady, sharp and ambitious. There was also a hint of aggression behind the stainless steel glasses that would come in very useful. Mark agreed to join for a salary of £8,500, and they shook hands. Then, next day, Colbeck Welch received a phone call.

'The thing is, I want to come in at nine and a half thousand pounds a year,' said Mark.

'But we agreed eight and a half, Mark. We shook on it.'

'Look, I know, but I'm taking a bit of a risk . . . and I want to see the bank making a commitment to me in its salary level.'

Colbeck Welch was dumbfounded. Surely, it was up to Mark to show his commitment to the bank and not the other way round. In the end he agreed. He was short of staff and there was no point in quibbling over a grand. The boy was obviously a bit of a chancer but that might not necessarily be a bad thing. And it seemed he had made the right decision when he found out that the bank was putting up a fight to retain Mark's services.

And so in January 1986 Mark joined the firm at their discreet-looking offices on the Esplanade in St Helier, working as a trainee Eurobond broker on one of the two main tables in the large, open-plan dealing room. There were five dealers to each desk with a support team of runners and secretaries. It was a demanding job: the day began at 7.30 a.m. and would often not end until past 6.30 p.m. The trick was to buy apples, sell oranges and somehow, through luck, alchemy or a careful understanding of the percentage movements, massage profit out of the transaction. Ultimately, no matter how much training is put in, a good broker is born and not made. From the outset it was obvious that Mark had flair and he worked all the hours God sent. 'He'll be burnt out when he's twenty-eight,' Elizabeth remarked proudly to Angela Barnes once.

It was the mid eighties and it was boom time. Crazy amounts of money were being made in the City and in Jersey it was little different. Mark's salary rose, as did his bonuses and status; he was on the fast track. But at home Mark's success only served to alienate him further from his father. 'Do you know,' confided Nick in hurt, whispered tones to friends one evening, 'that boy is making more money shuffling stocks around than I did after ten years' teaching.' Mark, like his Uncle Stephen, apparently had the necessary drive to be a success, and Nick didn't like it.

In the office Mark earned himself a reputation as a 'control freak'. He was a withdrawn, unemotional character who never smoked, drank or let himself go. He lived, breathed and ate the job. His only other real interests were martial arts and weight training and it was as if these provided an escape from the atmosphere of the Crow's Nest. He exercised religiously. A single-minded dedication showed itself in everything he did. His sudden interest in scuba diving was typical: rather than potter about in the local pool, he took a week's intensive training holiday in the Maldives and came back with an instructor's qualification. At home he would retreat into the small wooden chalet at the side of the Crow's Nest where he kept his collection of martial arts magazines and books on the occult. He never seemed to have any time for girls and was positively awkward in all but the most formal of settings. But a dark side to Mark Newall revealed itself at work. He displayed an overwhelming arrogance and disdain for other people. His attitude was even reflected in the pages of his address 'bible' – the book containing the numbers of the bankers he did business with. After each name and phone number was written his personal opinion of them: 'dork', 'fool', 'pratt', 'dickhead', and so on. This unpleasant side would also manifest itself in endless clashes with colleagues and the humiliation of subordinates in which he almost seemed to enjoy being cruel for its own sake. And there were split-second personality changes. One evening at a restaurant Mark started laying into a colleague. Another senior broker thumped the table angrily and shouted at him to lay off; in a second Mark was back to normal and chatting away. It was a transformation that was the talk of the office for weeks afterwards.

One day on the phone in the bond room Mark seemed to lose control completely. He began screaming down the receiver, 'You silly cow . . . you stupid bitch. How many times . . . ?' Colbeck Welch later discovered with a shock that he had been shouting at his mother. They had been arguing about her financial investments.

A certain lack of endearing human qualities aside, there were other aspects of Mark's behaviour that disturbed his colleagues: his insubordination was one. The boy would simply not do as he was told and demanded his own way every time. Office show-downs between Newall and his boss were frequent and noisy. The boy would tremble with rage, go white in the face and just refuse to budge on the tiniest of points. Some of their fiercest battles were caused by Mark's tendency to cut corners and take on what his boss called 'rubbish business' – business that had not been newly brought into the company but had just been shunted on from the Parish office. To Newall's fury he would be told to 'Go out and earn some real money' and pull in completely new business. Relations between Mark and his boss deteriorated until it got to the stage where Colbeck Welch regretted ever having heard of Mark Newall.

But his talents were undoubted. He had an intuitive grasp of percentage points, interest rates and an almost instinctive ability to juggle the currency and interest-rate fluctuations that affected the price of bonds. In most successful careers there is an identifiable point that marks the beginning of lift-off, and for Mark Newall that occurred in mid-1987 when the solid, blue-chip Sheppards was taken over by the Paris-based Arab bank Banque Arabe et Internationale d'Investissements. The takeover was signalled by the arrival in Jersey of John Ginsbury, a very big wheel at the bank and its director of capital markets.

Ginsbury had a reputation as a talent-spotter and Newall set out to get himself spotted as fast as he could. Ginsbury admired those who worked around the clock and Newall gave total loyalty. Weeks of ingratiation duly paid off and soon Mark was one of Ginsbury's boys – to the annoyance of his colleagues. His punishing work régime, his ruthless treatment of rivals, and his loyalty to his boss began to propel him through the ranks and ultimately he became a regular commuter between Jersey and the bank's Paris and London offices.

By the mid eighties the storm clouds gathering over the Newalls' lives were darkening: an unexpected threat to their savings had emerged from 3000 miles away. In America, courts across the land were being flooded by lawsuits filed by workers whose health had been damaged by exposure to asbestos. The Newalls' underwriter Richard Outhwaite had invested his clients' money heavily in American insurance cover which included long-term illness and his syndicates were dangerously exposed. He had taken on high-risk business that many other underwriters would not have touched. In the good years it was a strategy that had paid off and the Newalls, like thousands of others, were happy to sit back, pocket the money; but now the chickens were coming home to roost.

Like many reasonably well-off people, Nick Newall had invested in Lloyd's thinking it was about the closest thing you could get to a sure bet in this life. Certainly he seemed to be in good company. Fellow members of his syndicates included former prime minister Edward Heath and ex-tennis champion Virginia Wade. The notion that 'unlimited liability' might actually mean exactly that and that he might have to pay out had barely crossed his mind.

Trouble had been brewing for some time. Nick had been advised by his bank manager, then by Mark himself, to get out of Lloyd's but his usual complacency had prevailed. The thunderbolt struck in 1986 when Nick Newall, still half asleep in bed, tore open an envelope in the handful of mail he had been given by Elizabeth. What he read shook him so hard he shot bolt upright, hitting his head against the headboard as he did so. Stroking the bruise, he read the letter in disbelief.

Up until then the letters from his managing agents had included cheques for sums of around £20,000 – but not this time. Instead there was an explanation that his syndicates had incurred huge losses, and a request that he forward £60,000. Shortly afterwards this was followed by another demand, this time for £120,000.

43

These payments bit hard into the Newalls' depleted investments. By the summer of 1987, concerned at the way one cash demand was following another, Nick Newall had joined an Action Group which tried to put a stop on the losses and mount an investigation into why they had happened. It was only a foretaste of the disaster that was to befall many middle-class households in the years to come.

As if this wasn't enough, there was huge pressure on the Newall finances from another quarter. After another hammering on the stock market, Elizabeth turned up at Angela Barnes's house on the verge of tears. 'Nick is terribly angry with me, Angela,' she said meekly. 'I've lost a bit of money.'

Angela comforted her and assured her it didn't matter; but the next day Nick came in, sat down in the kitchen and sank his head into his hands in despair. 'That bloody woman,' he said. 'Do you know she has lost me sixty thousand pounds?' For nearly twenty years since hitting the jackpot with the Lesney toy car company shares, Elizabeth Newall had been unsuccessfully trying to recapture her form. But that early success was a fluke. Against all advice, the Newalls had borrowed against the Lloyd's deposit they had lodged with the bank. But even more desperate measures were needed: they sold off a small plot of land they had in Javea and planned temporarily to rent out the Spanish villa.

It was Elizabeth who finally realized what needed to be done if they were to hang onto what they had left. It led to one of the biggest fights she and Nick had ever had. As was often the case, the venue was Angela Barnes's kitchen.

'For the last time, Elizabeth, it's absolutely out of the question,' shouted Nick. 'There is no way I'm handing the money over to that boy. We'll just have to sell up and leave Jersey and live in the house in Spain permanently.'

'If you do that you're going on your own because I'm staying here,' yelled back Elizabeth.

Mark was not yet twenty, but he was already showing a financial acumen that was completely lacking in his parents. He had flown through his banking exams and it seemed logical to hand control of the family's financial affairs over to him and stop the Newall savings haemorrhaging away completely. From every point of view it made complete sense, but Nick Newall found the idea repellent. He simply did not trust his son and refused to even countenance the idea. But for all his bluster, it was usually Elizabeth who got her way when push came to shove, and this time was no exception.

Mark was finally given power of attorney over the family finances to invest as he thought best. It was a move that stunned friends, relatives and the Newalls' financial advisers. That Mark had taken on the responsibility from motives other than a sense of duty was obvious when Nick and Elizabeth let slip his hefty commission payments – thirty per cent of all profits accruing from his dealings. He took their share portfolio and made it more active, and, using his expertise and access to informed opinion in bonds and derivatives, he was soon making money for them. Of course, in the bull markets of the mid eighties, this was not a difficult task.

But even with Mark in control of the Newalls' money squabbles continued. Elizabeth, realizing that Roderick had no more financial nous than his parents, insisted Mark look after his savings as well. Reluctantly Mark eventually agreed to look after Roderick's share of the profits – ten per cent.

Mark had invested what was left of his parents'

money shrewdly and by 1986 he was making between £30,000 and £40,000 a year in profits, but unfortunately it was too late to save his childhood home: the Crow's Nest had to go.

CHAPTER 3

The moment Maureen Ellam parked her car outside the Crow's Nest and turned round to drink in the incredible view of the Grève de Lecq she knew her search was over. Down at the bottom of the bay she could see the rollers breaking onto the rocks off cliffs not more than a quarter of a mile away. For once the estate agent's boasts had been no exaggeration. She walked over to the door and pressed the button. Seconds later it opened and she was met by a smiling red-haired young man in his early twenties. Maureen explained why she'd come. 'Come in, come in,' he said, gesturing her indoors enthusiastically.

The side door led into a large kitchen surrounded on three sides by banquette seating. Another young man with dark hair and glasses leaned against the table who ignored the visitor. The red-haired one then threw himself enthusiastically into his sales pitch. He pointed out the fittings, then indicated the awful plastic-covered banquettes. 'And I bet you don't realize how useful it is,' he said.

You bet I do, thought Maureen, thinking that if she ever owned the place the first thing she would do would be to tear it out and stick it on a bonfire. A lifetime in the hotel business had given her an expert eye for the finer points of interior decoration.

'You can use it for storage,' said the youngster, lifting

off the plastic cover to reveal a large gap stuffed with yellowing newspapers. It was all Maureen could do to stifle her giggles. It was a splendid house but Maureen couldn't help but think how tatty it all looked. However, she instantly realized its potential.

Turning to look at the other youngster, she asked, 'Are you two brothers?' The dark boy looked up for the first time.

'Unfortunately,' he said in a bored tone of voice.

'Unfortunately? Unfortunate for who?' replied Maureen, intrigued.

The young man didn't answer, but she was aware that she should have said 'whom' instead of 'who', and for some reason she got the feeling that he had picked up on this.

The red-haired lad guided her through the house. He was helpful and friendly and made great play of the wonderful view from the vast picture window. At one point, when they were looking at the sloping garden, the brother strolled out to them and raised a finger in the air. 'There is one problem,' he said solemnly, interrupting them. 'That's the dog. Whoever wants the house will have to look after the dog because he won't be leaving.'

'Oh, that's a shame,' said Maureen firmly. 'I'm not too partial to dogs. The owners of the last house we wanted to buy wanted us to take their bloody airedale. So I don't think I'd want to know.'

'He won't be a lot of trouble,' he said, pointing to the hillside above the house. 'His grave is on that hill.'

Maureen looked at the lad's impassive face, then laughed. 'Well, I'm sure I could manage that.'

The other boy continued with his tour and eventually led Maureen back to her car, saying that if she wanted to see the house again she only had to ring. Even before she drove away Maureen's mind was made up. After a lifetime of hard work and scrimping and saving she had at last found a retirement home where she and her husband David could live in comfort and privacy. It needed a lot of work but the potential was obvious. And those striking boys! She wondered what their parents could possibly be like.

For two couples who were to become the firmest of friends the Ellams and the Newalls got off to a bad start. It was Nick Newall's arrogant manner that once again caused offence. David Ellam, a shrewd, intelligent, but typically blunt northerner from Blackburn, couldn't be doing with airs and graces and Nick's aloofness rubbed him up the wrong way when they first met. After that initial hiccup, however, the negotiations for the house drew the two couples together and an unlikely friendship blossomed. On the face of it they had little in common. While Nick Newall was lazy and impractical, David had worked hard as an engineer all his life and could turn his hand to anything. He was tall and bearded, spoke with a soft northern accent and was prone to dramatic outbursts. Elizabeth was loud, reckless and totally extravagant while Maureen had been a shrewd and successful businesswoman who had carefully saved all her life. She was small and fastidious and wore her blond hair in a pony-tail. In their irresponsible and rather selfish approach to life, the Newalls were the complete opposite of the cautious Ellams. Yet the two couples clicked and, as the sale negotiations got under way, the Ellams were completely won over by the sheer charm of the oddball couple.

During her visits to the Crow's Nest, however, Maureen Ellam became painfully aware that beneath the surface of this apparently happy middle-class family something was very wrong. There seemed to be no love lost between the couple and their son Mark. The deep mutual contempt was almost palpable when they were all in the same room. Often, as the two couples sat and chatted in the kitchen, Mark would come in. He would never stay for more than a few seconds or exchange more than a few words with his mother or father, yet Maureen and David could feel the tension between them. The boy was an enigma – a curious, buttoned-up character who spoke, acted and dressed older than his years. He seemed to Maureen well enough behaved and he held down a good job; in a funny way he seemed more grown up and mature than his parents.

Any cautious enquiries about either of their sons were brushed off by Nick and Elizabeth – not because they thought it was private; Maureen got the distinct feeling that they had many more interesting things to talk about.

One evening later that summer Maureen was carrying plates into the kitchen after dinner at the Crow's Nest when Elizabeth came up behind her. As usual she was in a tizzy.

'What's it this time, Elizabeth?' asked Maureen.

'It's that awful boy, Mark,' she replied. 'He wants to go and stay in the house in Spain and I've told him he can't and he just says, "Well, Roderick went, why can't I?"'

Maureen was puzzled. Well, why couldn't he?

As usual, Elizabeth was flustered and kept fiddling with the spectacles she kept on a thong round her neck. 'Well . . . it's just that Roderick is likable and fun but Mark just puts people's backs up. We've got such nice neighbours down there and I don't want them to know we've got such an unpleasant son.'

Maureen made polite noises but she was devastated.

No wonder Mark had turned out the way he had if this was how he was treated at home. She had grown very fond of Nick and Elizabeth but she just couldn't help thinking, poor Mark. The boy seemed to live a rather shadowy existence and was barely part of his parents' lives at all, although Maureen could see that they found him useful: he did the gardening, cooked many of their meals, looked after the upkeep of the house and paid rent on the chalet where he slept. Maureen often wanted to broach the subject of the divisions in the Newall family, but the passions seemed to run so deep that she always drew back at the last moment.

The sale of the Crow's Nest was to be overshadowed by the Newalls' financial problems, Nick explained to Maureen one evening in the kitchen. He and Elizabeth had found a modest bungalow on the south coast. It was much smaller than the Crow's Nest but as a base for spending the summers in Jersey it was fine. The elderly owner was seriously ill and wanted to return to England as soon as possible. Nick was reluctant to take advantage of a sick man but the house was going cheap. The couple's finances were in a parlous condition: the sale of the Crow's Nest was hampered by the fact they had no cash for the deposit on the bungalow. This was a problem Maureen was able to solve instantly – she wrote them out a cheque for £25,000 there and then on the kitchen table. 'There you go,' she said. 'Even if the whole thing falls through we'll make some money off the deal somehow.'

'I still feel I'm defecating on the old man,' Nick said, quickly scooping up the cheque and pocketing it.

The sale proceeded slowly. Matters weren't helped by Nick and Elizabeth, who were so disorganized they exasperated Maureen and David. Elizabeth became more and more manic; Nick was lazy and useless. It soon became clear that only young Mark Newall was blessed with practical abilities and slowly but surely he began to take over the handling of the sale. One day Elizabeth was jabbering excitedly as usual on the phone to Maureen. 'You've got to get your solicitor on the phone and tell him . . .'

'Now hang on, dear,' said Maureen firmly. 'I've got to tell my solicitor nothing. I'm paying him to tell me. Now come on, you two, stop worrying. Push off and leave the details to me and Mark.'

Even during the sale of the house the underlying family tensions were evident. 'I must apologize for the conduct of my parents,' said Mark in his typical pompous tones after his parents forgot some detail. 'They are highly negligent and deeply incompetent.'

There was a real edge to his voice and Maureen brought him up sharply. 'Now hang on, young man,' she said. 'They are not business-minded like you and me, they are academics.' Mark didn't reply, but again Maureen was left wondering what on earth had caused the loathing within this family.

As Maureen began to deal with Mark she became more and more impressed with him. Physically he still resembled a schoolboy but he was meticulous and diligent with a real eye for detail. When the sale was delayed because the car parking space had been omitted from the deeds it was Mark who rectified the error. With Nick and Elizabeth out of the way the deal went like clockwork and by June 1986 everything was ready to roll. Mark arrived at Maureen Ellam's house to finalize the details. Standing at the kitchen table he flipped open his notebook and ticked off various points. 'Wow, what a kid,' she said, looking at him in admiration. 'I could have done with a son like you.' She noticed he blanched slightly at the remark but she could tell he was pleased. Poor little bugger, she thought. It's probably the first time anyone's ever shown any appreciation of him.

Even by British mainland standards Jersey's property laws are arcane and complex. House sales are carried out in the Norman French language in the island's Royal Court at 2 p.m. on Fridays with both parties making a solemn pledge to stand by their agreement. The cheque is lodged with the bank and the actual 'flit' or transfer takes place the same day. There were hitches until the last minute. The first planned completion date was 18 July, but then David and Maureen were let down by buyer after buyer. The balance was given to Mark to invest. Early on the morning of 1 August 1986 a furniture removal van loaded with the Ellams' belongings lurched slowly up the steep narrow road that led to the Crow's Nest. After it was unpacked the Newalls' things were loaded up and the van set off for the bungalow. Nick took no part in the flit as he had decided he was 'feeling a bit off colour'. Typical, thought David Ellam.

At £230,000 Maureen was really paying well over the odds for the Crow's Nest. The bungalow at No. 9 Clos de l'Atlantique, however, cost the Newalls £84,500, of which £55,000 was raised on a mortgage.

That morning, when Maureen visited the Newalls at their new home, she decided to have a laugh at Mark's expense. 'Right, young man, I'm glad I've got you,' she said. 'Remember your parents – the "incompetent, negligent people" you were telling me about. They have just sold their house for more than twice what it was worth. They are home and dry.' She said it with a laugh, but Mark's reaction astonished her.

He stared at her, his eyes burning with contempt. Then, without a word he turned, strode out of the house, jumped into his sports car and drove off. Later, when Maureen told Nick about it his response was as strange as his son's. He sat, gripping the arms of his chair so hard his knuckles were white. He seemed to be almost in pain he was so angry. 'That bloody boy,' he murmured.

'Oh come on,' said Maureen. 'See the funny side of it. He is not some punk rocker you'd be ashamed to have walking up the High Street. He's not a drunk, not even out of work. He's a handsome, clean-cut boy. You should be proud of a boy like that.'

'Yes, Maureen, you are right, I suppose,' he replied, but there was no enthusiasm in his voice.

That night the two couples celebrated the occasion with a bottle of champagne and the Newalls gave the Ellams a special moving-in present – a sepia picture of the Crow's Nest identical to one treasured by Elizabeth.

A month later, on 2 September, David Ellam's birthday, Maureen and David strolled down the road to the Prince of Wales, a twelfth-century mill converted into a restaurant and pub. The millwheel still revolves behind the bar and the place provides one of the main attractions of the Grève de Lecq. The landlord told them he had owned a bit of land next to the Crow's Nest; a plan of his to build a chalet on it had been blocked by the Newalls. 'And do you know the worst of it?' he said. 'That boy that used to live in your place – arrogant lad – with glasses. He came in here and says to me, "You can do what you like with your field now, put a multi-storey block of flats on it for all I'm concerned. I've just sold the house for twice what it's worth" – arrogant little tow rag.'

David was indignant but Maureen was not at all surprised. She knew, could almost feel, that that side of Mark existed. Strangely, she didn't resent him for it.

But again she was taken aback by the strength of Nick Newall's reaction when she told him about the conversation. He rubbed his temples and was quiet for a moment. She wondered if he was all right, but then, at last, he said, 'God, Maureen . . . I hate that boy.'

The pure venom in his voice stunned Maureen. She tried to make light of the incident. 'Oh come on, he's not all bad, he'll get his come-uppance some day – and soon.'

But with his thumbs pressed hard into his temples, Nick just sat silently staring at the floor.

No. 9 Clos de l'Atlantique soon proved too small for both parents and son. Without the chalet Mark no longer had a bolt-hole to escape to and, cooped up together, the animosity between the three became unbearable. Like the Crow's Nest, it became a house of hate. In the late summer of 1986, while his parents were in Spain, Mark abruptly moved out and, with a colleague from the bank, into a flat in the nearby village of St John. When his parents returned from Spain later that year they were aghast. Mark had left the bungalow without a word, they complained to friends. 'He hadn't even bothered to mow the lawn.'

To many of their friends the Newalls – who were completely above board and open about their financial problems – seemed to be living life more and more on a knife edge. They made no attempt at all to rein back on their spending; indeed their life seemed to assume an even more hectic pace than before. On Christmas Day 1986 in Spain, seventy-eight members of Javea's expatriate British community gathered on the patio of Nick and Elizabeth's villa for a special occasion – the opening of their new swimming pool. The food was provided by outside caterers and the best wines flowed.

When she heard about the poolside soirée Angela

Barnes was taken aback. She knew how strapped for cash the couple were. 'But Elizabeth,' said Angela, 'that must have cost you a fortune. Wherever did you get the money to pay for it?' But Elizabeth merely brushed the question aside with an airy wave.

'Our boy Mark is a financial genius,' she later boasted to Joan and Alex Riches, who were good friends of the Newalls in Javea. 'He has been headhunted and he is going to restore the family fortune. Do you know he is one of only four people on Jersey who can handle Eurobonds?' Elizabeth had never spoken much about her younger son before but now that he was in charge of the family money the Newalls' friends grew heartily sick of hearing about him.

However, the problems that were troubling the lives of Nick and Elizabeth Newall were not only financial. To some friends it seemed as if they were careering out of control: Elizabeth began drinking more heavily than ever before and would often retreat to Angela Barnes's house in the middle of the afternoon and down a bottle of wine and smoke a whole packet of cigarettes. Underneath the appearance of carefree normality, all was not well between them. Friends were saddened to see a couple who had once been so devoted grow further and further apart. For some time they had been leading separate lives – a fact that was more apparent in the easygoing community of Javea than it was in Jersey. In Spain Elizabeth would go off and play tennis while Nick would take the boat out for long trips.

Nick had begun to wander. Always a ladies' man, he never hesitated to let a woman know if he found her attractive. He began taking women friends on discreet trips on his yacht. At one dinner party he was caught *in flagrante* with another woman. If Elizabeth knew about his infidelities she did not let on to friends. She maintained that if she caught Nick with another woman she'd kill him, but friends got the distinct impression that the couple were drifting apart.

Health problems also started to re-emerge: for years Nick had been dogged by a mysterious illness, in addition to back problems following a sailing accident some twenty years previously. He now began to take to his bed for days at a time. His doctor and various consultants were baffled by the illness and Elizabeth took to feeding him homeopathic lotions. 'You've never seen Nick when he is having one of his spells,' she told her friends the Matthews in Spain once. Strangely, his 'turns' would often come on before a social occasion and Elizabeth would turn up for dinner parties alone.

Something strange was happening to Elizabeth too: she began to suffer from blackouts. Sometimes in the middle of a meal or a conversation she would stop and stare into the middle distance. This could last for up to thirty seconds. Angela Barnes got so concerned about her that she phoned both Nick and Mark, who agreed that Elizabeth must see a doctor. But nothing was ever done.

One Sunday Nick and Elizabeth went round to the Clos de Hugh for lunch with Angela and her son Peter. They were about to settle down to eat when the doorbell rang. It was Mark. Angela was a bit put out. This unannounced appearance meant she'd have to set another place at the dinner table. But the moment he walked into the dining room she felt the tension between son and parents rise. Uh-oh, she thought, there's been some trouble here. The meal went smoothly enough until Elizabeth began enthusiastically regaling the company with the details of a book she had read.

Suddenly Mark interrupted. No, he insisted irritably, she had got it all wrong. He began to correct her, but as he spoke the edge of his voice grew stronger and his face got paler and paler. Then he abruptly switched to the subject of their latest cash windfall and Angela guessed that money was the real issue. 'You will just squander it just like you've squandered everything. There will be nothing left for me or Roderick.' Then he pointed at his mother and, in a low voice heavy with menace, snarled at her, 'I'm going to kill you one day, you know.'

It was too much for Elizabeth. She got up, fled the room in tears and locked herself in a bedroom.

Nick tried to brush the incident aside in his usual manner, calling Mark a 'stupid boy', but Angela was astonished. She had known things were difficult between Mark and his parents but never imagined that such seething fury lay beneath the boy's controlled exterior.

One day in early 1987, during Wimbledon week, Elizabeth drove up to the Crow's Nest and rushed in to speak to Maureen. As usual she was in a terrible fluster. 'That awful boy,' she began as usual. 'You'll never guess what it is now.' She paced around the kitchen, running her hands through her thick red hair. Maureen had become used to these melodramatic outbursts and asked calmly, 'What is it now, Elizabeth?'

'He wants to buy a house, of all things.'

Maureen couldn't understand what the fuss was about. Mark was old enough and sensible enough to know what he was doing: 'He is earning big money – let him buy before he gets the taste for spending it.' And besides, she pointed out, it would give him the necessary residential qualifications to stay on the island.

'Anyway,' said Elizabeth irritably, 'he's already got

his eye on a property and what's more he wants you to look it over and see what you think of it.'

Maureen was taken aback. She didn't think she had ever managed to pierce Mark's armour. Indeed, she thought the boy held her in contempt. 'My, what an honour from Lord Mark,' she retorted.

'No, he really respects you, you know. You're one of the few people he does.'

Maureen was intrigued and agreed to go and inspect the property. Later that week she and Mark drove out to see a large white-washed house with three bedrooms set in a cul-de-sac in the village of Noirmont in the district of St Brelade on the south-west coast. Maureen thought La Falaise was beautiful but surely too big for one young man on his own. Mark's mind was made up, however. The only problem was the money: the house cost over £100,000 – much more, she thought, than he was able to get his hands on at his age. But that was his problem; otherwise she was happy to give it the seal of approval.

In the summer of 1987 the Newalls were visited in Javea by their Lloyd's syndicate manager Alison Follis and her husband Michael, who were staying with friends near by. They were in the living room chatting when the phone in the hall rang and Elizabeth went to get it. Moments later they could hear her voice growing louder and louder. She was having a furious row. Nick tried to keep the conversation going but Elizabeth's shouts drowned out all speech. Alison and her husband shifted uncomfortably in their seats and exchanged embarrassed looks. Eventually Elizabeth slammed the phone down and came into the room, flushed, angry and animated. She explained she'd been wrangling with Mark: he wanted them to help him with the deposit for the house.

Alison Follis had met Mark. She remembered her astonishment when Nick Newall, more than a year ago, explained that his son would be handling all his finances from then on. The father had seemed awkward and slightly embarrassed, but nothing had prepared her for her first meeting with Mark at her London office. He was surly and aggressive to the point of rudeness and far from constructive in his attitude. And apparently he behaved in a similar fashion with his own parents. Now he was impatient with them for not getting on with the paperwork on his house. 'He expects us to be able to do everything from here at the drop of a hat . . . ' Elizabeth said in an exasperated voice.

That night over dinner Alison was chatting to Nick when she heard the tail end of an exchange Elizabeth was having with Michael. She was talking about the problems they were having with their sons: '. . . honestly, sometimes it gets so bad that we live in fear of our lives.' A stunned silence fell over the table for a second. Alison and Michael glanced at each other in disbelief. Elizabeth looked over at her husband for support. 'That's true, isn't it, Nick?'

Nick lowered his eyes, shamefaced, and for a moment it was as if the aloof, arrogant exterior had crumbled to reveal a broken and emasculated man. 'Yes . . . yes, it is,' he said.

The purchase of La Falaise was a transaction which marked the crossing point in the fortunes of parents and son. Helped by an £80,000 mortgage from Lloyds Bank, Mark Newall bought the house in August 1987 for £114,000 – £30,000 more than his parents' house in Clos de l'Atlantique. They were approaching the edge of the precipice.

*　　*　　*

A few scattered stones on a heather-covered hillside on a small Scottish island are all that remains of a turbulent and violent past. Once, centuries ago, the island of Shuna was a bitterly contested outpost of the lands of the clan MacAlpine – a place of murder, mayhem and betrayal. Today the quiet is disturbed by the cry of the curlew, the bleating of a handful of sheep, and the breeze. But though the castle has long since sunk into ruin there is one habitation left: a large, seven-bedroomed Georgian Scottish farmhouse, built five years before the Jacobite rebellion.

In the years following the Highland clearances the small community which lived on Shuna was dispersed. At the turn of the century it passed into the hands of John Craig, a father of the Clydeside shipbuilding industry. By the time Craig's daughter Gay married Stephen Newall the island had become a haven from the stresses of Glasgow life.

In May 1987, on the shore of Loch Linnhe a young girl, bent over with the weight of the hefty young man she was carrying on her back, staggered to the shoreline then, picking her steps carefully, began to enter the water. After ten yards she reached a rowing boat and, with a heave, Amanda Newall tipped her burden inside and the two cousins burst into laughter.

Roderick had not been to Shuna since he was little and had forgotten that waders were needed to get to the boat – the only means of access to the island. Taking the oars, he began to row and looked around in awe. The purple mountains that ring the Loch were at their spectacular best. It was a far cry from the primly mani-cured lanes of Jersey.

Amanda hadn't seen her cousin for years. Out of the blue he had phoned saying he wanted to travel to Scotland and visit Shuna, where Amanda had been doing her last-minute crash revising for her university exams. She had readily agreed but the request puzzled her. She had not seen much of Roderick since her family had left Hampstead and returned to Scotland in the late seventies. Throughout his teenage years Mark had continued to come and stay with his five cousins, but from the age of about fourteen Roderick had gone off on his own, frequently spending his holidays with Charlie Shaw and his family in the west of Ireland.

They had both changed in the intervening years. Amanda had inherited more than her share of the Newall good looks and had blossomed into a blue-eyed beauty. Three years in the army had filled Roderick out.

The moment he stepped on Shuna he was bewitched. It was a refuge, a haven away from the stresses and strains, a place for soul-searching. He said he was annoyed his parents had never shown him the Highlands before. Eagerly he threw himself into the simple routines of chopping logs, thumping a few fence posts in or cutting peat. One night, as they both sat in front of the fire chatting about their futures, Rod suddenly started on about the strains in his relationship with his parents; he had recently had a fight with his father in Spain. As was apparently frequently the case, several drinks had led to an angry exchange of words. This time the bone of contention was Roderick's career. 'You'll never believe what he said to me.' His voice was bitter. 'He said he wished he'd never had children at all.' He looked at Amanda and for a moment it seemed he wanted her sympathy.

She was stunned. If Roderick was not shooting a line it seemed an astonishing thing to say to your son.

Roderick returned time and time again to the subject of his unhappy childhood during his stay on Shuna.

Adulthood had not led to an easing of the family tension; instead it seemed to have grown and become a major preoccupation with him. The strains within her cousin's home were no secret, but he was surely overdoing it, thought Amanda; he wasn't a child any more and had left home long ago. She just couldn't figure it out.

During the stay Roderick pulled out an expensive camera, which he said had been a present from Mark. This surprised Amanda. She had witnessed at first hand the two boys' fights when they were younger. Invariably Mark would come off worst. Now they were apparently on good terms. It was very odd.

In May 1987, during the beating of the retreat in Whitehall, Roderick had been presented to Princess Alexandra as one of the regiment's most promising young officers. As far as his parents were concerned he was doing very well in the army, so when he suddenly arrived in Javea out of the blue and announced he planned to leave and join the Metropolitan Police antiterrorist squad there was uproar. The Newalls had not been happy about his decision to join the army in the first place, and the apparent casualness of his decision to leave left Nick with a profound feeling of disappointment in his elder son. It was a decision that puzzled his Aunt Nan in London too: she realized that ever since Radley Roderick had had problems with authority and she couldn't see how joining the police would be any different.

Roderick had already thought long and hard about his decision and had worried about how he would break it to his parents. He had a long conversation with Charlie Shaw's mother, in whom he had confided since his schooldays, at her new home in Lymington in

Hampshire. She advised him not to break the news on the phone but to go to Spain. His parents were, predictably, far from pleased but he argued his case persuasively to one family friend – Edward Jelinek. The army, he said, was top heavy and promotion was slow. The police were changing and offered much greater career opportunities. Jelinek agreed and told Nick his son had a point.

That spring Roderick had been home on leave. He was proving to be as hopeless with money as his parents and was having his own financial problems. As Elizabeth was to tell it later, she was in the kitchen, standing over the stove and stirring something one day when he suddenly announced he needed several thousands of pounds to pay off his mess bills.

'Can't help you, I'm afraid,' said Elizabeth dismissively. 'We've got nothing.'

Suddenly the young man's face flushed and his voice rose shrilly. 'Look, I really need the money. You have to help me out.'

She turned back to her pot. 'If we had any, Roderick, we'd give it to you but as it is –'

Suddenly a heavy blow to her back sent Elizabeth spinning across the room and against the kitchen wall, where she slid slowly to the floor. A searing pain shot through her arm and shoulder. She looked up in horror to see Roderick standing over her, his eyes gleaming with fury. Terrified, she fled from the house, shouted for Nick, jumped into the car and drove off with the sounds of father and son battling in the kitchen ringing in her ears.

At Angela's house Elizabeth sat, head down on the kitchen table, in great pain and almost hysterical. She wouldn't hear of getting the police involved, despite the massive bruise forming on her arm and back which prevented her from playing tennis for five weeks after the attack. When she attended a faith healer she claimed that she had tripped and fallen. But it was an act of violent fury that shocked Angela Barnes. Whatever forces had lain dormant in the Newall family were now out of control.

As before, Nick Newall responded to the crises and tension in his family by becoming more and more preoccupied with his health. As one baffling symptom followed another and his spells in bed grew longer and longer, more than one friend wondered aloud if he was trying to escape reality. A surgeon friend who had examined him told their friend Edward Jelinek that there seemed to be nothing wrong with his back. Occasionally Nick would hint that his mysterious viral complaint was more serious than previously supposed and mutter darkly about leukaemia. He would surprise strangers by introducing them to his wife, then adding, 'And you will have to look after her when I am gone.'

At the end of August 1987 the Newalls left Spain and, after a brief trip to Switzerland, arrived in Jersey on 5 September. Then came the news that was to transform the Newall finances. Uncle Kenneth on Sark was ill and wanted to speak to his two nephews urgently about his will. Kenneth Newall's unprepossessing appearance belied a sharp intelligence and an acute wit. He had once joked to a friend that he didn't want to go walking along the Sark cliffs with any of his relatives 'because they might push me off'.

This sudden unexpected summons threw Nick and Elizabeth into a fresh panic. There had long been disagreement about how Uncle Kenneth's estate was to be divided up. Nick and Elizabeth were terrified that he would be persuaded to divide his legacy equally between all his grand-nieces and -nephews. As Stephen had five children, it would mean that his family would get more than twice as much as Nick's. Nick and Elizabeth felt it would be much fairer if half the money went to Stephen's family and half to Nick's.

Stephen and Gay Newall were very close to Uncle Kenneth; indeed, they had bought back the house built on Sark by Stephen and Nick's parents many years before and used it for their family holidays.

But Kenneth's decision was to please everyone. He had decided to hand over £800,000 of his fortune, half each to both his nephews, to enjoy while he was alive. It was an extraordinary act of generosity and it was to completely transform the fortunes of Nick and Elizabeth. They immediately began phoning round the good news to their friends – their entire future, so bleak only days before, now looked rosy. Elizabeth was almost manic with excitement; when she phoned the Ellams she invited them over for a celebratory meal.

One evening at Clos de l'Atlantique Nick and Elizabeth already seemed rather high even though they hadn't had a drink yet. Only weeks previously they had been on the verge of ruin and now they could see a future free of money worries. Elizabeth had prepared a feast – crab pâté followed by a main course of ox-tongue cooked in a delicious sherry sauce. 'Oh, you haven't seen anything yet,' she said as the compliments flowed. 'Wait till you come round next time and I'll give you lamb's tongue.'

The Newalls seemed delighted that they were able to have Kenneth's money without having to wait for his unwelcome 'popping off' first. The alcohol flowed freely and as usual it seemed to have little effect on Elizabeth and Nick. David was drinking his half-litre can of Whitbread while Maureen was sipping a glass of her usual Asti Spumante. The two couples had spent many memorable evenings together but this was the best, given in the knowledge there would be many more. 'Thank you for a terrific night,' said Elizabeth with her arm around Maureen.

'It's amazing what a bit of money will do!' said Maureen to squeals of protest from Elizabeth.

Leaning back in his chair, Nick took a puff from his pipe and said, 'Elizabeth, it's amazing what good company will do.'

At the end of the evening, as the Ellams lurched out of the door Elizabeth rummaged around in a cupboard for a second and produced a small, wooden stool made by Roderick at school. Maureen, she said, could use it to reach the high cupboards in the Crow's Nest.

'Are you sure you want to part with it, Elizabeth?' said Maureen.

'It's no use in here, is it?' came the reply.

As they drove off Maureen leaned out of the window and said, 'I'll phone you tomorrow when you're sober. You'll probably want it back.'

'But I'm not drunk,' shouted Elizabeth as she hung onto Nick in the doorway and the Ellams' car disappeared down Clos de l'Atlantique.

Judging by the noise coming from the long table in the hotel function room, everyone was having a great time, and no one seemed to be enjoying the celebration more than the tiny figure seated in the middle.

It was mid-September and the occasion was the celebration of Uncle Kenneth's birthday. The entire Newall clan had descended from all points of the compass. It was the biggest gathering for many years because for once nearly all Stephen's children were able to attend; both of Nick's sons were there too. It was the best family get-together anyone could remember. Even

Elizabeth and her brother-in-law Stephen, who had a talent for winding each other up, appeared for once to be getting on. Uncle Kenneth's decision had brought unexpected harmony to the Newall family and it went beyond the parents: Roderick and Mark were laughing and joking and seemed totally relaxed in each other's company. The brothers' childhood enmity was the stuff of family legend but, for the first time, there seemed a real bond between them.

Later that September Nick and Elizabeth embarked on their annual tour of their relatives still full of cheer that their money problems were over. After taking the ferry over to Weymouth on 23 September they spent a couple of nights with Nan and Alaster in Clapham. With grudging approval, Elizabeth decided to mark the family's new financial stability by going shopping. Accompanied by Nan, she went on a spree in Harrods and bought presents for her friends in Spain: shoes, handbags and sweaters.

Meanwhile Nick visited the London School of Tropical Diseases for more tests on his mysterious viral illness. He also paid a visit to his Lloyd's underwriters to find out how the Outhwaite Action Group was getting on.

The couple then travelled up to Scotland for another annual family ritual: a visit to their mothers – Nick's in Argyllshire and Elizabeth's in North Berwick on the opposite coast. It was a glorious autumn and the hills were a blaze of purple heather as the Newalls drove down the Clyde coast. One afternoon while they were in Edinburgh Nick left the National Library, where he had been ploughing through books in the history department, and made for a 300-year-old pub in the heart of the city's historic Royal Mile to meet an old friend. Sandy McCall was a retired Scottish banker who was a neighbour of theirs in Javea. He had long been a close friend and had always taken an encouraging and indulgent attitude to Nick's writing ambitions. Like many of the couple's friends, Sandy had detected troubles within the Newall household, but now he noted happily that Nick seemed more relaxed than he had in years. Enthusiastically Nick outlined the subject of his latest play, which he felt was a sure-fire winner – Mary Queen of Scots.

While Nick was busy researching his play, Elizabeth made her way to an elegant town house in the heart of the New Town to visit her schoolfriend and bridesmaid Vanessa Prosser. The two women's paths had diverged widely since their schooldays in St Andrews more than twenty years before. Vanessa had met and married a barrister and, by the mid-eighties, Lord Prosser was a senior Scottish judge. But each time they met, no matter how long the gap, the two friends would laugh and giggle as if they were still schoolgirls. Elizabeth seemed just as noisy and full of life as Vanessa remembered – she never really changed: there was always a bit of the schoolgirl in her. Roderick was Vanessa's godson and she and Elizabeth had always taken a keen interest in each other's offspring. Now, Elizabeth chatted about the future with excitement; about how the boys were getting on and how much she was looking forward to her silver wedding anniversary later that year and would be returning to Jersey on 18 December especially.

The Newalls travelled back down to London and, after spending another night with Nan and her husband, on Monday 5 October they drove to Winchester to visit Roderick at the barracks and had dinner with him at the Lainston House Hotel, Sparsholt. They took the ferry back to Jersey the following day. The last time that Nan Clark spoke to her sister was on 7 October while Nan was staying with their mother in North Berwick. They chatted briefly and Elizabeth expressed relief that at least one family difference had been resolved: Roderick seemed to have given up his notion of joining the police. Instead he was up either for promotion or for adventure training in Canada. His decision had pleased his parents – especially his father, who had accused him of not applying himself. But as she put the phone down, Nan Clark had the distinct impression that something was worrying her sister. It wasn't anything Elizabeth had said but Nan knew from the tone of her voice that all was not well.

The next few days were busy ones for the Newalls – they bought bits and pieces for the house in Spain and packed for the long car journey. They had arranged to have dinner with their friends the Blayneys on Saturday 10 October, but at nine o'clock on Saturday morning Elizabeth rang the Blayneys with profuse apologies: she had to cancel the date, she told Bob, because her boys had arrived unexpectedly on the island to take them out to dinner; would they mind taking a raincheck? Bob said of course not, but he made Elizabeth promise they'd come round on the Tuesday evening. No time was fixed – the couples knew each other so well they could just amble round in their own time as usual.

Later that Saturday morning Elizabeth Newall, with Nick in tow, swept into the kitchen of the Crow's Nest. She was in a flap. 'What is it now, Elizabeth?' said Maureen with a smile.

'It's those awful boys,' she replied. 'You'll never guess – Roderick's come back unexpectedly and he and Mark are taking us out for a meal tonight because it's my birthday next week.'

Maureen and David laughed. It was typical of Elizabeth to turn such an event into a crisis. The two couples sat chatting for a couple of hours and as usual the Newalls took a keen interest in the progress the Ellams had made redecorating the house. It was Maureen's birthday and, just before they dashed off Elizabeth presented her with a tin of shortbread – a present from Scotland. As the Newalls got into their silver-grey Citroën Maureen shouted after Elizabeth not to forget their dinner appointment the following week.

'Oh for God's sake,' shouted Elizabeth. 'Don't worry, we won't.' And with a laugh and a wave the car disappeared down the road.

At 11.11 a.m. that morning a casually dresed, good-looking, fair-haired young man walked into Norman's Builders' Merchant on the front at St Helier and began piling up an odd collection of items on the counter. They included two trenching spades, two plastic tarpaulins (one green and one blue), two torches and batteries, two packets of red heavy-duty refuse sacks, a pick-axe, two small modelling knives, a saw, rope and a can of upholstery cleaner.

He paid the cash sum of £103.42. It stuck in the assistant's mind because it seemed such an odd assortment of items.

CHAPTER 4

Early on the morning of Sunday 11 October Maureen Ellam was standing in the kitchen at the Crow's Nest, surrounded by flowers, when she was struck by one of her frequent attacks of impetuous generosity. The day before, her forty-ninth birthday, she had been given a record eight bouquets from family and friends. She'd put seven in jugs of water, but was having trouble finding a home for the last one. Why not give a bouquet to Elizabeth? *Her* birthday was only four days away, and a premature gift would be a lovely surprise. Grabbing the last bunch of flowers, Maureen jumped into her car and set off on the four-mile journey across the island to her friends' home.

She remembered that the couple had been taken out to dinner the previous evening by their sons. The family would be feeling pretty fragile this morning, if the Ellams' nights out with the Newalls were anything to go by. At nine o'clock her car pulled up outside the modest bungalow. Alongside the Citroën was the flashy white Toyota MR2 Maureen recognized as Mark's. The curtains were drawn and there was no sign of life. Probably still sleeping it off, thought Maureen, pressing the bell. But when the door opened and an unfamiliar face looked out she was quite startled. This must be Roderick, the officer in the Royal Green Jackets who was now home on leave. She hadn't seen him since the day he showed her around the Crow's Nest more than a year before. He seemed to have changed out of all recognition – his face was marble white, his eyes sunken, almost hollow. God, you must have had a skinful last night, young man, she thought. She asked him, 'Is your mother up, son?'

For a moment the lad just stared silently. 'She's still in bed . . . they're both still asleep.' Roderick's hand gripped the door handle tightly and he seemed to be having trouble keeping his balance.

Maureen laughed and pressed the bouquet on him. 'That's all right, son, you place these flowers on her pillow and when she wakes up she will think she has died and gone to heaven.' She ran back to her car, jumped in and drove off. On the road a strange thought stuck her. Nick and Elizabeth were notoriously early risers, no matter how much drink they had put away the previous evening. But that boy's face! It must have been some night they had.

At three o'clock that afternoon Roderick Newall caught a flight from Jersey Airport to Gatwick and made his way back to the barracks at Winchester. Later that same afternoon his brother Mark left his house in Noirmont and flew back to his flat in London, where he was working for Sheppards.

Three significant events took place on the following four days: on the Monday 12 October, Elizabeth Newall missed a dentist's appointment. The next day both Nick and Elizabeth failed to turn up for a tennis match or for dinner at the Blayneys'. And then, on 14 October, the eve of Elizabeth's forty-eighth birthday, the winds began to blow. The most violent storm ever to hit Britain struck without warning and in the space of a few hours it left the worst trail of death and destruction the south of England had seen since the war. On the mainland eighteen people died, and countless houses and buildings were destroyed. The next morning massive trees and heavy vehicles blocked roads and most of the rail networks were brought to a standstill. The entire South-East of England was blacked out. When it was all over a shellshocked population emerged and looked around, aghast. Six million trees had been felled in the winds and the face of much of southern England had changed for ever.

On Jersey all was chaos. The island had been caught in the teeth of the storm as it roared in off the Bay of Biscay. Eleven people were rushed to hospital with serious injuries and in one village a man lay trapped in his car by a fallen tree. Two children had narrowly avoided death when a chimney came flying through a window. Roofs were torn off buildings and eighty people were evacuated from their homes. In one village a fire engine rushed to a house that had been crushed by a falling tree. Another tree suddenly fell over, injuring two of the firemen. Guests at one hotel had only just been evacuated when the wind tore off the hotel roof and deposited it in a field a quarter of a mile away. The south-west corner of the island, where the Newalls lived, was completely cut off. The limited emergency services were soon overwhelmed by the sheer volume of calls.

At the Crow's Nest Maureen Ellam was phoning the Newalls but receiving no answer; she was growing concerned. She had had no contact with the Newalls for five days; it was not like them. Elizabeth especially was a compulsive caller who often rang several times a day on the slightest pretext. And Maureen was sure she would have got in touch to thank her for the flowers. The next morning, 16 October, Maureen phoned again before nine o'clock just to make sure she hadn't been missing them when they popped out. But again there was no answer. When the Newalls failed to turn up for dinner that evening – a date that had been arranged long beforehand – Maureen decided it was time to do something.

'David, you're going to have to go there and find out what's happened.'

But David Ellam had his own problems at that moment. He was clearing some of the felled trees that blocked the drive and needed to go to his engineering factory to repair some broken windows. 'Can't it wait?' he said. 'I'm sure there's no problem. They've probably just popped back to London to see relatives.'

But his wife was insistent. 'No, David, they've only just been there. Anyway they were planning to head off to Spain at the end of this week. They wouldn't have gone without saying goodbye.'

Maureen was clearly genuinely worried. David didn't think anything was wrong, but to set her mind at rest he promised to investigate immediately. This proved to be easier said than done. The road from their home on the north coast of the island to the Newalls' on the south-west was blocked by fallen trees in many places and three miles down the road a huge tree made further progress impossible. Parking his car on the verge, David cursed inwardly and began to pick his way towards the bungalow. There was no apparent damage to No. 9 and the family saloon was still parked outside so they couldn't be far away, he thought; the front of the house was secure but he was surprised when he went round the back and found the patio doors unlocked.

The moment he slid back the rear door and stepped inside a gust of warm air greeted him. The central heating was turned up far too high, he thought, stepping inside. All was quiet and, goodness, it was warm – far too warm for a mild October day. In the hall David discovered that the thermostat governing the heat for the entire house had been set at maximum, and when he went to the control box he saw that the heating had been set on manual instead of automatic, meaning the time-switch mechanism had been overridden. The temperature would be at maximum twenty-four hours a day until someone switched it off. Strange, thought David.

Gingerly he stepped around the room. There was a pile of letters behind the front door. The car keys were on the sitting-room table. There was no sign of life in the kitchen either and no response to his shouts. He phoned his wife from the house. 'Look, you'd better contact the boys to come and sort this out. There's no sign of them and their car is here.'

David found a note of Mark's ex-directory London number in the house and that evening Maureen phoned Mark at his flat. No, he had no idea where they were but he would phone around the relatives and see if they knew. After a frantic flurry of phone calls, Mark phoned Maureen back. Neither of his grannies nor any other relative had any idea where they could be; nor did any of the family friends in Spain. He couldn't raise his Uncle Kenneth on Sark but that wasn't unusual 'as he does imbibe quite a lot'.

Maureen was worried. 'I don't want to cause unnecessary bother or worry, Mark, but I really think one of you should come back. It's just not like your parents to go off like this.'

Mark explained that he was tied up, but Roderick, who was staying with him, would be able to fly over. He handed the phone over to Roderick and Maureen agreed to pick the older brother up at the airport. Maureen was surprised to hear that Roderick had been staying with his brother because Elizabeth had often told her there was no love lost between the two boys.

At 2.30 in the afternoon of 18 October Maureen peered into the crowd of passengers thronging the arrival hall at Jersey airport. Roderick saw her at the same time she saw him and he flashed a smile of recognition. He was a strikingly good-looking young man of about five foot eight, slim and broad-shouldered; he walked with the easy gait of the extremely fit. A rucksack hung casually over his shoulder and he wore the same red pullover he had had on when he opened the door to her the Sunday before. Red hair, red face, red pullover – that boy should not wear red, thought Maureen. He shook her hand, apologized for putting her out, and asked if there was any news; nothing yet, she said. He was soft spoken and surprisingly polite for someone of his generation. His accent instantly gave away the public-school background. That the boy took after his mother was obvious: same red hair, blue eyes, high cheekbones and easy charm. The resemblance was so marked that Maureen wondered what on earth prompted the daft thought that had flown into her mind the day before: What if the young man who had met her at the Newalls' door was not Roderick at all?

She laughed at her own stupidity. 'Thank God it really was you who opened the door the other day,' she said as they walked.

Roderick stopped and turned. For a second the blue eyes seemed to flare. His voice was low but insistent: 'What do you mean by that, Mrs Ellam?'

'Nothing, Roderick, just that I've only met you once and I wasn't sure if it definitely was you.' They walked on in silence. It was an awkward moment and Maureen was puzzled to see how upset such an innocent remark had made him. She could see in his eyes that she had hurt him somehow.

David was waiting with the car and Roderick slid into the back sat. Maureen tried to keep the conversation upbeat: 'You hang onto that flight ticket, lad, because when that pair turn up you are going to get them to repay every penny.'

'Too right, Mrs Ellam,' came the reply. 'That's exactly what I'm going to do.' Maureen tried to keep the chat going but Roderick was understandably distracted. Suddenly he spoke up: 'I really must thank both of you. This is terribly kind of you to go to so much trouble.' There was that politeness again – and at such an awful time.

Maureen twisted round. 'Look, lad, they are our friends and we'll do anything to help. Now, if they have gone wandering off and got stuck at the bottom of a cliff or something then we have to move fast.' Maureen went through a few possibilities. The Newalls were great walkers and could cover several miles in an afternoon. The island's coast was dotted with the remains of German bunkers left over from the war. They could be holed up in one of those. Maybe Elizabeth – a bit of a mountain goat – had fallen and Nick was scared to leave her and they were waiting for help.

But even as she spoke Maureen looked out of the window at the devastated countryside and could not resist a growing feeling of foreboding. The island had taken such a battering from the storm that in places the previously well-manicured Jersey lanes and hedgerows were almost unrecognizable. Everywhere she looked there were felled trees sprawled across roads, hedges and fences. Their huge branches had snapped like twigs; roots lay exposed to the air like gaping wounds. Telephone poles had been torn out of the ground and stone walls knocked flat. There was hardly a building undamaged and workmen and repair vans were everywhere. David asked over his shoulder how bad the storm had been in Winchester. Worse if anything, as it turned out; the soldiers at the depot had been deployed to help the civilian authorities and Roderick had spent two days clearing trees from a railway line.

The car motored down the narrow road that clung to the coast and onto the peninsula of St Brelade towards La Pulente where the Newalls lived. To the right the sea was purple and calm. It was a crisp autumn day and a strange post-storm stillness hung in the air, yet only a few days earlier the bay of La Pulente, one of the most beautiful on Jersey, had been the scene of incredible violence as huge waves smashed into a couple of dinghies, leaving them in pieces.

At the foot of the peninsula the road suddenly turned away from the coast and switchbacked up a steep cliff. A smaller side road on the left led to the row of small detached bungalows. No. 9 Clos de l'Atlantique sat in the middle of a row of five. It was, Maureen noted again, a very unassuming little house that symbolized the sad decline in Nick and Elizabeth's fortunes in recent years. But if the Newalls had ever been conscious of the come-down, it didn't show. Life for them was one big party. David pulled up beside the Citroën and Maureen turned and handed Roderick the set of house keys Elizabeth had left with her in case of emergency.

Even before the car had finally rolled to a halt Roderick had leapt out and run over to the door of the utility room that abutted the main house. Seconds later he disappeared inside. Poor lad, thought Maureen, he's putting a brave face on it but he's worried sick. The couple followed on together and stepped inside the utility room that led directly into the main passage which stretched the length of the house.

Inside, it was all so impersonal it could have been rented accommodation. The Newalls had spent only a few months of the year in Jersey, preferring to spend most of their time in their villa in Spain. So the bungalow was functional rather than homely and there were no family photographs or any other personal touches. Even though the couple had lived there a year they hadn't done much decorating.

The Ellams followed after Roderick through the hall and straight into the large living room. The moment Maureen stepped inside the living room she knew something, somehow, was wrong. At first glance there seemed no logical reason for this. There was no damage or disarray. There was no sign of entry, forced or otherwise. The living room was tidy and everything seemed in order. On one side of the fireplace was a wall cabinet, containing a television set and a large number of videos which the couple would swap with their neighbours in Spain. On the other side was a much-utilized small drinks table stacked with a variety of wine and spirit bottles. Only a small pile of pound coins on the dining table behind two armchairs and an empty bottle of Macallan malt whisky on a small table in the middle of the room struck a vaguely incongruous note. Yet Maureen felt – and she couldn't find a better word for it – that the room was definitely *wrong*, and it was a feeling that was growing stronger by the minute. 'Roderick, this room is . . . different somehow.'

His blue eyes met hers. 'What do you mean, Mrs Ellam?' he said.

She looked around, speechless for a second, searching for some sensible comment. 'David,' she said, looking over to her husband, 'this room is too tidy, it's been cleaned, it's been scrubbed; look at the walls and the ceiling.'

The other two followed her eyes. Stepping back, David could just make out the faintest whorl of wipe marks on the wall above the fireplace. And then there was the choking heat. How warm the house was! What on earth had Nick and Elizabeth been thinking of, leaving the heating on high?

In the kitchen there were oatcakes, marmalade and sugar on the table, and milk, eggs and bacon in the fridge. Some vegetables in a rack had shrivelled with the heat. The ironing board had been set up in the back porch and through the window Maureen could see a couple of Nick's shirts fluttering on the washing line. In the bathroom cupboard lay Nick's shaving things and a pair of matching toothbrushes. There was no sign that the Newalls had left without planning to return shortly. So where the hell were they?

Plans had been made to return to the house in Spain for the winter: in the small box room at the end of the passage there were a dozen cardboard boxes containing the supplies they were taking back with them – things that were difficult or expensive to get out there, from tinned soups to DIY equipment – all neatly packed and labelled. Elizabeth used the smaller bedroom to keep her clothes in and the remnants of the Harrods shopping spree had seen scattered around.

Maureen made her way through into the main bedroom. Like the rest of the house it was simple and functional – two large wardrobes set into one wall, a dressing table, a double bed, a chair, and that was it. It was the usual tip: a pair of Nick's casual trousers lay concertina'd on the floor as if he had just stepped out of them. Typical, thought Maureen. But there was one strange thing: while the bedroom was a mess, the bed itself had been carefully made. This was unusual because Elizabeth was the untidiest person alive. Beds would often be left unmade from morning to night. The Newalls were, not to put too fine a point on it, slobs.

'What do you see, Mrs Ellam?' asked Roderick, who had stepped into the room behind her.

'The duvet cover, Roderick,' she said, fingering the crinkled blue cotton. 'It's not been laundered properly. It's been washed and put back on but it's not been ironed or tumble dried. You can still smell the soap powder. You have to sleep a night in it before that goes away. No one has slept in this bed.' Then something on the bedroom carpet near the door caught Maureen's eye. It was a large, dark stain.

'What is it, Mrs Ellam?' said Roderick, following her gaze.

'It's a mark on the carpet, Roderick; it's virtually brand new. I helped your parents to pick it and now Nick's gone and spilt coffee on it or something.' The three of them stood in the middle of the floor, looking at the grey smear on the carpet. Maureen bent down and felt it. 'But someone's made an awful clumsy attempt to clean it. They've soaked it, and brushed it hard and forgotten to vacuum. Look at this fluff.' She knelt down and fingered tiny balls of material that clung to the carpet surface.

David bent down and felt the material. 'It's been lifted and replaced clumsily with tin tacks – they wouldn't have done that, would they?'

Roderick flitted from room to room, pulling out drawers, opening cupboards. The questions poured out of him: Mrs Ellam, do you see anything different? Does anything in the kitchen seem strange? Is there anything unusual here, Mrs Ellam? Anything that strikes you as odd? Anything at all?

On a table in the hallway were a couple of newspapers dating from the previous Saturday. David scooped up a pile of mail on the mat and began leafing through the letters. 'We should be able to tell the last time they were in the house from the postmarks,' he said, passing them over to his wife. One had been posted from Dover on the Friday. 'Well, I suppose it's possible that it could have got here on the Saturday. I wonder who Elizabeth knows in Dover.' Roderick tore the envelope open. It was a friendly note from Elizabeth's sister, Nancy.

At a loss as to what to do next, Maureen filled a jug of water in the kitchen and went round watering the house plants. Roderick darted from room to room, raking through drawers, throwing open cupboards; he would just not sit still. Finally David Ellam took charge. He announced that they'd done all they could but they still had no idea what had happened to Nick and Elizabeth. They had no alternative but to report their disappearance to the police.

Later the same afternoon at Jersey police headquarters in Rouge Bouillon in St Helier Maureen and Roderick were shown into an interview room to file their missing persons report. Roderick sat at one end of the room and dictated his statement to a WPC. Maureen was asked to write hers out by a police sergeant. From the outset Rod's attitude was petulant and unhelpful, almost as if he were trying to intimidate the young woman taking the statement. When she asked him how he would describe his mother he snapped back, 'Jolly hockey sticks,' leaned back in his chair with folded arms, and stared at the bemused girl. Later she asked, 'How would you describe your mother's voice?' and he was almost cheeky: 'Would you care to give me a few adjectives from which to choose?'

Maureen, both puzzled and amused at this attitude, reproached him. 'Oh, come on, Roderick, you sound just like your father. Now come on, be helpful.'

As they struggled to piece together the events of the last few days Maureen suddenly reached over and asked Roderick, 'What did you have for your Sunday lunch, son?'

Roderick whipped round in his chair in astonishment. It was the second time she had seen that look of hurt puzzlement in response to a perfectly innocent enquiry. 'What's that got to do with it, Mrs Ellam?'

'It's just a detail, Roderick. There was no leftover food, no joint or veg. I just wondered what you all had for dinner.'

'Oh, it was scampi . . . provençale, I think. And some smoked salmon.'

They finished giving their statements around six. David and Maureen invited Rod to come home and have some supper with them but he declined, saying his brother Mark had asked him to check on the storm damage to La Falaise.

'Don't forget, son,' said Maureen as they dropped Roderick off at the bungalow, 'don't go hungry. There's plenty of food back at our house.'

'I won't. Thank you very much, Mrs Ellam.'

Maureen Ellam's heart went out to the boy. He was trying to appear in control but, again like his mother, what Roderick was feeling inside was clearly written on his face. He looked very vulnerable and confused. She wished he would let her do more to help. Despite appearances, Maureen knew that the Newalls were not like other families and it must have been difficult for Roderick having to grow up in such a strange environment. And now, as if he hadn't got enough to worry about, he had been landed with this, poor lad.

That night the lights burned long at 9 Clos de l'Atlantique, and inside subtle alterations were taking place: in the living room the whisky bottle on the table was washed, dried and replaced; the faint imprint of wipe marks would disappear from the walls and the newspapers would be thrown out; in the master bedroom the crease in the badly lain bedroom carpet would be straightened out, the fluff on the dark stain vacuumed away and the faint smell of soap would fade from the stiff, badly dried duvet. For on his first night home after his parents' disappearance, Roderick Newall slept in their bed.

By the morning of Monday 19 October the Newalls' good friends Bob and Anne Blayney had learned from Roderick that his parents were missing. He asked them if they had any idea where they could be but, like everyone else, they were at a loss. They had been slightly worried by the couple's failure to appear for dinner on the previous Tuesday, and had even driven by the house itself on Thursday evening to find it in darkness. Like Maureen Ellam, Anne had made several calls and had intended to investigate further but, like the rest of the island's inhabitants, they had been distracted by the need to clear up after the storm. It had wreaked havoc in the vineyard. The La Mare was totally cut off by fallen trees and Bob Blayney had spent most of the weekend with a chainsaw, cutting his way through the roads leading to the farm.

At eleven o'clock on Monday morning Anne drove up to No. 9 Clos de l'Atlantique and went in through the front door, nearly tripping over Mark as she did so. He was on his knees in the hall with his sleeves rolled up, as if clearing up after something, and Anne's sudden appearance produced a fiery reaction. 'What the hell are you doing here?' he snarled.

Anne, taken aback, said, 'I'm not here to see you, I'm here to see your brother.' She was indignant: Mark had always been an odd boy but there was nothing to justify such hostility. Then Roderick suddenly appeared in the sitting room doorway. Shutting the door firmly behind him, he made his way across the hall and into the kitchen. Anne followed after him, brusquely sweeping past Mark.

Roderick certainly did not look well. He was white-faced and seemed distracted. He tried to make Anne a cup of tea but didn't seem to know his way around the kitchen, which was not surprising as he would have barely known the bungalow. Anne took over, saying, 'I'll have to think like your mother about where everything might be.' There was nothing untoward about the house, but some flowers were soaking in the sink.

Detective Inspector Graham Nimmo didn't know quite why, but he got the distinct impression that the young man, despite being twenty years his junior, was talking down to him. He was polite and well spoken, but there was no mistaking the contempt: it was as if he thought it beneath him to answer any questions from mere policemen.

The missing persons report on the Newalls had not reached the CID until Monday 19 October and that afternoon Nimmo and Detective Sergeant Jimmy Adamson were met at the front door of 9 Clos de l'Atlantique by both the Newall sons. The policemen had already had their busiest week in years. The island was still reeling in the aftermath of the storm and they had been swamped with calls requesting urgent police assistance.

From the outset the case didn't fit the usual missing

persons pattern. There was no teenage runaway or errant spouse, no trail of angry debtors or pursuing employer; only an ordinary comfortably off middle-aged couple last seen by their sons the night after a happy family celebration. The brothers were apparently at a loss and unable to throw any light on the matter. The dark-haired son, bespectacled and wearing a suit, did most of the talking. He spoke thoughtfully and carefully. The other, the red-haired army officer, paced anxiously up and down the room. Even if he hadn't seen the half-empty bottle of Macallan whisky placed prominently on the coffee table, Detective Inspector Nimmo would have guessed that he had been drinking.

No, Mark explained, a hint of impatience in his voice, they had no idea what could have happened to their parents. No, they had had no plans to travel back to Britain. No, they had no financial or health problems. It was unlikely they had just gone off on a whim to visit a friend or relative without taking the car or even locking up, said Mark; besides, they had already spent hours on the phone checking with friends and relatives from Scotland to Spain.

Certainly it didn't look as if the couple meant to be away from the house for long. The family saloon was parked outside; the house had been left open. And it was highly unlikely they would have left for Spain and forgotten to switch the central heating off.

When the Ellam's and Roderick first entered the house it had been almost unnaturally tidy, but by the time the police got there it was in complete disarray. The boys had turned it upside down, apparently trying to find out what had happened to their parents. In the main bedroom clothes had been flung about anywhere and drawers up-ended, leaving a vast pile of documents and private papers on the desk in front of the bedroom window.

In accordance with routine procedure Nimmo needed to take separate initial statements from the brothers, but when he asked to do this they exchanged a glance of concern and became strangely reluctant. Their tone was condescending, as if to ask why they had to go through this tiresome rigmarole. Why weren't the police out searching for their parents? Why couldn't they *do* something? Roderick was eventually persuaded, with great difficulty, to wait outside the sitting room while Nimmo took a brief statement from Mark. But the detective had only just flipped open the pages of his notebook when the door opened and he came back in. Why couldn't he stay? Roderick asked. Nimmo eased him out again, saying he wouldn't take long, but seconds later the door opened and in walked Roderick yet again. What where they talking about? he demanded to know. What were they saying? When this happened a third time Nimmo said in exasperation, 'Look, son, I'll get to you in a moment. Will you let me speak to your brother alone, please?'

Briefly Mark outlined the events of the previous ten days. He had been working at his stockbroker's London office but had flown to Jersey on Friday 9 October to finish off shifting his belongings to the house he had recently bought at nearby Noirmont (his father had hired a Renault van specifically for that purpose), and to celebrate their mother's impending forty-eighth birthday the next night. The sons had taken their parents for a meal at the nearby Sea Crest restaurant and returned to the bungalow. Later both brothers had spent the night at Mark's house before returning to 9

Clos de l'Atlantique for breakfast and lunch the next day. Their parents seemed cheerful enough when they left. Sure, they had a bit to drink on the Saturday evening, but nothing too excessive. They were both healthy and fit and keen walkers who would often wander the coastal pathways for miles. Both sons caught separate flights for London that same Sunday afternoon.

Roderick's account seemed to tally. On the Sunday afternoon he had been dropped off by his brother at the airport and had flown back and rejoined his regiment at the depot in Winchester.

And that, apparently, was that. In the vast majority of missing persons cases the errant individual turns up within forty-eight hours with a red face, ready for a stiff dressing down from worried family members. This would probably be the case this time as well. But as they left the Clos de l'Atlantique and drove back to St Helier the detectives agreed that something could have happened to the couple during the storm. The house itself had only lost a few roof tiles but they could have gone over a cliff or got trapped by the tide on the beach. The storm had created a forty-foot swell, so there was a strong possibility that the bodies would have been swept out to sea. The numerous coves and rocky inlets that dotted the coastline only ten minutes' walk from the bungalow would have to be scoured either way. It was sure to turn out to be straightforward enough.

Nevertheless, Nimmo thought there was something wrong about those boys – especially Roderick Newall. He seemed totally on edge. Nimmo could smell whisky on his breath but it was more as if he were high. That he should be tense and worried was understandable, but there was something else. More than twenty years

89

as a detective had taught Nimmo the telltale signs that
someone was lying, and as he talked to the red-haired
young man he could see one clearly – a tic in Newall's
neck pulsating furiously.

CHAPTER 5

On the night that Elizabeth Newall died her sister, Nancy Clark, saw her for the last time with Nick, sitting in a long black hearse flanked by outriders and moving slowly along. As it stopped Elizabeth got out and Nan, astonished, went to ask what on earth they were doing, but before she could speak Elizabeth turned and – although her mouth was not moving – Nan imagined she could hear her voice quite clearly: 'There, I told you he meant it and I told you it would happen. But let the matter rest.'

A moment later she was jolted awake and in the gloom of the bedroom found her husband Alaster gripping her shoulder. He had never known his wife to suffer such a dreadful nightmare.

When the news came through the Clarks were at Case Fidra, their villa near Alicante. Nan's mind had been in a whirl of anxiety. Early on Sunday 18 October Mark had phoned her from his flat in London and asked if she knew where his parents were. He had been unable to raise them and Roderick was already making his way back to the island. After a further flurry of calls Nan and Alaster realized that something was seriously wrong and set off for Jersey straight away. Just before they left they spoke to Roderick, who had found the bungalow deserted. His voice on the phone had been halting but Nan found one comment mystifying and deeply worrying: 'It doesn't look as if there is much hope.' It was a strange thing to say.

Although the elder by five years, Nan was very close to her sister. They could not have been more different: Elizabeth was loud and boisterous whereas Nan was calm and phlegmatic; Elizabeth was a bit of a day-dreaming romantic while Nan was the hard-headed realist. She exerted a kind of protective and calming influence over her younger sister and despite the geographic distance between them they spoke to each other most weeks. The Newalls, for all their impetuousness, were creatures of habit. It was not like Elizabeth to go off without letting someone in the family know. Nan didn't know why, but she felt – could almost sense – that something was very wrong somewhere and, as the car sped along the Spanish highway, her mind kept going back to the awful nightmare she'd had a week previously. On Tuesday, from the French port of St Malo Nan and Alaster caught the Hovercraft to St Helier, where they were met by Nimmo and Adamson.

The Clarks assured the police that it was completely out of character for Nick and Elizabeth to go off without telling anyone. They knew of no reason why they should not be there. They certainly had never gone off like this before.

As they arrived at the police station car park Nan met Mark leaving. The boy was tense, almost stiff, and when she approached him he leaned over and whispered conspiratorially into her ear, 'Don't tell them about the two sets of passports.' By rights Nick and Elizabeth shouldn't have had two passports each, but it had apparently made travel between Spain and Jersey that much easier. In any case, it was just a little thing. Why on earth that should have worried the boy at such a time she had no idea. Just tension probably, she thought.

Nimmo explained that the island was still recovering from the storm and that it was possible that something might have happened to the Newalls while they were out walking the winding clifftop paths. If so, the police faced a formidable task: searching all the innumerable coves, inlets and hundreds of concrete German fortifications could take weeks.

While Alaster returned to St Malo to pick up their car, Nan Clark met up with Stephen Newall, who had flown down from Scotland. The police had booked them into the Atlantic Hotel which was situated only a few hundred yards away from the Newalls' bungalow. The two detectives accompanied Nan to 9 Clos de l'Atlantique. They were met at the door by Roderick, and the first thing that struck Nan was the red sweater he was wearing. Elizabeth had bought it in Harrods and it had been intended as a present for a friend in Spain, so what was Roderick doing wearing it? Nan didn't mention it, but it played on her mind.

The anonymous bungalow in the drab little lane puzzled Nan. She had not had a chance to visit it since her sister and brother-in-law moved in the previous year, but she thought it was completely out of character. It was poky and, however hard she tried, she could not imagine her sister in it at all. The place had a temporary atmosphere, reflecting the couple's recent life on Jersey. It was hardly a home at all compared to the Crow's Nest, Nan thought.

In the kitchen she was slightly startled to be met by a middle-aged couple who were there. They introduced themselves as the Ellams; they had bought the Crow's Nest. 'We were very good friends of Nick and

Elizabeth,' said Maureen. Nan was slightly puzzled: her sister had never mentioned them.

That night Nan hardly slept with worry and the next morning, with her mind in a whirl of anxiety, she had to go for a walk in the hotel grounds to compose herself before she could sit down for breakfast with her nephews. Whatever strains the disappearance had brought, it had not affected Roderick and Mark's appetite: both were tucking into large platefuls and chatting easily with their Uncle Stephen. Mark was explaining to him in detail about the computers he was using at the bank. As she sat down Nan was struck once again by the resemblance between Stephen and her brother-in-law Nick. They were completely identical and even shared the same gestures. Stephen was more sanguine about the whole affair. 'I'm sure they will turn up shortly,' he said.

Later that morning, again accompanied by the two detectives, the family party walked down the hotel drive and turned left up the access road that led to No. 9. This time Nancy got the chance to examine the house in much more detail. In the middle of a back wall in the lounge stood a large sideboard; on top of it stood two three-pronged candlesticks and on the wall above hung four of Elizabeth's prized Russell Flint seascapes. Two cheap black armchairs were jammed into one corner and there were another two armchairs opposite. On an onyx table in the middle of the room stood the half-full bottle of whisky. A bookcase housed a collection of books and videotapes and a large table stood in front of the picture window that looked out onto the garden.

At Rouge Bouillon, an incident room was set up on Tuesday 20 October. The first priority, Nimmo and Adamson decided, was to discover what clothes were missing. That way they might be able to put a time on the disappearance. Nan knew Elizabeth's wardrobe intimately for the simple reason that she usually ended up buying her sister's clothes for her. Having picked her way through the piles in the bedroom and the hangers in the wardrobe, she thought that the only things missing were a long dark skirt and an orange top. A solitary dark-blue waistcoat on a hanger suggested that Nick had been wearing a dark-blue suit.

On the bedroom wall hung a portrait of Elizabeth, painted in 1958 when she was eighteen. In the box room at the end of the long main corridor sat several cardboard boxes and tea chests destined for the couple's home in Javea. There were dirty dishes in the sink but both Roderick and Mark said they had been eating in the house since they returned.

But the inconsistencies were apparent from the outset. If something had happened to Nick and Elizabeth while they were out walking, why were their walking boots still in a closet along with their raincoats? There was no sign of Elizabeth's handbag or of Nick's wallet or credit cards. It was Maureen Ellam who pointed out that a hearth rug was also missing. In the bathroom Nan spotted another curiosity: no towels. Nick always insisted on having lots of clean towels but there were none on the bathroom rails, none in the airing cupboard, on the clothes line, in the washing machine – or anywhere else.

And another thing: no Sunday newspapers. The couple always bought a huge bundle every week and would spread them over the floor and spend the whole day poring over them, drinking mug after mug of coffee. The boys insisted there were newspapers in the house when they left their parents; so where were they? Behind a chair Nan found a crumpled piece of paper and eventually realized it must have been used to wrap the flowers that Maureen Ellam said she had given Roderick at the door the week before. But, as untidy as she was, it wasn't like Elizabeth just to throw it down and leave it there.

Later the next day Stephen Newall had to fly back to Scotland and Elizabeth's mother arrived on Jersey and booked into the Hotel Atlantic along with her daughter, son-in-law and grandsons. When Nan went back on Thursday 22 October the bungalow was transformed: there were police officers everywhere. Nimmo leaned down and picked up a poker from the fireplace. Nan, glancing over his shoulder, saw a speck of red about the size of a fingernail with a long, dark-red tail near the tip. The two detectives looked at each other ominously.

As the days passed a sense of unreality had settled over the family group sitting in the lounge of the Atlantic Hotel. This was heightened by the presence of a BBC television crew filming a scene in the hotel grounds for the popular detective programme *Bergerac*.

Only days before, Nan and Elizabeth had been chatting excitedly about their plans for a family Christmas together in Scotland. Now, as Nan was only too painfully aware, with the passing of each hour the chances of the Newalls having come to harm increased. But that simple fact did not seem to have sunk in with her nephews. They seemed curiously detached and it became clear that they did not take the police seriously. One evening in the hotel lounge Roderick offered to get his Uncle Alaster a drink. The hotel bar had no single malts so Roderick, loudly dismissing their range of blends, said he had some good stuff in his room – a bottle of eighteen-year-old Macallan. It was a typically arrogant remark and earned a rebuke from his uncle

Alaster for his rudeness in front of the hotel staff. But Alaster became even angrier when he discovered where the whisky had come from: Roderick had taken it from the bungalow.

'Roderick, for God's sake,' he remonstrated, 'you know the police asked us not to touch anything in the bungalow. What the hell do you mean by taking that bottle away?'

Petulantly Roderick sloped off to sulk in a corner of the hotel lounge until a young and striking blond girl who had joined the brothers in the hotel went and fetched him back to the main group. With her cropped fair hair and high Scandinavian cheekbones, Elena Irrgang was an arresting sight. She had been a colleague of Mark's at Sheppards and had shared the flat with him in St John but there was no romantic attachment between them. Instead she was an occasional girlfriend of Roderick's and was never far away from his side while they were at the Atlantic Hotel.

Eventually, on Thursday 22 October, the detectives, annoyed by the boys' refusal to stop moving things around in the bungalow, asked them to hand over the keys and move into the Atlantic Hotel with their aunt and uncle. No. 9 was now officially sealed off.

Nan and Adamson went on a tour of dry cleaners in St Helier to find out if by any chance Elizabeth had dropped some of the missing clothes off. The Newalls did not have their papers delivered but a check with local newsagents seemed to confirm they had not called in to buy any on Sunday 11 October. The visit to their Uncle Kenneth on Sark, planned for the fourteenth, before they returned to Spain, had not materialized, and a trawl through the ferry manifests and the airport passenger lists drew a blank. The Newalls had booked tickets on the St Malo ferry on 20 October for the journey down to Spain.

Gradually the police were able to piece together the Newalls' last movements. On the morning of Friday 9 October, while the boys flew over from the mainland, Nick had picked the Citroën up from the local dealer where it had been serviced. In the afternoon, between three and five o'clock, the couple visited their optician and then went home. That evening Roderick had arrived on the island at 8.30, his brother half an hour later. On Saturday morning the Newalls had spent a couple of hours at the Crow's Nest visiting the Ellams, and then Nick had helped Mark shift some of his belongings from the flat in St John, where he'd been staying, to the new house. The brothers had already been in the bungalow on Saturday but had gone back to Mark's house at 3 p.m. to change.

Roderick arrived at the bungalow at eight o'clock; Mark turned up about thirty minutes later. A bottle of champagne was already chilling and Roderick and his parents – Mark was driving – drank it before going on to the Sea Crest. At the restaurant they ate lobster thermidor and drank several bottles of wine. During the meal there was an altercation. Witnesses at a nearby table remembered Elizabeth suddenly getting up and running to the toilet. Mark drove both there and back in his father's car, though he had driven the hire van to the house as his own sports car would not start. Back at the Clos de l'Atlantique they drank from an eighteen-year-old bottle of Macallan malt whisky. Roderick and Mark left at 2.30 a.m. and spent the rest of the night at Mark's house in Noirmont three miles to the east.

The next morning the brothers returned to their parents' bungalow at 8.30, had breakfast and then lunch with their parents and left at around three o'clock to catch their flights. After returning the hired van, Mark dropped Roderick at the airport then went back to his house to get some clothes and caught a later flight to Gatwick, leaving his sports car behind in the airport car park. Mark said he hadn't been able to get it on the ferry that day, so he flew back to Jersey the following Tuesday and at 8 p.m. returned to his house, where he picked up more clothes, collected his ferry ticket from his firm's offices at the Esplanade, and took the car back over to the mainland on the ferry. He had been back on Jersey for less than an hour.

Angela Barnes went into No. 9 Clos de l'Atlantique on 26 October, but was unable to tell the detectives anything. Bob and Anne Blayney had also wracked their brains to come up with an explanation for their friends' disappearance; all Bob could come up with was money. Nick was always going on about the precarious state of his finances and had mentioned problems with his Lloyd's syndicates. Bob thought it very possible that he had been in much deeper trouble than he had admitted and that the couple may have found it necessary to 'disappear' for a while. But whatever it was, it would have to be something very serious for such drastic action. One afternoon Mark Newall had phoned Bob Blayney and had mentioned that he was having the Newalls' credit cards cancelled. 'Oh, don't do that,' said Bob. 'They might need them.' It had seemed a rather premature and unnecessary thing to do, especially if the Newalls had merely gone off for a short break. But there were a number of things about the boys that didn't add up.

There was still no real sense of emergency. Roderick particularly behaved in a distracted and puzzling manner, but the Blayneys had no impression of panic or any of the emotional turmoil or despair that Bob imagined would overtake him if, God forbid, his wife or one of his sons ever went missing.

'Come on, Roderick, we've got to organize a search,' he urged some days after the disappearance when Roderick turned up at the farmhouse. The two men were standing in front of the fireplace in the sitting room. Bob asked if Roderick had been in touch with his parents' GP to see if they may have been suffering from any hidden illnesses.

'No, I hadn't thought of that,' replied Roderick. Bob was surprised. It seemed an obvious thing to do. It struck him that the boy was showing a tremendous lack of initiative for an army officer. He didn't seem to know what to do next; he seemed naive. And at that moment Bob was struck by another thought: Roderick was almost being too naive. From that moment something began to stir in the back of Bob's mind. 'This just does not add up,' he said to his wife later.

The police had been told that the Newalls were keen hilltop walkers. Nick Newall in particular was a frequent sight striding along first thing in the morning with his pipe clenched between his teeth. In the past he had thought nothing of setting off from the Crow's Nest along the clifftops, down to the deep ravine to the east known as the Devil's Hole near the Blayneys' farmhouse, before returning – a round trip of six miles. An incident room had been set up at police headquarters and as each day passed more and more officers were drafted in to help. Search parties were scouring huge tracts of the island – from the sand dunes of St Ouen to the hidden rocks and coves of the Corbière peninsula. A sixty-man team using helicopters and inshore boats scoured the coves, bays and rocky inlets that dotted the coastline and the miles of winding cliff paths near the bungalow.

It was obvious there was nothing the rest of the family could do for the moment. On 27 October Nan and Alaster, together with Roderick and his grandmother, returned by ferry to Weymouth. Roderick returned to the regimental depot in Winchester, the Clarks and Mrs Nelson to London. They all promised to keep in touch daily about developments. By 29 October, when Nan and Alaster travelled back to Jersey with Roderick to check on the progress of the investigation, there were sixty officers working on the case full time – a huge deployment of resources for such a small force.

In November, the Clarks flew back to Spain and, after meeting Adamson and Nimmo, they made their way to the modest villa that had been Nick and Elizabeth's principal home in later years. The town of Javea, fifteen miles north of Benidorm, has become a fashionable retirement resort amongst North Europeans seeking to flee the bleak northern winter. Of the 12,000 population, 4000 are British; there are also sizeable German and French communities. It is quiet and peaceful and the expatriates tend to mix only with their own nationality. It is a world apart from the tourist hotspot of Benidorm just down the coast.

The Newalls had made many good friends in Javea. Joan and Alex Riches had lived there since the sixties, when Alex retired from his job as a director with Lipton's, the tea firm. They had been sailing companions and bridge partners to the Newalls for years. The first that Joan knew of the Newalls' disappearance was when she got a call from a mutual friend – Mrs Jane Matthews – in late October. The police in Jersey had already asked Jane if she could shed any light.

'You mean they must have fallen off a cliff or something?' said Joan.

'Er . . . no. It's not like that.'

Together the two women had gone to the villa and searched around to see if any of Elizabeth's clothing was still there. On the kitchen table they found a note in Elizabeth's handwriting: 'Must remember to remind R. to take the van over.' Since the visits by the Jersey detectives at the end of October they had heard no more.

On this trip to Javea, one of the police's main concerns was that they still had not found the couple's passports. After a fruitless search of the villa, Alaster and Nan stayed to have lunch with Jeff and Jane Matthews. They then tidied up the house and arranged for it to be looked after and for the pool to be kept clean. Nan emptied out the wardrobes and cupboards. Over dinner, again with the Matthews, they tried to come up with an explanation by sorting out the pieces of the jigsaw – the unlocked house; the previous night's celebration; the overridden timeswitch and the thermostat set at maximum. It didn't make sense.

A small speck of horror in the midst of the middle-class clutter in the sitting room was the first clue to the terrible things that had happened in the Newalls' bungalow. It had been spotted by Nan Clark and the detectives on the stem of the poker on that day at the outset of the inquiry. Despite the frenzied efforts to clean the house, the real story of what happened was still waiting to be found on the walls, on the ceiling, and on the pictures and ornaments in the sitting room and in the bedroom. But all this wealth of evidence was to be missed completely. It was the biggest bungle of the investigation. Any missing person investigation is potentially a murder inquiry, and in any murder the scene of the crime becomes a shrine to be preserved and protected, for later reference.

The tragedy of the Newall inquiry was that from the outset the scene of the crime was not treated with the respect it deserved. The scene of crime team, who were initially charged with looking after the bungalow, for teasing and winkling out any clues, completely failed to notice the dozens of minute blood droplets that had been sprayed from floor to ceiling and had eluded the cleaner's efforts. At this crucial stage of the inquiry, the essential momentum and direction were lost, and the investigation quickly faltered. Without any evidence to prove otherwise, the case remained essentially a missing persons inquiry. The detectives had no facts to guide them – only vague hints and clues from the family and friends of the Newalls.

The official line of the inquiry may have been 'missing persons' but bit by bit, as the door-to-door searches continued, as more and more people were interviewed, a more sinister scenario emerged. There was the old lady who lived in Noirmont Lane. She said she saw two young men passing parcels between a van and a car outside Mark Newall's house at a time when he said they were asleep. And someone else further along the lane had received a visit from a young man who had asked if she knew of anywhere they could burn rubbish. It was an odd request.

From the outset Angela Barnes never had any doubts. She had witnessed at first hand the family bitterness and loathing. All she could think was that she was not in the least bit surprised. For Maureen Ellam the first lurking suspicion had emerged within twelve hours of Roderick's return; within twenty-four it had hardened into certainty. Bob and Anne Blayney had also soon worked out that nothing was right with the boys' story. The only question was not who, but why? In private the Newalls' friends began to talk about the couple: the history of hatred in the family, the squabbles over money; the recent violence – and it all seemed to point in one direction. Yet outside this close-knit circle their suspicions went unvoiced. It was as if the enormity of what had happened was too great for any of them to grasp; as if a blanket of middle-class discretion had settled over the whole affair. It was no ordinary crime. If guilty, the brothers had carried out a moral transgression of such magnitude it apparently also defeated the imagination of those charged with investigating it.

On 29 October Chief Inspector Martyn Le Brocq was still able to say publicly that 'We are not sure whether we are investigating a crime or not.' And Maureen Ellam, one of the few people to speak to the police of their suspicions, was furious when one very senior policeman sat in the lounge of the Crow's Nest and said with a laugh, 'Surely you don't believe those two brothers murdered their parents, do you, Mrs Ellam?'

As the days passed, speculation about what happened to the couple became the chief item of fare on an island with a voracious appetite for gossip and scandal. There was talk of financial frauds, sexual intrigue, and drugs. Nick and Elizabeth's faces stared out from hundreds of posters all over the island. Television and radio coverage was unrelenting.

The search was still inching its way across the island through the gorse and bracken, but Nimmo and Adamson were getting their first glimpses of the hatred that existed within the Newall family, and their attention was beginning to move from the search to the brothers themselves. Slowly, as they uncovered the details of the Newalls' lives, the two detectives began to eliminate the possibilities. Years before, the Newalls' boat *September Tide* had been sold to a Dutchman who turned out to be involved in drug-smuggling. Then there was the disastrous New Mexico land deal in which they'd lost so much money. But as all the leads dried up, one possibility began to emerge and totally overshadow everything else.

In late October Adamson and Nimmo drove along the road that skirts the shoreline of the Firth of Clyde west of Helensburgh and turned off onto a private road just before the small village of Rhu. The road led up a steep brae to an imposing grey house set in acres of grounds with a commanding view of the Firth of Clyde. Rowalleyn had once been the home of Madeleine Smith, the beautiful daughter of a eminent Glasgow businessman. More than a century ago she had been tried and acquitted of murdering her lover – and strangely enough he was a Frenchman who came from the island of Jersey. It was a lurid tale of sexual impropriety, betrayal, explosive letters and poison, set against the background of nineteenth-century mores, but it caught the public imagination for years to come and eventually spawned a Hollywood film. It was a story that seemed perfectly in tune with the imposing stone walls of the house. For many years Rowalleyn has belonged to the Craig steel dynasty. It became Stephen and Gay Newall's home when they left London to move back to Scotland in the late seventies.

As they cradled their glasses of whisky in the large living room, Nimmo and Adamson could see that what they were suggesting was deeply upsetting to Stephen Newall. The idea that his own twin brother could have been done to death by his nephews produced profound inner conflicts.

'I can see what you are getting at, I know what you are saying,' he explained. 'But you must understand, they are my flesh and blood. I owe it to them and Nick and Elizabeth to keep an open mind on this.'

Over the next few days at Rowalleyn Nimmo and Adamson travelled back into the family history. There were obviously tensions – all families have tensions – but, according to Stephen, there was never anything to indicate that this could happen. However, he said he would do what he could. On the subject of the brothers' relationship with their father, he thought it was Mark who had more problems; Roderick had always been a kind of 'golden boy'.

The two detectives moved from relative to relative and, though all told the same story, they did make one discovery that threatened to complicate matters. In North Berwick Mrs Sarah Nelson, Elizabeth Newall's mother, began to maintain she had spoken to her daughter on the telephone on Sunday 11 October. If true, this almost certainly ruled out the boys' involvement in their parents' disappearance. Or could the seventy-nine-year-old grandmother have been mistaken?

CHAPTER 6

Most disappearances are characterized by tearful appeals by relatives for information, but as the days went by the wall of silence from the Newalls' family was driving reporters to distraction. The sole response was 'No comment'. It was almost as if the shame of the whole business overwhelmed the need to find out what happened. At the end of October Guy de Faye, a newsreader with Channel Television, got a call from a friend saying that Mark Newall had a problem he wanted to discuss over lunch. Guy was intrigued. He had met Mark a few times on the periphery of the island's fast young social set. Mark hadn't made much of an impression; Guy remembered a rather dour, buttoned-up individual who had little small-talk. He didn't have much to say for himself until he got onto the subject of his job; then his conversation really took off. Guy had been impressed with the sums of money he said he was moving around. Mark had also boasted about how he had organized the sale of his parents' house and how he handled their finances. And there was another curious remark: Mark said that at Christmas his parents had given his brother a Fair Isle sweater, while he had received nothing. 'I run their show and get no gratitude for it,' he had said resentfully.

Guy did remember one other encounter very vividly. Every Friday night Mark kept a table at Victoria's restaurant in the Grand Hotel, probably the best on the island. Friends and colleagues from the bank would be there. One night Guy tagged along and remembered sitting with a group of braying yuppie types and their sloany girlfriends. They were all behaving badly and making a tremendous noise, eating and drinking away. Mark seemed a rather distant, quiet figure at the end of the table, occasionally sipping his glass of orange juice. At the end of the night when the bill came Mark paid for everyone, and Guy remembered thinking how sad it was that the bloke had to buy his friends in this way.

At lunch Mark seemed unchanged; he was neat, tidy and self-contained. He came straight to the point. He was being relentlessly pursued by the media and didn't know how to handle them. What should he do?

Essentially, said Guy, he had two options – one was to pull up the drawbridge and tell them to mind their own business. On the other hand, he could completely open up and be totally up front with them. Maybe he should also think about launching an appeal to find his parents.

Mark thought for a moment, then said, 'I think maybe I should give an interview.'

Most murders are domestic and most are solved within minutes and ninety per cent of the time the identity of the murderer is obvious. But this one had all the ingredients of a classic mystery and, after twenty-two years in Fleet Street, Gerry Kemp, a senior reporter with the *Sunday Express*, knew a winner when he saw one: the mystery disappearance of the well-off couple; the deserted house on the holiday island; the dark cloud of suspicion hanging over the two good-looking sons who stood to inherit: it had all the makings of a great story. The day he flew into the island Kemp met Superintendent Martyn Le Brocq and Inspector Graham Nimmo at the Sea Crest for a late lunch. The officers were keeping their cards close to their chests, but insisted there were three options: one – that the couple had absconded; two – that they had been kidnapped; or three – that they had been murdered. They were keeping an open mind, they said, on all the possibilities and did not favour one or the other.

Kemp had already spoken to Nan Clark, making repeated requests for an interview. 'Look, the family have got to say something,' he remonstrated. But she had declined. Eventually Mark agreed to an interview. It took place over coffee and biscuits in the lounge of the Hôtel France in St Helier on 1 November, three weeks after the disappearance. From the moment he met Mark, Gerry was struck by the young man's formal manner and almost condescending tone. He felt he was being patronized, and it rankled slightly. They went through the bare outlines of the story again:

'When did you last see your parents?'

'On Sunday, about three in the afternoon. Maybe a bit earlier. They were wearing casual clothes. Roderick and I then went back to my place. The evening before my father and mother were drinking eighteen-year-old malt whisky. I was driving and I do not drink. The rest had a bottle of champagne at the bungalow and they had wine with the meal.'

'What did you have for lunch on the Sunday?' asked Gerry.

Mark hesitated. 'I can't clearly remember. It was, I think, parma ham or scampi.'

Strange, thought Gerry. Surey the details of the last meal you ever shared with your parents would be indelibly stamped on your memory.

'My father was wearing a dark-blue suit but I can't remember what my mother was wearing, though I think it was a two-piece suit. The blue suit is missing but there is more than one outfit missing from my mother's wardrobe.' His parents, said Mark, had no financial worries of any kind and were devoted to each other. His mother, especially, was very close to her family.

'What did you talk about that Sunday morning?'

'Oh, general talk – which opticians they had been using.'

'What about the Ellams?'

'I don't know the Ellams,' said Mark – rather too sharply, thought Gerry. 'I wouldn't class Maureen and David as friends of mine; they were more friends of my parents.' That his parents were around after the Sunday was definite, said Mark. He claimed they had been seen on the Monday and besides, his grandmother in Scotland had spoken to them that day as well.

'Where did you go the next day?'

Mark then briefly ran through the same account he had given to the police. The interview went smoothly. Mark thought before he spoke and it was only when Gerry asked him a question towards the end that Mark became flustered: 'You are very interested in martial arts, aren't you, Mark?'

The boy hesitated and stared back. 'I don't know what you mean?'

'Well, you've got a book on martial arts.'

'I don't have any books on martial arts . . . '. He shifted uncomfortably in his seat.

'But the police have got one of your martial arts books. It was found in the house. I saw it at the station.'

Mark stared at Gerry silently for a moment. 'I have about ten books on unarmed combat. It is a subject which interests me . . . I can't do much sport since I had a knee injury. I do some fitness training.' There was an awkward pause. Gerry was puzzled by Mark's barefaced U-turn.

'Did your parents have any enemies?'

'No, not as far as I know.'

'What about Spain?'

Mark hesitated slightly. 'I know very little of their life in Spain, but if there had been a problem I would have been the first to know about it. The police have not suggested to me that I might know what happened to them.'

'What do you think happened to them, Mark?'

'Well, if you look at the available facts none of them fit any one scenario. They do not fit any of the theories of accident, kidnap or murder. Any explanation I have heard does not fit the facts. The answer has to be something completely illogical.'

'How do you think it will work out?'

'Well, people don't just disappear and walk in through the door three weeks later . . . If we are to look at it realistically the chances of them being alive are slim.'

The boy was calm but as the interview progressed Gerry noticed Mark's knuckles getting whiter and whiter as he tightened his grip on his car keys.

Subtly, gently, Gerry decided to apply some pressure while all the time giving the appearance the interview was over. It just might shake the boy up a bit. 'I can't really understand it, Mark,' he said, pulling on his coat. 'If it was my parents I'd be having nightly appeals, offering rewards and organizing searches.' He was heading for the door but suddenly stopped and turned.

'But you do know what has happened to them, don't you?'

Mark hesitated again. 'If someone intimates that I have some knowledge of what happened to them because I was the last one to see them . . . ' He paused and began again: 'Well, that's not a line of conversation I would like to pursue.'

As they made their way to the hotel foyer Mark turned to shake hands with Gerry. 'I am awaiting your story with a great deal of trepidation, Mr Kemp,' he said. 'The last thing I want at the moment is sensationalism. I'm only hoping that what you write will be a credit to your profession. I don't think what happened in Jersey . . . I want to keep my personal exposure to a minimum over this.'

What a strange boy, thought Gerry as the white Toyota drove out through the hotel gateway. But he had no doubt. He's done it all right.

Before Gerry arrived at the Crow's Nest to meet the Ellams, Maureen and David had a thorough discussion about how they were going to handle the interview. One thing they must not do, they decided, was voice their suspicions about the boys. No matter how definite their views, they felt it was just not their place to make accusations. So when Gerry struggled in through the door, took off his raincoat, sat down and said, 'I've just talked to a boy who has topped his parents,' they just looked at each other and burst into relieved laughter. It was finally out in the open – Gerry Kemp had openly voiced what they had thought all along.

When Maureen mentioned dropping off the flowers on the Sunday morning Gerry was amazed to discover that since Maureen's first brief visit to the police station they had not been asked to give a full statement. 'They have never been near us,' said Maureen. 'Strange, considering we were such good friends and had been involved in a financial transaction with them.'

'It's more than strange, it's almost negligent,' Gerry commented.

In late November a group of the Newalls' closest friends on Jesey gathered in the Blayney's farmhouse at La Mare vineyard. Detective Inspector Graham Nimmo wanted a confidential chat about the case to see if together they could come up with anything to help the inquiry. Present were Angela Barnes, Maureen and David Ellam and Michael and Ann Munx-Jones. Briefly Nimmo outlined some of the police's findings: that the bungalow's central heating had been left set to maximum, and that the time-switch had been over-ridden so that it was on all day. 'It is my belief that this was done to dry out the house after an extensive clean-ing of the house had taken place,' he revealed. 'I'm going to come out in the open here,' he said, glancing from face to face. 'We are working on the principle that the boys were involved in some way in their parents' disappearances.'

Nimmo was unsure how they would react to this. He thought it entirely possible that there would be anger and indignation at such a suggestion but, as he paused for a second to let his words sink in, he looked round and caught the eye of Bob Blayney, who was nodding in agreement and said, 'I think you're right, you know.'

Then Michael Munx-Jones thought for a moment and he too began to speak. 'Yes, thinking it through, I have to say it is quite possible.'

Slowly and hesitantly each person in the room voiced agreement and then all of a sudden everyone was talk-ing at once. It was as if a spell had been broken. 'I have no difficulty in believing those boys have murdered their parents,' said Angela. They all agreed that it had to be Mark – so buttoned up, so strange and difficult – who had done it; his brother would be covering up for him. The group began to ask questions. How had they done it? Why had they done it? Which brother had taken the lead? And, most important of all, where were the bodies?

'Have you tried searching up around the Crow's Nest?' Bob Blayney asked Nimmo, and expressed surprise when he was told that they had not. It was about the first place the police should have looked, he thought. 'Because of that wooded slope, those trees and gulleys – you could hide anything up there. The boys were always digging tunnels when they were little. What you should be looking for is a kind of lair or a burrow.'

'You mean like a den?' said Nimmo.

'Exactly,' said Bob. 'Something like a den.'

The friends were in no doubt that if the boys had murdered their parents they would have to pay the price – all except for one dissenting voice which emerged as they talked. Maureen Ellam was defensive and almost protective of the brothers. She conceded that they knew a lot more than they were saying, but she spoke as if there could be a justification for what they had done; as if the Newalls themselves were in some way responsible for what had happened. It was a theory she would come to believe in more and more as time passed – to the considerable anger of the Newalls' other friends who had known them a lot longer than she had.

Maureen was concerned about Roderick, who began to display the reckless bravado that had been such a feature of his school and army life. He would tear around the island's narrow roads, deliberately ignoring the forty m.p.h. speed limit and the police cars who were tailing him.

As the autumn drew on, a wax-jacketed figure could often be seen striding along the pathways that criss-crossed the gorse- and bracken-covered slopes of the Grève de Lecq. Rod would return time and again to the cliffs he had known so well as a child, as if drawn there. Once, when he was visiting the Crow's Nest, Maureen mentioned that she had seen him on the opposite cliffs, observing the house through his binoculars. 'What were you looking at, Roderick?' she asked.

'Oh, nothing, I was just looking at Timmy's grave,' he said, pointing to the stone marker in the back garden where the family pet was buried. But Maureen felt there was much more to it than that.

Angela Barnes also found herself in a rather difficult position. Although convinced of the boys' guilt, she was nevertheless a close family friend and had known Nick and Elizabeth since they arrived on Jersey nearly twenty years before. She was torn between anger at Roderick and Mark and protectiveness towards the boys themselves. She'd known them since they were knee-high and played with her own children. Indeed, Roderick and Mark had often been dressed in her own slightly older sons' cast-off clothes. Angela had realized they were in a sense surplus to their parents' require-ments; she had felt desperately sorry for them and had gone out of her way to be kind. So it was only natural that both brothers would gravitate to her house at Clos de Hugh.

In the weeks that followed his parents' disappearance Roderick frequently visited Mrs Barnes. Unlike Mark, he had never had a chance to make a life for himself on the island since he knew virtually no one there.

Often he would just sit and chat, enjoying Mrs Barnes's hospitality and pouring himself tumblerfuls of whisky. Sometimes he seemed quite cheerful and at ease. At other times he would sit, whisky glass in hand, and mumble to himself, 'I feel so sorry for Mark . . . so sorry for Mark.' He obviously wanted company, but Angela suspected there was an ulterior motive. Some days he would rush into her house and ask anxiously, 'What's the gossip, Mrs Barnes, what's the gossip?' He looked to her for feedback: her son Peter was a lawyer and was a co-executor of the Newall will; he would naturally hear a lot in St Helier about the progress of the police investigation.

Occasionally Roderick seemed to be in the grip of almost manic mood swings – as if he were getting a big kick out of the whole business. His eyes would sparkle with excitement and Angela wondered if he might be on drugs. She knew about his previous drug-taking because he himself had bragged to her about it in the past: one day the previous summer he had been chatting after lunch and had suddenly produced a small tablet. 'It's a new kind of hallucinogenic drug, Mrs Barnes. It's called Ecstasy. You can take it if you like,' he said.

Angela's sons Peter and William looked at each other in horror, but she just screwed up her face in disgust and handed it back to him. 'How can you, Roderick?' she said. But the boy just grinned broadly, obviously feeling very proud of himself. 'Does Mark do any drugs?' she asked him.

'No, not really, they don't agree with him, though he does do a bit of coke at the weekends,' Roderick replied cheerfully.

One day Roderick came round for lunch and Angela decided to drop a less than subtle hint. 'Tell me,

Roderick,' she said, 'do you think there could have been a third person involved?'

The boy didn't even flinch. 'Oh no,' he said, 'just one or two.'

'But it would have been terribly difficult shifting two bodies, wouldn't it? Your father was a big man and your mother was no lightweight either.'

'No, not at all.' Roderick shrugged. 'Just heave them over your shoulder and off you go,' he said, distractedly wolfing down his food.

On another occasion he was sitting in the dining room of the Clos de Hugh. Angela had become increasingly nervous about being alone with a boy whom she was sure was a double murderer, so she had asked a friend to pop round and keep an eye out. When the doorbell rang, Roderick's reaction was startling: he shot out of his chair and bolted across the room, out through the sun lounge doors and across the lawn. He'd got halfway across the grounds before Angela's shouts brought him back. Trembling, he was brought back into the house and made to sit down. Angela wondered again if he was on drugs and asked him, 'Roderick, what on earth did you do that for?'

'I thought it was the police . . . ' he said limply, and sat, shaking, in his seat. The remark went unexplained.

Mark Newall would also call in at Mrs Barnes's house. As ever, he was noticeably more controlled than Roderick and during one visit Angela decided to steer the conversation into deeper waters. She tried to clear up a few of the inconsistencies that had bothered her – especially one: the boys' explanation for taking the hired van to Clos de l'Atlantique on the Saturday evening. Mark's brand-new Toyota, they said, refused to start.

'I've never been able to understand why your car was

117

not able to start at nine in the evening but was able to start at nine in the morning,' Angela said.

Mark merely brushed aside the question with some remark about the engine being cold.

On another occasion when Mark was visiting, Angela brought up the subject of Nick's jacket. 'It had a wonderful red lining, Mark,' she said innocently. 'Do you suppose he still has it on him wherever he is?'

Mark went white but said nothing.

Before their first trip to Spain Nimmo and Adamson had forgotten to take the rather obvious step of informing the local police that they were coming. This had unfortunate consequences. While they were sight-seeing in Javea, the detectives began taking photographs of each other outside the local police station, unaware that Spain was in the grip of a terrorist alert. They found themselves being bundled into the cells on suspicion of being Basque terrorists. After much shouting they were released but it was an embarrassing episode.

They did, however, get a much clearer picture of the Newalls' complicated financial affairs: in Javea they discovered a vast quantity of documents and a personal computer on which was kept much of their financial information. In addition to their Lloyd's syndicates the couple had a far-flung portfolio of accounts in America, Switzerland, Australia, Andorra and Hong Kong. And, in addition to their own finances, they managed money offshore for some of their relatives.

Detective Sergeant Charles MacDowall was put in charge of trying to make sense of the Newalls' complicated financial transactions. MacDowall came from one of the wealthiest families on the island, and his clipped public-school accent set him apart from the rest of the

Jersey CID. He had initially turned up for work in a Porsche, but it was gently suggested to him that this was not appropriate. On his first Christmas he gobsmacked his colleagues by presenting everyone on his shift with a silk tie.

MacDowall quickly discovered that, in December 1984, the couple had illegally applied for two extra passports, saying their previous ones were missing.

By possessing two sets of passports and cleverly juggling between them, the Newalls were able to conceal which dates they had been in Jersey or Spain and thus evade the local Spanish tax. If the Newalls were resident in Spain for more than ninety days at a time they would have been liable to pay Spanish taxes and MacDowall guessed they had two sets of passports to show they had not breached the time limit.

Just over a month after the Newalls went missing, on 21 November, the family was overtaken by another tragedy. Uncle Kenneth Newall, whose gift had so delighted Nick and Elizabeth, died suddenly at his farm on the island of Sark. He had been poorly for a long time and the Newalls' disappearance had hit him hard. Earlier the police discovered that Roderick had travelled to Sark to see him only days after the disappearance. What did the old man know? On 28 October the detectives had interviewed him over a meal at a hotel in Guernsey. He was a curious and sad little figure. Jimmy Adamson felt that the old man carried a dreadful burden; that he knew something of what lay at the dark heart of the Newall family but could not bring himself to talk about it, no matter how much he wanted to.

The detectives decided to attend the funeral, which took place on Guernsey on 26 November, to see if there were any more relatives to be interviewed. The behaviour of the Newall brothers at their uncle's funeral was in sharp contrast to the attitude they had struck during the search for their parents. They seemed distraught and grief-stricken. Roderick in particular was red-eyed and subdued and, at one point as they left the church, Mark slipped his arm through his brother's and walked him outside. The sight of the two detectives caused Roderick to explode with anger and he screamed abuse at them outside the crematorium, accusing them of harassing his uncle and even of bringing on his apparent heart attack. Stephen Newall had to step in and calm things down.

The disposal of Kenneth Newall's remains was to be a source of recrimination both within the family and the police. Mark had arranged for his uncle to be cremated as soon as possible, so there was no time for a post mortem to be carried out on the body. Alaster Clark had even tried to stop the cremation taking place. Suspicion surrounded the whole affair, but went unvoiced.

Roderick's covert interest in the activities of the police search teams had been noticed by Maureen Ellam when they started to concentrate on the Grève de Lecq headland opposite the Crow's Nest. But Rod needed to know more and, dressed in his wax jacket and tartan shirt, with his binoculars around his neck, he made his way up a lonely winding track to see what they were doing. A message was passed to Nimmo that Newall wanted to speak to him, but the detective was having none of it. He wasn't going to have 'that little tow rag' thinking he was at his beck and call. 'Tell him to get lost,' said Nimmo. He turned his back on the boy standing further down the hill, and continued with the search. For a moment their eyes met over the heather and Nimmo could feel the boy's hatred, but he was determined to keep his distance and to make sure all contacts were purely official. He wanted the boys to know that he knew they had done it.

The relationship between the brothers and the police went from bad to worse. Nimmo cultivated a distant and hostile presence, but Jimmy Adamson, a more easy-going personality, played the role of the 'good cop', ferrying messages between the boys and Nimmo and talking to them informally. As far as the boys were concerned, Nimmo was Mr Nimmo, while Adamson was always Jimmy.

The treatment by the police of the prime suspects was to astonish many who looked at the case afterwards. Despite the mountain of circumstantial evidence, the boys were never detained, never cautioned, never given a hard going over. At any point they could have been pulled in, given a thorough grilling, released 'pending further inquiries', then pulled in again. In 1987 the Police and Criminal Evidence Act governing the treatment of suspects did not apply in Jersey. The detectives could have detained the boys and even denied them access to their legal representative. So their powers were very wide-ranging: Article Three of the island's police laws says that, 'Where a police officer with reasonable cause suspects that any person has committed, is committing or is about to commit, an offence, he may arrest that person.' Given the fragility of the boys' state of mind in the immediate aftermath of the crime, there is no saying what the result might have been.

Instead, something very different happened: the detectives' access to the Newall brothers was dictated entirely by their effective advocate, David Le Quesne, who had also acted for their parents, and it was he who set the terms and conditions whereby the police could speak to the brothers. It was a strange situation and it affected the whole course of the investigation.

The phrase 'tax haven' is greatly frowned on in Jersey. The locals much prefer to describe their island as an 'international finance centre'. However it is styled, a combination of light regulation, confidentiality and low taxes have proved irresistible to thousands of wealthy individuals, companies and financial institutions.

There is little evidence of this at first glance. As the ferry pulls into St Helier harbour the visitor is faced with a charming little port flanked on one side by Elizabeth Castle and, to the east, West Mount and Fort Regent. It is a pleasant but unremarkable town which, apart from the French street names, could be anywhere on the south coast of England.

But behind the sleepy winding streets hums enough financial activity to rival the City of London. Among the banks to have opened shop there in recent years are the Chase Manhattan, the Bank of Bermuda, and the Bank of India. The offshore business has been good to Jersey and in the last twenty-five years the amount kept on deposit there is thought to have grown to a a staggering £45 billion. The rows and rows of brass plaques that adorn offices and banks throughout the town are proof that, despite the rural image, financial services have long overtaken agriculture or tourism as the biggest earner.

There is no VAT, no capital gains or capital transfer tax, no death duties, no wealth tax and no gift tax. Residents pay income tax at a flat rate of twenty per cent, no matter what they are worth, and corporation tax is set at a flat rate of £300 a year. Exchange controls are non-existent, allowing for the fast movement of funds throughout the world. More than 2,000 companies are nominally based on Jersey and company laws are tailored for the kind of company that wants to have as little to do with the law as possible.

Located fourteen miles off the coast of France, Jersey is not constitutionally a part of Great Britain; nor is it even in the United Kingdom; only partially does it belong in the European Community. It is a 'bailiwick', giving nominal allegiance to the British Crown.

A turbulent history marked by repeated invasions by both the French and the English has helped to foster a sturdy and jealously guarded sense of independence amongst Jersey's native inhabitants. Not since the islanders sunk a British customs boat in the 1600s has there been any serious attempt by London to interfere and the island has been self-governing ever since. The island is nominally run by a bailiff, a deputy bailiff and the lieutenant governor, the Queen's representative, and the electorate of 80,000 votes in its own parliament consisting of senators, deputies and constables. It proclaims its freedom from party politics but, like all such communities, is deeply conservative.

This insularity is not unnatural, given Jersey's location and history, but over the years this has manifested itself as a particularly small-minded nastiness. As late as 1969 a twenty-one-year-old Portuguese worker was expelled because she was about to become an unmarried mother. Male strippers have been sent off the island and the local authorities refused to allow the Monty Python film *The Life of Brian* to be shown. Today abortion is not available on demand and a debate still rages about whether the Jersey-born offspring of Portuguese residents should be allowed the vote. Strangers to the island occasionally detect a note of smug complacency.

The relationship with the mainland has traditionally

been edgy: UK politicians grumble about the privileges and immunities accrued over the years and complain that Jersey does not pay its way. The islanders have retorted that they are totally self-sufficient and pay for all their capital projects; the only benefit the UK could bestow – defence – wasn't much good last time it was needed, during the Second World War. While unemployment reached record levels in the UK, in Jersey it is still much lower. There is no public debt and a healthy capital surplus.

On the down side, Jersey supports a rigid social division: there is literally one law for the rich and another for second- or even third-class citizens. Like South Africa's erstwhile apartheid system, the divide is rooted in the island's rigidly enforced residential qualifications. Only a few people a year, each worth an average of £10 million, are granted full residency qualifications. For the rest it's not so easy. Professional people working in the financial arena may be allowed to rent or even buy a home for a limited period of time. But once their work on the island is over, so too is their entitlement to stay. For the Portuguese, Irish and Scots itinerant workers who do so much to keep the wheels of the island's tourist industry turning it is even worse. They are not allowed to buy property and once their seasonal work is over they often have no choice but to leave.

And Jersey's financial success story has its dark side. Some of the names to have channelled funds through the island in recent years read like a roll call of international crime and fraud: Asil Nadir, Roger Clowes, Robert Maxwell, the failed BCCI bank and Colombian cocaine barons have all taken advantage of the island's lenient financial arrangements. In 1983 bars of gold bullion from the infamous Brink's Mat robbery turned up in Jersey and, in 1987, it was revealed that Ferdinand Marcos had found the Channel Islands a convenient route for the disposal of some of his wealth. The incidence of money-laundering has been over-emphasized, according to the island's financial community – who rightly point out that there is not a financial community in the world that can be immune. The fact remains that the two qualities most prized in a bank – confidentiality and respectability – are often in direct conflict. That fraudsters can use the island's financial arrangements with apparent impunity is a constant source of embarrassment but, in terms of policing, it has created a distinctly schizophrenic attitude.

Despite the image created by the popular TV series *Bergerac*, there is little violence on the island. The last celebrated crime involved the infamous 'Beast of Jersey', who terrorized the island between 1960 and 1971. Child-molester Edward Paifnel was eventually found guilty of horrific sex crimes and sentenced to life imprisonment. It was a sensational case and it showed up the shortcomings of the island's policing with problems rooted in its feudal past.

There are two sorts of police on Jersey: in addition to the ordinary full-time uniformed force based at headquarters in Rouge Bouillon, St Helier, there are a number of unpaid, volunteer 'honorary' officers based in each of the island's twelve parishes who have the right, enshrined in law, to stop a suspect. The 'Beast of Jersey' investigation was hampered by the fact that only an honorary policeman had the power to carry out a search or formally charge a suspect. The case led to a complete overhaul of police procedures.

Unlike mainland forces, the Jersey police are not overseen by any kind of police complaints authority;

they were not obliged to undergo regular Home Office inspections until 1987. Internal feuding in the States of Jersey police erupted in mid-1987, the year of the Newalls' disappearance, when three of the island's most senior detectives were placed on trial accused of fabricating evidence against a man convicted of robbery. It was a spectacular and lurid case, set against a backdrop of vicious office politics and in-fighting between a reform-minded chief officer from outside the island and an old guard of detectives. The three were acquitted but immediately resigned from the force, depriving the island, in the opinion of some Jersey politicians, of three of its most effective detectives.

The trial did nothing to dispel public disquiet about standards: it emerged that one of the cleared detectives had left the police while facing more than thirty serious charges, including blackmail and attempting to smear a senior colleague in a sex scandal. Even more sensationally, the trial revealed that another of the force's senior detectives – the head of the CID Martyn Le Brocq – had, against police regulations, altered his notebook and then lied about it in court. For the head of the CID to lie under oath in the witness box would be reprehensible in any force in the UK; for him to get away with it with only a mild reprimand was staggering. The Attorney General Philip Bailhache, had inexplicably refused to prosecute Le Brocq on the grounds that it was 'not in the public interest'. This fact alone was to have great implications in the Newall inquiry which Le Brocq was to lead.

If all this wasn't enough, only months before the Newall disappearances a murder trial had fallen apart specifically because of errors in the investigation. It was against this backdrop that the Newall investigation exploded onto the television screens and front pages.

At the time, it seemed to some serving police officers that the island's police and legal establishments were completely traumatized by the affair.

It was a cold and blustery day on Jersey on 27 November 1987, but inside the office of Detective Inspector Graham Nimmo at Rouge Bouillon temperatures were rising. 'I don't see why I should answer these questions,' snapped Mark Newall. 'I'm not cooperating any further.' The police were carrying out a long tape-recorded interview with each Newall son under caution. Nimmo desperately wanted their accounts on the record, but even setting up something as straightforward as this had been like getting blood from a stone. From the outset David Le Quesne had blocked every police move against the brothers. He had insisted that at no point must any accusations of guilt or wrongdoing whatsoever be put to Roderick and Mark. His approach had succeeded in intimidating the senior police officers to the point where they let up the pressure on the boys and even negotiated the terms of the interviews. Following the previous investigation, which had proved so disastrous, Nimmo and Adamson were taking a very softly, softly approach.

Adamson sat quietly in one corner while Nimmo went through the brothers' stories in minute detail. The results were taped on a reel-to-reel recorder by the side of Nimmo's desk. By agreement the boys had also brought their own tape recorders.

Yes, Nimmo told them, they were suspects, as were their relations and the Ellams and anyone else who had known their parents. As in all his previous contacts with the boys, his tone was polite, gentlemanly and non-accusatory. Restrained by the agreement with the boys' legal representative, Nimmo could only bite his

127

tongue as discrepancy after discrepancy came tumbling from the boys' lips.

During the interviews the brothers had cut very different figures: where Mark was cool, calm and calculating, Roderick was emotional; where Mark would become condescending, Roderick would lose his temper; and where Mark would attempt to out-psyche the detectives with his ill-concealed contempt, Roderick would go into a huff and refuse to co-operate. Mark was especially careful before answering questions. He would stop and think for a moment, considering his answer. His habit of saying 'absolutely' in answer to questions irritated Nimmo intensely, so Mark would repeat the word even more frequently. The dislike between the two was palpable, but eventually Nimmo managed to rattle him. Mark insisted he had been in bed asleep early on the Sunday morning, but Nimmo revealed that he had been spotted outside his house at 6 a.m. by a neighbour. This prompted an indignant outburst: Mark's face coloured and then he clammed up. The two sat staring at each other in stony silence for a moment, then Nimmo resumed his questioning.

Nimmo used insinuation and inflection to unsettle them, and occasionally one would get flustered and ask what the other had said. The two marathon interviews lasted seven hours each; Roderick went first. At midday the brothers indicated they wanted to have lunch together, but Nimmo was determined to stop them conferring. 'You can have lunch where you like but I'm not having you talk about the interviews,' he told them. So the boys offered to take the detectives to lunch at Mark's favourite haunt, Victoria's restaurant at the Grand Hotel. A stilted meal followed, and Mark paid. His interview ended at 1 a.m. the following morning.

Nimmo knew from past experience that no matter

how much effort is put into concocting a story there are still gaps. When he and Adamson had finished analysing the tapes they counted more than forty discrepancies in the boys' stories. They could not agree who slept where when they went back to Mark's house early in the morning of the Sunday. Their recollection of the Sunday morning conversation with their parents was widely off. They could not even agree on what they had had for Sunday lunch. When they listened to their own tapes, the boys must have realized they had made serious errors. The next day Mark phoned Nimmo to say that Roderick had been drinking before his interview, that he had made some serious errors and wanted to correct them.

Nimmo had no doubt that Roderick was the weaker of the two. The boy was highly strung and clearly very frightened, the opposite of his brother. Nimmo was sure that a good hard talking-to might snap him, but the detective's hands were bound. So not only was it never put to the boys that they might be responsible for whatever had happened to their parents; they were never even asked to explain the glaring inconsistencies in their stories. There was no doubt that they were lying, but the evidence was still circumstantial.

CHAPTER 7

Something dark and hideous had flown through Nan Clark's mind the moment her nephew Mark told her of his parents' disappearance. It was a notion she at first dismissed out of hand, but in the days that followed it would return again and again. By the time she knew all the facts it had become a fully formed conscious thought: suspicion.

Nothing about Nick and Elizabeth's disappearance seemed to make sense. They had no reason to vanish and surely bodies would have been discovered by now if they had had a mishap on the cliffs. As far as Nan could see, the only clothes that were missing were the ones they had been wearing at the restaurant, so where had they gone so formally dressed, and why were the boys so vague about their parents' clothes? Why was Roderick wearing a sweater that Elizabeth had bought for a friend in Spain?

And Nan's nephews were acting so strangely. While she was distracted with worry, they seemed vague and somehow disconnected and their odd behaviour had started before the Newalls went missing. She remembered Elizabeth's surprise at discovering that Mark, after so many years of being at daggers drawn, had visited Roderick at the barracks the previous Easter. What had prompted the sudden reconciliation?

In the past there had been so many fights: Nick's

mother had once returned from a trip to Jersey with a horrific story of a battle between Nick and Roderick during which fists had flown. And Stephen Newall, too, had in the past been concerned at the 'awful' childhood his nephews were undergoing. Elizabeth had always had a tendency to over-react and Nan remembered with amusement the time when Roderick failed to get a part in a play at Lockers Park Prep School – she had phoned the school in a flap, worried that he might be on the verge of killing himself!

But on one occasion when she phoned Nan in the mid-eighties she had just had a dreadful row with Mark. It was while he was still at school and was about a trivial matter – Nan forgot the reason. But Mark's reaction! He had stormed out of the Crow's Nest but had returned later, apparently subdued but no less angry. Then, in a quiet voice, he had threatened to kill his mother one day. Nan had tried to play it down; it was all part of growing up, she said, thinking of her sister's tendency to over-dramatize.

But Elizabeth would not be mollified. 'Oh, but he means it, I'm sure he does,' she said.

And when Angela Barnes told her of the threat Mark had uttered to his mother at her own dinner table Nan began putting things together. It was only many years later that she detected a distinctive pattern beginning to emerge. When Elizabeth had described how savagely Roderick had attacked her Nan began to think there might be some basis for her sister's concern.

Then there were the inconsistencies in her nephews' stories. They said they'd gone back to the bungalow for breakfast because they were out of milk at Mark's house, but she knew the boys didn't usually even like milk. And why so early if they'd been late the night before? And why the sudden surprise birthday dinner –

Roderick had never organized such a thing before.

For no apparent reason, in recent months Nan had received a flurry of visits from both nephews. After they left school in 1982 and 1984 Nan had seen little of Roderick and Mark. They were both apparently busy with their careers and the last time she had seen Roderick was when he became ill at Sandhurst in 1984 and came to stay with her. On these recent visits their behaviour could only be described as odd – Mark's especially. Nan got the distinct impression that he wanted her to confirm for him that he had had an unhappy childhood. It was not until much later she came to the conclusion that, psychologically, the ground was being prepared for what was to come.

On the evening of Monday 26 October Nan phoned Angela Barnes and asked her to come and see her at the Atlantic Hotel. Nan was red-eyed and clearly distraught when Angela entered her room. Her first words were, 'You know who has done this, don't you? It's those bloody boys.' Angela nodded silently in agreement.

One night over dinner at the hotel, as Nan looked at the faces of the two boys she had known since they were born, she wondered, How had they done it? In the days after the disappearance, Alaster had realized that the boys knew more than they were saying, but for Nan acceptance was to be a painful process: that her sister could have been done to death by her own flesh and blood – by the two sons to whom she had given life and love – the horror of the very idea sent her mind reeling. As the enormity of it began to sink in, Nan began desperately to think back, to look for a reason hidden somewhere in the past.

Night after sleepless night the faces of two angelic-faced little boys would smile out at her from the flickering film reel of her memory: playing on the beach in Jersey; attending parties with her own sons; on holiday in Scotland; opening Christmas presents. Only minutes after the birth in the Glasgow hospital, Nan had held the baby Roderick and passed him to his exhausted but delighted mother. And she had been there too when Mark arrived prematurely at the Newalls' farmhouse, North Dron. Nan had washed them, played with them, bounced them on her knee, dried their tears and lulled them to sleep with bedtime stories. The possibility that those same boys had turned on their parents was almost too much for her imagination too comprehend. On one level she could not, would not, believe it. On another, the suspicion had formed the moment she learned that the couple had gone missing. But what on earth could they – or anybody, for that matter – have done to deserve such a thing at the hands of their own. Had something evil lurked within those boys all along? Or had it been triggered by something outside their control?

What made things much worse, as far as Nan was concerned, was that, as time went on, it became clear that this was no spontaneous explosion of violence. For a while the Clarks thought that perhaps a drunken argument had got badly out of hand; that sickened, scared and deeply ashamed of what they had done, both boys had sought to remove the evidence and now lived in complete denial, blanking the memory from their minds altogether. Unfortunately, everything pointed to something much more terrible.

'I have absolutely no doubt it was premeditated, Mrs Clark,' said Detective Inspector Nimmo. The more they looked at the evidence, the more it made sense. How else could they have covered up the act, disposed of the bodies and cleaned up the house? And there was the van. Why was it conveniently taken to the bungalow on the night of the murder? It all pointed to a crime planned well in advance.

The police investigation had revealed a long history of hatred within the family. The teachers at Radley College had told of the boys' fights and of Roderick's detestation of his parents. From John Ridgway at the outward-bound school they learned of his vicious temper, carried on into adulthood. Many of the friends and relatives had now opened up and revealed their fears. Indeed, Nimmo was convinced that not only was it pre-planned but that the boys might even have drugged their parents beforehand. Extensive forensic examination of the bottles they had been drinking from produced nothing, but that did not mean anything. The boys had had more than enough time to wash them.

For hour after hour Nan and Alaster would discuss it. They remembered Nick and Elizabeth, carefree but loving, impetuous but happy; the two squabbling boys, healthy and attractive. Which brother, had planned it? Which one had done the deed? What had they done with the bodies? Had the parents suffered? Did they know what was happening in the last few moments or did they not feel a thing? And always they came back to the same question – why? The boys had been given a stable and privileged environment, expensive private education; their parents had ensured they were given opportunities others could only dream about. It had apparently been a gilded youth in every sense. They had grown up healthy, intelligent, able, and with the world at their feet. And there was nothing in their background to indicate they could have been capable of such a thing. Had something dark and evil been lurking in the heart of the household?

Roderick was headstrong and feisty, not shy of putting up his fists. He had had his problems at school, but then so did many boys. Mark was very different. As a little boy he had been clumsy, shy and uncommunicative and things had got worse when he reached adolescence. Nan dated it from the rugby accident he had been involved in when he was fifteen or sixteen. He injured his leg badly and from that point he had seemed to fold in on himself. He became sullen and cold – much more so than most moody teenagers. Roderick had been the macho one; Mark had turned more and more to martial arts after his rugby injury meant he could no longer play ordinary sports. The Clarks had no doubt Mark was capable. Of the two, only he had the capacity and application and the sheer ill will to put such a plan into action. As to Roderick, they were more puzzled. He was the archetypal golden boy, and he and his mother had always been on good terms.

But whatever the whys and wherefores, as time went on Nan began to suspect the boys might get away with it. Neither she nor Alaster could figure it out: officially, the senior police officers were insisting it was still a missing persons investigation, yet Nan had been to the bungalow with Adamson and Nimmo and had seen the bloodstain on the poker herself. What on earth were the police playing at?

In the months to come Nan's communications with the police were to grow strained. Superintendent Bob Le Breton always seemed too busy to see her or speak on the phone. Eventually he even stopped replying to her letters. The only inside information Nan was getting from Jersey came from Angela Barnes but there were so many rumours flying around it was not easy to figure out what was going on.

Despite her certainty of the boys' guilt, Nan

135

remained in contact with them – especially Mark. Her suspicions remained unspoken in all their future conversations. She could not forget that they were her own flesh and blood, her sister's sons, and she felt she was bound by loyalty to her sister to keep in touch with them. She was haunted by her dream foretelling the two deaths and by her sister's last apparent wish to 'let it rest'.

That Christmas a subdued family group gathered round the dining table in Clapham. Roderick and Mark had joined Nan and Alaster and their grandmother for Christmas dinner. As the turkey was carved the conversation was stilted, but the four put a good face on it for the sake of Mrs Nelson.

As time went on, while Roderick was never shy about keeping in touch with his relatives, Mark became a much more distant figure as far as the Clarks were concerned. But the following year, on 27 February, Mark phoned his aunt and tried to find out if she had any news about the forensic tests she had been asking the police about only a few days before. She was continually pressuring them for information about the inquiry. Somehow this always got back to her nephew. Later Mark came round to Liberty Mews for lunch. 'Heard anything from Jersey, Auntie Nan?' he would ask, half-distractedly, fork in hand.

'Oh, nothing so far, Mark. I don't know what's happening but I'll let you know when I do.'

Early in 1988 the Clarks returned to the house in Jersey, where they made their way to the Newalls' old home, the Crow's Nest. They had met Maureen and David Ellam only briefly in passing at the bungalow, but after only a few minutes of conversation Nan said, 'Well, at least we know you're not the guilty parties anyway.' And so the talk turned to those who were.

Nan said she thought something had happened to the boys the previous Easter when Mark visited Roderick at the barracks. Then they started to speculate: where did those boys bury their parents? Nan and Alaster had visited the police in order to go over the investigation. The detectives insisted that there could be no progress until they had found the bodies; certainly no arrests could be made.

At the foot of the cliffs of the Grève de Lecq directly across from the Crow's Nest a cave cuts through the rock deep into the cliffside. It was used by smugglers long ago and was still accessible at low tide. Alaster had a theory that the bodies could be there. 'Well, it's worth a try,' said David Ellam.

They didn't know what they were looking for, but grimly the two middle-aged couples made their way into the gaping darkness. By the time they got halfway down, Maureen had had enough and turned to retrace her steps; David and Alaster went on a bit further but drew a blank.

Not all the Newall relatives knew about the circumstances of the disappearance. Stephen Newall had deliberately tried to shield his daughter Amanda and had told her only the sketchiest details, so when she went to visit her cousin in his flat in London early in 1988 she knew nothing of the suspicions. The last time Amanda had spoken to him had been in mid-October, after Uncle Kenneth had phoned her from Sark asking if she knew where her uncle and aunt were. His voice had seemed very quiet – almost as if he were on the verge of tears. Subsequently Mark had phoned and she was puzzled by his line of questioning. 'What did Uncle Kenneth say?' he asked insistently. 'What did he tell you?'

In London Amanda saw that Mark was leading a typically city 'yuppie' existence, living only for his work. Although he was obviously not short of money, he had a real bachelor lifestyle: there were piles of unwashed laundry everywhere and he even ate his meals off paper plates. She was shocked at how gaunt and thin he looked. She got on well with her cousin and the air of premature cynicism that put so many people off him did not bother her at all. She suspected she was one of the few women he found it easy to talk to, but even from her he resisted any personal probing. Apart from work he seemed to live an empty life. She could remember only one girlfriend – a colleague at Barclays, so she asked him, 'Are you seeing anyone at the moment, Mark?'

She expected her query to be rudely sidestepped as he usually did with all personal inquiries, to her surprise, he said quietly, 'I'm not like Roderick, I don't find it easy making relationships.'

Meanwhile, far away on a mountainside in Switzerland, Roderick was living life to the full. With the snow rushing inches past his helmet at a speed of seventy m.p.h., he clutched the side of his toboggan as it barrelled down the slope. For those with a taste for danger, there is nothing quite like the Cresta: guaranteed to satisfy the most relentless thrill-seeker, the world's most famous downhill toboggan run was tailor-made for Rod Newall – after the previous three months it was just what he needed to take his mind off things.

It was January 1988 and Rod was one of the eight-strong Royal Green Jackets Cresta team who had driven from Winchester to Switzerland for a week's 'training' in St Moritz. Three quarters of a mile long, the Cresta runs from the 200-foot 'leaning tower' in

St Moritz down a steep gully, corkscrewing its way through ten corners past the village of Cresta, and finally streaking into a finish in the village of Celerina. In the best traditions of the regiment the young men worked hard and played hard, with the daylight hours spent on the slopes and the evenings devoted to serious carousing. It struck some of Rod's fellow-officers that, considering the trauma of recent events, he was not nearly as subdued or quiet as he might have been. Indeed, he seemed curiously detached and unemotional – and even more willing than usual to take risks. One day on the ski lift another officer, Lieutenant Andy Purvis, asked Rod if he had had any news about his parents. 'I'd rather not talk about it, if you don't mind,' had been the curt reply, and that was the matter closed.

When the news first broke about Rod's parents the regiment could not have been more supportive. His recruiting officer, Major Tim Hartley, had stopped him at the gate, placed a hand on his arm and offered his sympathies; his adjutant, Captain Jamie Athill, told him he could take as much time off as he wanted; his best friend, Patrick Saunders, had even taken him home to his parents' house in Basingstoke to escape the barrage of media enquiries. One night in a pub they discussed the disappearance. Newall looked devastated, according to Patrick. He later remembered his friend as appearing 'gaunt, hollow-eyed and completely at a loss as to what could have happened'.

On the evening before the team were due to return to the UK, eight figures emerged unsteadily from their chalet and lurched across the snow, each with a tin tray under his arm. The climax of the trip was a night-time toboggan run down a closed road illuminated by street lamps. Well-fuelled with alcohol and dressed in bow ties and dinner jackets, the riders sat two to a tray, the back riders locking their legs around the man in front, then snaked down the road at high speed, scattering unwary pedestrians and singing at the tops of their voices.

Although many of Newalls' fellow officers were supportive, others had growing doubts. By early 1988 rumours in the regiment about his drug-taking had been adding to the unease about him. And there had been the continuing unpredictability and the violence. Some months before the disappearances Rod Newall had been attending an exercise training camp in Brecon when his car suddenly caught fire and was gutted. At first the detectives thought this in some way could be connected to the disappearances but some in the regiment thought it might have been an act of revenge wrought by one of the many enemies Newall had made during his time in the army. Newall's conduct was deteriorating and when the very real suspicion of patricide and matricide was added to his history of insubordination and violence, the regiment found it too much to stomach. Many of his fellow officers were openly saying that he should be flung out. So when, in late February, he walked out through the gates of the depot at Winchester for the last time, a collective sigh of relief was heaved in the officers' mess. His resignation had saved them the trouble of booting him out.

On Jersey the investigation had become well and truly bogged down: the police had interviewed 300 people, taken over 200 statements, and the incident-room filing cabinets bulged with more than 700 reference cards, but they were no further forward than they had been on the day the Newalls were reported missing. But then, on 29 February, Roderick Newall caught a late-afternoon plane from Southampton to Jersey and flew into a whole load of trouble. After landing, all the passengers were asked to wait in the holding lounges at the airport passenger pier while two sniffer dogs checked the luggage. Roderick was stopped in the green 'no goods to declare' channel and asked to step aside. It was possibly the first time that sniffer dogs had been used at the airport, and possibly it was no accident that customs officers were waiting when Roderick came through; but nothing could alter the fact that he was caught with three small packages of cannabis resin and a small pair of scales.

From the moment he was arrested Roderick was co-operative and helpful. His explanation – according to his advocate, David Le Quesne – was that he had taken to smoking dope because he was 'unhappy at his personal bereavement'. Roderick told customs officers he had bought ten grams of cannabis for £7 in Amsterdam on the way back from his Swiss holiday and had also taken some into the island on a previous trip on 15 February. He was taken into custody, and in court two days later, handcuffed to another prisoner, was charged with importing cannabis and possessing scales with a view to committing an offence.

The news that Roderick had been arrested devastated Mark. He immediately phoned his Aunt Nan on 1 March from Paris and demanded to know what she was doing to help. He needed to speak to his impetuous brother urgently and tried to get a message into La Moye prison, but the authorities wouldn't pass it on. In desperation he then phoned Angela Barnes and asked her to convey a message to Rod to phone him as soon as possible. 'Oh, I don't know, Mark,' said Angela reluctantly. 'I'm not sure I want to be involved.'

'You don't understand, Mrs Barnes,' he said. 'I have complete and utter control over Roderick.' It was a startling thing to say. What Mark meant and why he said it she had no idea, but the phrase stuck in her mind. She finally agreed to pass the message on and, against her better judgement, went to visit Roderick in La Moye. Far from being cowed by his experience, Roderick was cocky and full of himself and seemed to be taking prison in his stride. It's that childish bravado again, thought Angela. Leaning back in his seat, he said, 'You know, I could get out of here easily if I wanted to – no sweat.' He later presented the same arrogant exterior to Maureen Ellam when she visited him. Once again, he boasted about his drug-taking: 'It's the second best feeling you can get.' To the anticipated question, he replied, grinning, 'Sex.' Maureen told him not to be so stupid.

Roderick was released on bail and he was told to report to the police station twice a week. The detectives were elated. At last they had something with which to 'put pressure on the little bastard'. A picture of Newall looking dishevelled and distracted after his court appearances appeared in the *Jersey Evening Post* the next day. News of the arrest set the island buzzing.

On 3 March Nan and Alaster met Mark and Roderick in David Le Quesne's offices in St Helier to discuss the administration of the Newalls' estate. Over the previous few weeks the Clarks had come to develop a deep dislike for Le Quesne. They just could not understand how the man who had represented the Newalls could, without a blush, now represent the prime suspects in their murder.

Later they called in at police headquarters to discuss the progress of the inquiry. All four were led into Nimmo's office. Slowly he drew a large handful of photographs out of an envelope and handed them round. The photographs were of large, shapeless dots, mostly in the shape of a teardrop with a tail. 'It's blood-stains,' he said. 'They were found on the walls and ceiling.' What it all meant, he continued, was that there had been two violent deaths in the bungalow. 'Now, do any of you have any explanation to offer for this?'

Nan and Alaster sat in stunned silence. Roderick and Mark stared at the pictures but Nimmo noted they didn't betray even the slightest emotion. Come on, boys, he thought. Make an effort. The least you can do is put on an act. 'Naturally, we will want blood samples from all four of you,' he said.

Nan and Alaster agreed but the brothers were furious: 'I'm not putting up with this charade any longer. This whole inquiry has been a damn disgrace. You're incompetent, all of you. Why aren't you trying to solve this, instead of bothering us?' The sheer venom in Mark Newall's voice startled Nancy and Alaster. Nan knew the boy could be nasty but she had never seen him as vicious as this. Seconds later Roderick joined in, his voice merging with Mark's in a long, angry tirade about the police's incompetent handling of the affair. Nan sensed that he was trying to intimidate the detectives; the complaints spewed out thick and fast: Why hadn't a mysterious pink Mercedes, apparently seen near the bungalow, been found? What about the couple who had defrauded their parents of thousands of pounds? Why hadn't they checked out the mysterious crash in Spain of a plane rumoured to have been on Jersey round about the time of the disappearance?

The brothers firmly refused to give blood samples and accused the police of trying to frame them. Their manner was loud and aggressive and their tone insolent and condescending. Shrewdly Nimmo realized they were trying to make him lose his temper, and he went to fetch his superior officer, Bob Le Breton. Le Breton stormed into the room in a fury, shouting that if he did not get more co-operation from the brothers he would shut down the investigation altogether. Again, the boys' reaction was astonishing. They just clammed up and would not speak to the officers.

Later Nan and Alaster broached the subject of the blood tests with Mark. 'Why on earth won't you do what they ask?' asked Alaster.

'I'm not having anything to do with them,' came the indignant reply. 'Anyway, they might find I've got AIDS and if I do, I don't want to know.'

Roderick invited his aunt and uncle back to Mark's house, where he was staying, for a cup of tea. Nan and Alaster were intrigued. They had never seen Mark's home before. La Falaise, the large white-washed house in a cul de sac, seemed a terribly large commitment for such a young man. Roderick ushered them in cheerfully and led them through the bare house to where Mark was sitting slumped in a chair looking exhausted. No effort had been made to cheer the place up; instead it felt like a students' house. During the Clarks' brief stay Roderick was his usual animated and friendly self and seemed totally unaffected by his experience; but Mark got quieter and quieter and slumped deeper and deeper into his chair. The events of the past few days seemed to have taken a tremendous psychological toll. Alaster noticed that his hands were clenched tightly, the knuckles white. When they rose to leave he did not say a word; instead he sank back into his chair without even looking at them. That evening, in the discreet and elegant surroundings of Victoria's, only Roderick turned up for dinner. 'Mark's feeling a bit under the weather at the moment,' he said airily. 'Now, what are we having?'

Later that night Alaster told Nan that Mark

reminded him of several suicidal patients he had treated in the past. 'I don't think he's long for this world,' he said. 'He obviously can't live with what he has done.'

On 4 March – two days after Roderick's release – the police went public with the new evidence confirming the existence of bloodstains in the bungalow. At a press conference the police announced for the first time that they had launched a murder inquiry. 'Determined efforts had been made to clean the scenes, thereby making examination extremely difficult,' Detective Chief Superintendent Bob Le Breton told the assembled reporters. Several items were missing, he added, including a hearth rug and some books. Detective Inspector Graham Nimmo confirmed that there now appeared to be a definite connection between the determined efforts to clean the house and the fact that the central heating was on manual override at its highest setting. Again they emphasized that they wanted to trace the clothes the couple were wearing the last time they were seen in public at the Sea Crest restaurant.

The disclosures about the bloodstains came as a revelation to the island, but were no surprise to the Newalls' close friends and relatives. They were taken aback for a different reason. 'We could have told them there were bloodstains in the house in October,' said Maureen Ellam to her husband bitterly.

One day in March Bob and Anne Blayney, together with Angela Barnes, were summoned to police headquarters at Rouge Bouillon and there the detectives handed them several large black-and-white photographs. At first they seemed to be some kind of abstract patterns. Angela and Anne stared at them curiously. 'They're bloodstains,' said Nimmo abruptly. 'Found on the walls and the ceiling in the bungalow.'

The forensic scientist from Aldermaston, David

Northcott, had carried out a thorough examination of the house at 9 Clos de l'Atlantique and had revealed the full extent of the bungling at the scene of crime. Using ultra-violet and laser technology, he had detected the minute traces of blood that were scattered around the sitting room and master bedroom and had remained there despite the efforts of the perpetrators to remove them. He was also able to reconstruct much of what had happened on the Newalls' last night. Everywhere he found the small, heart-shaped, tailed traces of blood which gave the first indication of a heavy bludgeoning: on the walls, above the fireplace, on the ceiling, on the coal scuttle and on the pictures above the fireplace. One shot, taken underneath the wash basin in the bathroom, showed long streaks of blood that had remained – presumably after bloodstained clothes had been washed there. Anne Blayney stared with a kind of fascinated horror as the clearest possible evidence of what had happened to the Newalls was placed before her. As the photographs were handed round, she realized uncomfortably that Nimmo and Le Breton were looking at them and gauging their reactions with a kind of hungry intensity. It was an eerie moment. She knew they were just doing their job and that technically they could not afford to rule anyone out as a suspect, but it was an uncomfortable moment and thinking about it made her shiver for a long time afterwards.

As well as the bloodstains in the house, Northcott also found two tiny bloodstains in the back of the red Renault van which Nick Newall had hired for Mark to move belongings from his old flat to his new house. Could the car have been used to ferry the bodies to their graves?

The forensic evidence put new impetus into the

inquiry and trained 'sniffer dogs' were flown to the island to take part in the search. Butch the Alsatian and Winston the black Labrador had made their last public appearances in Lancashire a year earlier, when they had scoured the bleak hillside of Saddleworth Moor for the child victims of Moors Murderers Myra Hindley and Ian Brady. But, by any standards, their task on Jersey was a formidable one. The long line of searchers had combed the bracken-and-tree-covered slopes near the Grève de Lecq headland, where the Newall brothers had spent much of their childhood. The big break came on 8 March. La Vallette is a popular picnic site with fine views, and it was here, in some grass and bracken next to a parking area only a few hundred yards from the Crow's Nest, that the dogs found the first solid evidence of the fate of Nicholas and Elizabeth Newall after they left their bungalow. Dog handler Sergeant Philip Kirkham was guiding Winston along a stone wall that led up a steep part of the headland. Suddenly the dog burrowed into a piece of bracken and emerged holding something black and misshapen in its mouth: it was a black leather handbag – partially scorched but still recognizable. Inside were various personal effects, including a one-pound coin. Alongside the handbag there was a blue lipstick-holder a small compact, and a Schaeffer pen which, the police discovered, had been given to Elizabeth by a family friend in Belgium the previous May. Nearby was the remains of a small fire. The top of a perfume bottle was found further down the track and, lying amongst the daffodils, was the stemless head of a pipe and the lenses from a pair of spectacles. There was also a singed cookery book, given to Elizabeth by her mother-in-law, and the remains of two shoes, together with some unidentified pieces of material. Ten yards away, in amongst another clump of daffodils, was the remains of a smaller blaze and here the police found a Bissell carpet sweeper and some pieces of J-cloth. Some distance from the fire was discovered an unidentified metal object. It was an iron bar with four metal links attached to it.

The area was taped off and the precise location kept a secret. Nan Clark and Stephen Newall were able to confirm that some of the items belonged to Nick and Elizabeth. It was clear that they had been dumped long after the Newalls had left the Grève de Lecq. Forensic examination of the items by David Northcott at Aldermaston proved beyond any doubt that the items had come from 9 Clos de l'Atlantique and, moreover, that a frantic clean-up operation had taken place there. Tufts of fibre from the sweeper showed them to be of similar composition to the carpet in the sitting room where Nicholas Newall's bloodstains were found. Other fibres matched up with those from the fawn carpet in the master bedroom where Elizabeth's blood had been found. Fragments of a J-cloth found in the fire were identical to pieces Northcott had detected in the house.

The discovery overjoyed Nimmo and Adamson and they felt that progress was being made at last. The bonfire helped explain one curious witness statement obtained at the outset of the investigation: Maureen Bickerton, a neighbour of Mark Newall's in Noirmont, said that at about 2 p.m. on Sunday 11 October 1987 a young man had asked if she knew where he could burn rubbish. She wasn't sure about his appearance, but the request had stuck in her mind. The pound coin helped to explain another anomaly – the small pile of coins on the onyx table in the Newalls' front room. They were still rare on the island in 1987 and Nimmo thought they had probably been brought back by the couple after their mainland shopping spree. He suspected that after the murder Elizabeth's handbag had been upended and the coins had dropped out – all except one.

The fact that the bonfire was so close to the Crow's Nest only reinforced Nimmo's belief that the bodies had been buried somewhere nearby, and on Friday 11 March, searchers and police dogs continued to comb the north coast near the bonfire site. They concentrated particularly on a dense thicket below the bonfire. The dogs were taken further up the valley to search a wooded area 200 yards from the Moulin de Lecq pub on the north-east side near a small brook, but found nothing.

Through the large living-room window of the Crow's Nest Maureen Ellam could see the long line of policemen in their blue search overalls, making their way slowly up the brown slopes of the east coast of the Grève de Lecq. It was the uncertainty that was getting her down. As her mind struggled and failed to comprehend what had happened in the Newall family, the disappearance of the bodies was an added and cruel twist. In a coded appeal in a local evening newspaper she appealed to Roderick to reveal where the bodies had been buried:

> The thought of who might have murdered them is of much less importance to me than the absolute necessity of finding their bodies and laying them to rest in the decent manner which society demands. People might find it difficult to believe, but the identity of those responsible and the reason why such a terrible thing was done is secondary in my mind at the moment. All I want is for them to be found and given a decent funeral.

But there was no response.

Meanwhile Roderick was living at Mark's house in Noirmont. Unlike his brother, he seemed totally unperturbed by the recent painful turn of events. On 11 March he appeared in the St Helier police court and pleaded guilty to three charges of importing cannabis, being in possession and also having a set of scales in order to commit a crime. Most people would have taken the hint after that first brush with the law, but not Roderick. Casual sex and soft drugs were too much of a way of life for him to give up. Two weeks after being fined in court Roderick was sitting cross-legged on the living-room floor at La Falaise rolling another joint. He'd been given it by a young Irish girl who was also staying there. She had fallen for Roderick and when he asked her to get some dope off a friend she readily agreed. He had just lit the cigarette when the door opened and the police walked in. 'Oh shit,' he said, looking up into the grinning faces of the two detectives. It wasn't the first time that sex and drugs had led Roderick Newall into trouble, and it would not be the last.

The following day Nan Clark had a phone call from Mark. 'Aunt Nan, you've got to do something to help Roderick,' he implored her. He had just checked into Inverlochy Castle Hotel in the Highlands near Fort William; it is one of Scotland's best hotels with extensive facilities for shooting, fishing and riding. Mark had been looking forward to a break after the strains of the previous few days when he was rudely interrupted: Roderick had been re-arrested.

'What are you going to do?' he asked Nan, and his voice was panic-stricken. It was almost the first time Nan had heard him lose control. He had been infuriated to discover that the police were going to use his brother's arrest as an excuse to search his house, La Falaise.

The police confirmed to Nan that Roderick had been found with a small quantity of soft drugs hidden in an aerosol. She phoned the prison doctor, who said he was in good health. The next day she alerted David Le Quesne and then talked the whole business through with Angela Barnes.

Again Nan returned to Jersey, and again she visited her nephew. His second spell in prison had left him noticeably more subdued. He now seemed to be taking the whole matter much more seriously. But he was also deeply angry and, gripped by a strong persecution complex, he responded in typically headstrong fashion – by going on hunger strike and refusing to eat for four days over the Easter holiday weekend.

In court on 7 April the prison officers allowed Nan to sit in the waiting room with her anxious nephew who, to her relief, had called off his hunger strike. Le Quesne argued that Newall should be allowed to return to the UK: 'dwelling on the family tragedy' alone in his brother's house was not healthy. He had taken to drug use, said the advocate, 'of late' to escape the sadness resulting in the disappearance of his parents. Newall was under intense pressure from the media and was being subjected to 'constant police pressure for various reasons'. Le Quesne was exasperated by his client's stupidity, but angered by the police, who he felt were harassing Roderick. Roderick was flung back in jail but released two days later with another stiff fine.

Nan stayed at Angela Barnes's house and the two women went through the background to the case. They discussed the Newalls and their financial problems; then they discussed the boys. 'You know,' said Nan in a distant voice, 'they were such lovely little boys. I still cannot take it in.'

'For God's sake, Nancy,' said Angela briskly, re-filling her whisky glass, 'can't you see it's obvious those boys have done it? It's as clear as the nose on your face.'

The day after Roderick's second court appearance, Nan flew back to London. She later came to ask herself how deeply involved Roderick had been with drugs. The question echoed round her mind. He had been charged with possessing only small amounts of cannabis but it had been found in an aerosol container with a false compartment designed so that it would always weigh the same as the real thing. It was not just the paraphernalia of a casual cannabis smoker, the police later told her: it was the sort of thing used by a serious drug-trafficker.

On hearing this, Nan thought back. When Roderick started taking an interest in drugs she, like many adults, had thought it was just a phase he was going through in his mid-teens. When she learned it had persisted throughout his army years she was surprised. Then she remembered that Roderick had always seemed to be dashing around Europe; even his mother did not always know whether he was in Switzerland or Holland or Belgium or West Germany. Nan wondered when he got time to carry out his army duties and how such a financially constrained young man could afford it. Could it be that her nephew was much more involved in the world of drugs than she had ever suspected? The morality of it wouldn't have bothered him, and the fear of being caught might even have provided a kick. Laundering the proceeds would not have been a problem: Mark could have provided the financial expertise. Was this the bond that had drawn the boys together?

And then Nan remembered something even more disturbing: Nick and Elizabeth's missing seven days. Before embarking on their last trip from Spain to Jersey in August 1987 – just before they visited the mainland – Elizabeth had phoned Nan at Casa Fidra and told her they would visit the Clarks before leaving for Jersey. Then there was another call announcing a last-minute change of plan. Elizabeth said they were going straight to Jersey because they were in a hurry and would come over and visit the Clarks at their London home straight afterwards. Nan had expected a delay of only a couple of days, but it wasn't until a full week later that Nick and Elizabeth eventually turned up at the Clarks' flat. Nan had later pressed the police to investigate the matter, but they had drawn a blank.

It was just not like the Newalls, and Nan had waited for her sister to launch into an animated account of the dramas they had encountered en route. But instead, she was curiously subdued and just mumbled something about avoiding the returning French holiday traffic on the main roads. Nan anticipated the usual lengthy description of the places they'd visited and the food they had eaten, but none was forthcoming. Elizabeth was never usually so cagey.

When the police finally traced the Newalls' movements through their credit card payments they discovered that, far from taking to French back roads for those few days, they had travelled to Switzerland, then through Holland and Belgium, across northern France to St Malo, and by ferry to Jersey. It was a bizarre journey and Nan could make no sense of it. The Newalls had no friends or relatives in those countries; the only connection with Switzerland was their bank account there, but they didn't have to *go* there.

As the Clarks tried to come up with an explanation they found more and more pieces that just did not fit. If Roderick was seriously involved in drug-running, then why the problem over his mess bills? Could Nick and Elizabeth have been unwittingly inveigled by their sons into abetting them? It was a terrible thought.

Thinking back Nan also remembered curious events from the last time she saw her sister. Elizabeth had gone on a shopping spree and, to Nan's astonishment, had bought six handbags and seven pairs of matching shoes!

Then there was the curious business about Roderick's career. Elizabeth had been very worried about it and, on 5 October, while she was staying with Nan in Clapham, she had spent a whole evening on the phone to Winchester trying to get hold of Roderick at the regimental depot. Both she and Nick had been particularly on edge that evening, putting away a large quantity of whisky. Eventually she got through to Roderick and after a brief chat had replaced the phone in a very crestfallen mood. Roderick had failed to get an instructor's job he had applied for. The news cast the couple into a deep gloom that struck Nan as disproportionate. She wondered why they were so despondent.

Then Nan discovered that when Roderick was arrested on Jersey his court appearances had been held up to allow time for him to be interviewed by the army's Special Investigation Branch. What was that all about? To all enquiries she got a firm brush-off, which only increased her suspicions

Nick and Elizabeth had always been scatty about their financial affairs, but some of the details amazed Nan. The couple had accounts not only in Hong Kong and Switzerland, but also in Madeira, Andorra and Japan. Could the two sets of passports have held more significance than they knew? Could Nick and Elizabeth have become involved in something that went badly wrong?

For hour after hour Nan and Alaster would agonize over each scenario, taking it apart and following it through; but each one led to a dead end. The more they thought it through the more they began to suspect there was much more to the whole story than met the eye.

Two days after his release, Roderick was back at his childhood home, the Crow's Nest, having a cup of coffee with Maureen Ellam. As he left and climbed into his hire car, Maureen leaned in at the window. She glanced at the outline of his face – the red hair, the blue eyes so like Elizabeth's – and said, 'Young man, you look like your mother.' He looked up but said nothing. Maureen guessed he still had drugs on him. 'I don't know how you could do this, Roderick. As if you don't have enough problems with the police. First of all, let me have a look at this stuff. I've never seen it. Come on, let's have a look.' Roderick sat still for a moment, pulled a face, then dug into his pocket and took out a small tin-foil package and unwrapped it.

Maureen stared at the small brown lump. 'Christ, fancy getting into trouble for that,' she said. 'You haven't got parents around to tell you off but you need reprimanding. You know it was bloody stupid of you to use that stuff.'

'It should be made legal, Mrs Ellam.'

'Whether it should or shouldn't isn't the point, Roderick. It isn't, and you are breaking the law.' Roderick sat back in his seat and put on his little-boy-lost expression. Maureen looked into his blue eyes. 'You really are like your mother,' she repeated softly. He blanched slightly. She went on, 'You know it's a shame you didn't get to know them better. They were bloody marvellous people.'

'I know, Mrs Ellam,' came the soft reply. 'It is a shame.' Then he put his car into gear and drove off.

CHAPTER 8

Only a few months into the inquiry, at the beginning of April 1988, it was obvious that the local CID were well out of their depth. What was needed was a fresh, more experienced pair of eyes. Detective Chief Superintendent John Saunders fitted the bill perfectly. A high-flying detective in his early forties who, despite working in what many would have thought was the rural backwater of Sussex, had earned a reputation as one of the country's top detectives. In 1987 he had headed ten murder inquiries, eventually getting a result on every one. His soft-spoken manner belied a fiercely driven nature, and in the incident room he submerged himself into the case, absorbing every statement, scrutinizing files, listening to the taped interviews, and re-examining the forensic evidence. Skilled investigation is more art than science, and what John Saunders had was the ability to examine a seemingly straightforward sequence of events through a variety of mental prisms. He also had a mind like a steel trap.

Soon he was requesting that various gaps in the investigation be closed off, that statements be checked, witnesses re-interviewed, and time-sequences tightened up. One day he looked up from a deposition and asked Jimmy Adamson why the Newalls' gardener who, apart from the sons, had been the last person to see them alive, had not been interviewed. Adamson was stunned. He didn't even know the Newalls had a gardener! And, like all good detectives, Saunders would return to the scene continually. For hours he would sit in his office replaying the police video of the interior of the house. The poor quality of the picture only heightens the sinister implications of what is being seen. The opening shot shows the sitting-room sideboard with the two three-pronged candlesticks. There are four pictures on the wall behind it, and between them the forensic scientist had placed markers to point up the position of the bloodstains that had been missed by the scene-of-crime team. The camera moves towards the back of the room: two black easy chairs, side by side, are pressed hard up against the wall. In front of the chairs is the small onyx-topped table. A wall-mounted cabinet in the corner contains some pieces of Elizabeth's Rockingham china. Hanging on the wall are two ornamental ducks. Panning around the room, the camera lens sees what the killer would have seen: the TV, standard lamps, a video case, and then alights on the main table in front of the picture window. On it there is a driving licence, a watch, some keys, a pile of one-pound coins, the couple's passports – eventually found hidden behind a bookcase weeks into the inquiry – cigarettes, matches, and a letter-opener.

Sitting in his office, Saunders tried to see the same scene through the eyes of the killer. Nick Newall may have been standing in front of the fireplace and perhaps had leaned over to refill his glass from the bottle of Macallan on the coffee table when the attacker struck. A heavy blunt weapon probably smashed into the side of his head, sending him crashing to the floor immediately. He was nearly six feet tall, and a powerfully built man of around fifteen stone, so the first blow had to be hard enough to fell him. As he lay slumped and groaning on the floor, any realization of what had happened would have only lasted a moment before he sank into unconsciousness. The life was probably battered out of him during a sustained pounding of the head and upper body with the weapon: there would have to have been at least four or five blows to complete the job successfully. As the weapon thudded down the skin would be broken only after the second or third strike. There would have been no arterial spray; instead the blood would have been spread by the action of the bludgeon as it arced through the air, and centrifugal forces acting on the weapon would have sent blood droplets flying off to land on the ceiling, the walls and the carpet. Eventually the groaning would have stopped and the killer may even have hesitated to check for a pulse. He may have been exhausted by the exertion and the shock, but the job was only half done.

The camera followed in the killer's footsteps, out of the sitting room, past the large yucca plant standing beside the front door, then down the gloomy narrow passage to the main bedroom. It was a small room with a bed, wardrobe, desk and not much else. It was not possible to say whether Elizabeth would have known what was happening to her, but almost certainly within minutes she had lain dead on the floor beside the door. The room is a total mess: clothes are strewn everywhere. The camera pans over the three-sided dressing table. On a free-standing hanger are some of Nick's shirts. In the corner is a seven-drawer cabinet and a tartan pouffe. On either side of the bed stands a bedside table complete with reading lamp. The bloodstain markers can be clearly seen at the bottom of the bedroom door near the hinge and underneath two prints on the wall to the left of the door. On the wall there are six bloodstains next to the mirror and three more higher up. There is a footprint on the bedroom door.

At that stage the killer may have been in a state of shock-induced euphoria and the frantic rush to dispose of the bodies and clean the house would have helped to block off the reality of what had occurred.

At the end of every week of the inquiry the detectives would gather to discuss their findings in a setting known as an 'Open Forum'; the idea was that every rank could speak freely and exchange ideas. During these meetings they ran through endless scenarios. Could one of the parents have attacked the other, then killed him- or herself? Could the boys, in disgust and fear, have then buried their bodies? Were both boys involved? Couldn't one have committed the murders, and the other have covered up for him? If so, which way round was it? Was it really premeditated? And did something go wrong? To be seen so publicly with their parents before the murders and then to leave the bloodstains seemed extremely haphazard? Could they have planned to do the murders elsewhere?

At the end of April Saunders handed in his report, containing the results of his review, to the Jersey Chief Officer David Parkinson. He had asked the Jersey detectives to close off various points, which they successfully did, and now he felt there was enough evidence to charge the boys.

The police put a brave face on it for public consumption. Saunders, said Chief Officer Parkinson, had been called in 'at his own officers' request'. His appointment 'did not in any way cast doubt on the ability of the investigating officers'; the same team would continue with the inquiry. But what Saunders had seen when he read the file on the Newalls' disappearance led him to make serious criticisms. The forensic examination was a farce and the scene had not been sealed off. Certainly when he interviewed Nan and Alaster Clark they got the strong impression that he thought the boys would be behind bars if this had happened in the UK.

In a press interview Saunders tiptoed around his findings diplomatically. He said that he had not uncovered any inefficiency, inadequacy or incompetence. But he had suggested new lines of inquiry. He did have his criticisms:

> These are particularly in the scientific and technological field . . . there are other suggestions as well which not only apply to this incident but to the handling of future incidents . . . there are certainly some things which I might have considered doing from the outset which were not done and which I might have done . . . (but) it's a big learning process and we all learn from each other.

Though his criticisms were sound and his presence had boosted the inquiry, it was no further forward: the case against the brothers was still largely circumstantial. In theory the police might have been able to sustain a conviction without any bodies – it had been done in the past – but it would be a very risky trial. In April Nan had again pleaded with Martyn Le Brocq for action, but was told: 'It's all hearsay and without new evidence we just can't do anything.'

One day at the end of April the Ellams received a visit from Detective Superintendent John Saunders at the Crow's Nest. He admired the superb view from the garden and was given a guided tour of the house and grounds. He said he wanted to roll around a few ideas. As they sat chatting and drinking coffee in the sitting room it became clear to Maureen that the police were no nearer solving the disappearances. Saunders sipped his coffee, put the cup down in its saucer and looked up. 'You've been seeing a lot of that boy lately, haven't you, Mrs Ellam?' he commented.

Maureen nodded. 'Well, I suppose I've virtually taken the place of his mother. He doesn't know many people on the island. I've gone on at him for this drugs business, for instance.'

Saunders stared at his coffee cup for a moment, then looked up at her again and asked, 'Do you think you could ever ask him if he did it?'

David leaned forward and said, 'I'd rather she didn't.'

Saunders continued, looking firmly at Maureen, 'Would you?'

'I could,' said Maureen, 'but I'll have to think about it.' However, her mind was already firmly made up.

The next morning at 8 a.m. she telephoned Mark's house in Noirmont where Roderick was staying and left a message on the answering machine: 'Mark or Roderick, whichever one of you is there, could you phone me as soon as possible? I need to speak to you urgently.' Her call was returned within the hour and, to Maureen's delight, it was Roderick's voice at the other end. 'I'm so glad it's you, Roderick. Could you come and see me right away?' she said to him. But he wasn't keen. He pleaded pressure of appointments. He had to see his lawyer and had not even had his breakfast yet. Maureen was not easily dissuaded: 'Come straight up here, lad. I'll make your breakfast. I'll put the kettle on.'

Within an hour the roar of a car engine in the driveway of the Crow's Nest announced his arrival. Roderick bounced into the house he had known so well as a child, wearing his brother's posh cashmere jacket and his usual big, disarming smile. The kitchen had been virtually transformed since he and Maureen first met there and he complimented her on the improvements. As she placed the coffee cups on the tray to take through to the living room, she said, 'You know, Roderick, you have never asked me what I think happened to your parents.' She lifted the tray and turned round. She thought for a moment that he hadn't heard her.

Roderick picked up another saucer, and said, 'I'll carry the biscuits.' He followed her into the sitting room, took off his cashmere coat, and dropped it carelessly onto the furry hearthside rug.

'Careful, Roderick,' said Maureen. 'Your brother will be very angry with you if you get his coat covered in hair.'

The lad looked up and flashed another of his smiles. 'Oh, Mrs Ellam, you've got Mark completely wrong, you know. He's not nearly as bad as you think he is,' he said, cradling his coffee cup and relaxing in an easy chair in front of the picture window.

'Oh, I know he's not bad, Roderick,' said Maureen and looked at him firmly. 'Now, my lad, I want you to sit there and listen while I talk. And I want absolutely no comment from you.' She was silent for a moment. Outside in the Grève de Lecq it began to drizzle down. The sound of the waves crashing into the bay could be heard quite easily. It was a speech she had rehearsed a thousand times but now, at the crucial moment, her mind went blank. Then, clutching her coffee cup, she began to speak: 'There was a family fight –'

Roderick switched his gaze to the view of the bay and interrupted, 'Oh, Mrs Ellam, there were so many of those –'

'I know that. You just sit there and listen. Don't talk. Now, I think the over-disciplined pent-up Mark just snapped and it all got out of hand.' She could feel her voice breaking but went on, 'Now I don't know what to advise you, son – don't know what you should do next, but from what I've read, under Norman law, you could both get forty years. I don't know what to tell you to do, love, I just don't know. The only thing I can suggest is that you get off this island and never come back.' As she finished Maureen could not stem the flow of tears. She wiped her eyes and felt a comforting arm around her.

Roderick patted her shoulder gently, whispered, 'Oh, Mrs Ellam . . . ' in her ear, then picked up his cashmere coat and left.

In the course of 1988 the case was featured on BBC TV's *Crimewatch*, but despite a flood of calls there were no solid leads: one person said he had seen Nick Newall on the island of Shuna, but it was his twin, Stephen.

Meanwhile the Jersey detectives were so desperate for evidence that all they could do was grasp at straws: this proved almost disastrous. Someone at Rouge Bouillon had the bright idea that, if the brothers could be covertly tape-recorded, then some kind of confession could be obtained. The Avon and Somerset Police were asked if they could lend out the skills of their covert surveillance unit but they dragged their feet, so the detectives decided to mount their own freelance operation.

One day both brothers were invited to the police station on some pretext and, while Roderick's van was parked in the station car park, it was broken into. The operation was unprofessional in the extreme: instead of a discreet radio microphone, the 'buggers' placed an ordinary mini tape-recorder under the bonnet and merely left it running on the off chance that the brothers might say something to implicate themselves on the road home. The only problem was retrieving the tape. This was solved by again breaking into the van late at night when it was parked outside La Falaise, but even that part of the operation was bungled: the van bonnet accidentally slipped and slammed down with a clang loud enough to waken the entire neighbourhood. Tension was running high when the recovered tape was played back at police headquarters, but all they could hear was shifting gears and the roar of the engine. It had been risky and irresponsible. If uncovered, it could have seriously affected the chances of a successful conviction in any future case.

On another occasion the officers planned to carry out forensic tests on Mark's Toyota. Permission had always been refused by Mark, and there was a suspicion that the bodies could have been driven away in the boot of the rear-engined car. An arrangement was made to have the car impounded by customs when it was shipped to Southampton and then, overnight, to have it secretly driven to Aldermaston where the relevant tests could be carried out. It was an arrangement that stretched to the limits the relationship between the police and customs as the testing took more than a day. Mark Newall was furious at the delay. And again the police drew a blank.

At the beginning of June 1988 a bearded Roderick, his hair now long, bounded up to a villa in Javea, into the open arms of an old lady standing in the doorway. He hugged Joan Riches so hard that for a moment she thought her bones might break. The Riches had always been especially fond of Roderick. To him, they were surrogate grandparents. To them, he was a fine and

165

upstanding young man. He had never been afraid to show his emotions but this was an unusually intense display. Suddenly he broke off and became, if anything, rather more controlled than usual and unwilling to talk about his parents. What most exercised him, it seemed, was his recent treatment at the hands of the police. Roderick was very angry indeed. He explained how he'd visited Amsterdam, where marijuana smoking was quite legal, and had forgotten about the dope in his bags when he came through the airport. On the second occasion, said Roderick, he'd been framed: the police had got someone to slip him the stuff. 'It was a complete fit up,' he told them indignantly.

He also told the Riches that, to get over his parents' disappearance, he had travelled to Scotland and once again had spent some time on Shuna. The weeks of reflection had helped him come to terms with what happened. 'You know, motoring back, I looked at the countryside. It's so beautiful it almost makes you cry,' he said to Joan quietly.

Poor Roderick, she thought. He's being very hard on himself and controlling his emotions. But though their hearts went out to the boy, his attitude of calm resignation at his parents' fate puzzled the Riches. If something had happened to my parents, thought Alex, I wouldn't rest until I'd found out who'd done it and made them pay. He mentioned this to Joan later.

'Oh, that's because he's so strung up,' she said. 'He thinks that if he does show any emotion at all he'll break down completely.'

The Newalls' neighbours Jeff and Jane Matthews were alarmed at the sight of Roderick when he sat down in the basket chair in their sitting room. He looked awful – with red sunken eyes and a thick stubble on his chin. He could not furnish them with any explanation about his parents. He was relaxed, and admitted quite candidly that he thought they were both dead. 'All I can imagine,' he said, 'is that they might have seen something they weren't supposed to see . . . ' His voice tailed off, and he went on to hint vaguely that while out walking they may have come across a drug-smuggling operation. But he knew no more than the police.

Even then, as he retold his story, there were things that did not gel with Jane Matthews. Roderick said they had gone to the bungalow early on the Sunday for breakfast; but she thought the boys never ate breakfast as they were allergic to milk. These suspicions were further aroused, when later that year, in August, the Matthews received a visit from Mark Newall. They were surprised because they had barely met him: latterly he had never been part of his parents' life in Spain, although all their friends knew and were fond of Roderick. Sitting himself down in the same wicker chair that his brother had sat in two months earlier, Mark repeated Roderick's explanation of what had happened. 'All I can imagine,' he said, 'is that they might have seen something they were not supposed to see.'

The Matthews looked at each other in amazement. It was not merely a similar story to the one Roderick had told them: it was the same one repeated exactly word for word.

During the rest of June the Matthews and the Riches saw little of Roderick. He seemed to spend all his time holed up at the villa working on his father's yacht, the *Chanson du Lecq*. One day Joan and Alex Riches were doing some repairs to their own boat and they happened to pass the *Chanson du Lecq*. They were dismayed to see that the painted name had almost completely flaked off. 'You know how strict the harbour police are about names being prominently

167

displayed on the side of the boat,' said Joan, leaning down to talk to Roderick. 'I hope you're not thinking of changing it. It's such a lovely name.'

He went quiet for a moment, then gripped the side of the railing. As he did so, Joan could see that his eyes were brimming with tears. 'You're right,' he said. 'It's such a lovely name.' For a moment it was as if all the happy memories of that boat had come flooding back. Then he turned away; the moment had gone.

The next time Rod came up to see the Riches it was a stifling hot summer's day and the sound of crickets floated in through the large open windows. He sat in an armchair, holding a tumbler of whisky. He seemed very tired, though more relaxed, and he was able to talk about the disappearance more calmly. He speculated about what had happened again but had no explanation.

As she leant over to refill his glass, Joan said, 'You know, Roderick, when I heard about this I thought you boys had got into trouble and wanted your parents out of the way for a bit and that something had gone wrong . . . ' It was a well-intentioned remark and she said it good-naturedly enough, but the moment she looked up at him she realized she had said the wrong thing. He was glaring back at her and gripping the tumbler so tightly she thought it might break. 'Things do go wrong, don't they, Roderick . . . ?' she said in a calm, reassuring voice.

The room was silent for a moment. Roderick stared into his glass and took a sip of whisky. 'Yes,' he said, 'they do go wrong.' For a fleeting moment Joan felt she'd come very close to an explanation for everything. Then, just as quickly, it was gone.

*   *   *

On 13 June 1988 there was a knock at the door of Nan and Alaster Clark's villa, Casa Fidra. She opened it to find her nephew Roderick on the doorstep. She greeted him warmly and invited him in. Long before, despite her knowledge of his crime, she had decided she was not scared of him, nor ever would be: she still felt protective towards the boys and would never turn them away.

To Nan's eyes he was his usual affable self. She and Alaster invited him to attend a party they were having; he did so and helped to clear up afterwards. The wine flowed, and Roderick seemed in terrific form – as charming and affable as always. He revealed his plans to take the boat on a long journey. Alaster then apologized and said he had had a long day: would Roderick mind if he retired? Declining his aunt's invitation to stay, Roderick insisted on driving home, despite having drunk a fair bit. En route he came across a car crash and was later to tell Nan that it was only his first aid skills that had helped save the life of one of those involved.

Underneath their calm exterior the strain was beginning to tell on the Clarks. As if they didn't have enough to worry about, Alaster's father died in Scotland three days later. On 17 June at Valencia Airport the couple boarded a flight back to London and were amazed to see in the first-class section a few seats in front of them, a familiar red-haired figure. It was Roderick. He explained he was on his way back to London to catch a connection to Jersey where he was going to get a driving licence before embarking on his travels. They travelled into London together and parted at Baron's Court tube station. Rod said he would be staying the night at his brother's Docklands flat. Just before he left them Rod had turned and hugged his aunt. She didn't know then that that was the last she was to see of him for four years.

Alaster and Nan travelled on to Scotland and the next day, after her father-in-law's funeral, Nan phoned her mother and was told that Roderick had gone straight back to Spain. She was puzzled and phoned Mark to find out what was going on. He was agitated. 'I just put Roderick straight back on a flight to Spain, Aunt Nan,' he told her. 'I'm not having him wandering around Jersey and getting himself framed by the police again.'

At the age of twenty-two, with a failed army career behind him, Roderick Newall was at a loose end: he had no prospects, no plans and, apparently, no ambitions. Money was no problem – Mark would always see to that – but there was the question of what to do with the rest of his life. It was during his Spanish sojourn that he had finally realized what he wanted to do. Throughout the rest of June and July Roderick threw himself into the business of getting the boat ready for a long haul. During this time a transformation had taken place: the pressed trousers he had arrived in were replaced by old sea-dog jeans; he began growing his hair long and he stopped shaving. It was almost as if he were slipping out of his army officer skin and settling into a new one.

One afternoon he came running into Joan and Alex's house in a very excited mood. The previous day he'd been sailing off the Costa Blanca and had just dropped anchor when a sharp wind got up. 'And do you know, I made myself take the *Chanson du Lecq* off by sail alone – no engine – because if I'm going to do this journey I've got to be able to do things like that on my own.'

For the first time the Riches realized that Roderick was serious when he said he planned to take his father's yacht across the Atlantic. He had always been a competent sailor – though not in his father's league. But surely he didn't have nearly enough experience for such a risky undertaking. Roderick realized this himself, and took a series of sailing lessons from an old friend of his father's. Like Nick Newall, Duncan Macmillan had been a teacher and, like Nick, favoured the old-fashioned Calvinistic approach of learning by rote. He barely knew Roderick but, aware of the rumours surrounding the boy, he was intrigued. When he turned up at the Newalls' villa to give Roderick his first sailing lesson, he immediately thought Newall was either ill or on drugs. Roderick looked shattered and for a moment seemed to have forgotten his sailing lessons or even having met Duncan before. He mumbled a few words before pulling himself together.

Roderick proved to be a capable sailor and a quick learner, and after a few days he had mastered some of the more advanced sailing techniques. But the Atlantic was another matter. Gently Duncan Macmillan tried to dissuade him. 'Stick to the Med for a year, Roderick,' he said. 'Just hop around the coast. Then maybe you could try the big one.'

But Roderick would have none of it. It was almost as if he had something to prove to himself.

CHAPTER 9

On a hot summer's day in 1988 a smart young man in a pin-striped suit with a newspaper folded under his arm emerged from Piccadilly Circus tube station, made his way through the teeming crowds along Shaftesbury Avenue and then down Denman Street towards an Italian restaurant – the Estoril.

The restaurant was run by old friends of Nan and Alaster Clark's and held many happy memories. In the past, when Nick and Elizabeth had come to London, they would all invariably make a night of it there. Now, on 23 July 1988, they were meeting their nephew Mark for lunch.

'Hello, Uncle Alaster, Auntie Nan.'

Looking up from their menus, Nan and Alaster barely recognized him. The glasses had been replaced by contact lenses, his hair was styled and gelled in the latest fashion, and he was wearing a sharp new suit. Maybe he's trying to carve out a new identity for himself, thought Nan.

Just over a fortnight earlier Detective Sergeant Jimmy Adamson had visited the Clarks at their flat in Clapham. He had with him a psychological profile of Mark and Roderick carried out by a forensic psychiatrist from Broadmoor Hospital. Professor David Hamilton was an expert in the study of the psychopathic mind and had interviewed Peter Sutcliffe, the Yorkshire Ripper. At the request of the Jersey detectives he had flown to the island and spent hours going over the material. He had listened to the tape-recorded interviews, visited friends, read the depositions and the account of the family's tortured home life, and then produced a profile of each of the brothers. Jimmy Adamson handed the report to Alaster Clark, who had read it in silence for a few moments then, with a grave expression, handed it back.

The professor had emphasized that without detailed study of the brothers he was unable to come to a firm conclusion; however, he thought that at least one and possibly both exhibited strong psychopathic tendencies: they could have murdered their parents and shown and felt no hint of remorse for what they had done.

Now, as she sat studying the menu, Nan couldn't help glancing over at the smart young man sitting opposite and wondering what on earth her sister had done to deserve a son like this. It was the first time they had seen him since Roderick's trouble on Jersey but he seemed to have regained his composure. He was preoccupied with work and his conversation was full of obscure financial jargon she barely understood. He explained that the villa in Spain had been let to a friend of Roderick's, but he was vague as to his brother's actual whereabouts.

After lunch his goodbye was short and sweet – 'Better get back. I'm worked off my feet at the moment' – and, with the usual stiff handshake, he turned and soon disappeared back into the Shaftesbury Avenue crowds.

It was the chance discovery of a discarded shovel near a pond not far from Mark's house in Noirmont that had kickstarted the inquiry back to life. In late June 1988 the police announced they had traced it back to a hardware store in St Helier which had sold it on the morning of 10 October the previous year – the eve of the Newalls' disappearance.

The breakthrough delighted the detectives. Here at last, eight months on, was the possibility that someone had purchased equipment with which to dispose of the bodies. It could well tie the brothers to the disappearances – if only they had the bodies.

The discovery sparked a fresh wave of speculation. The shop assistant failed to identify either of the brothers as the purchaser, but had been adamant that the fair-haired man had been alone. Mark had an alibi for his own movements at about the time the tools were bought. He was at his house in Noirmont, having a telephone installed. Maybe Roderick did it alone and his brother was covering up for him.

The news, with its gruesome implications, turned Nan Clark's stomach: night after night she tried to block out the horrific images it conjured up. Had one of the brothers calmly gone and bought what amounted to a murder kit with which to dispose of the bodies just before they treated their parents to a celebratory dinner? It beggared belief.

After weeks of kitting out the boat with charts and fitting automatic steering equipment, in late June Roderick was ready. The sextant on the *Chanson du Lecq* was the same one that his father had on the *Rodmark* when it set sail from Scotland for the West Indies. Now, nearly twenty years later, it was to be used on the journey it was originally intended for. He set off on a fine morning with a light westerly breeze punching at the sails. At last he was on his way. The moment when any seaman takes control of his yacht for the first time is sweet and at the same time frightening. Like most lone sailors, Roderick was simultaneously filled with satisfaction and apprehension about what lay ahead. For the first time he was truly free of the institutions – at home, at school, and in the army – that had provided the framework and meaning for his life. Out there on the sea, with an infinity beneath and above, Roderick began to learn the secret language of the ocean. He came to understand the washing of the waves against the keel, the whisper of the wind along the sails; he listened to the silence. He was now a man in charge of his own destiny.

His first port of call after Gibraltar was Morocco. From there he sailed across to the Cape Verde islands, then rode on the back of the trade winds to the Caribbean, landing in Barbados. Two months after he left, Joan and Alex Riches received a postcard at their home in Javea. Roderick, sounding jubilant, said the crossing had taken him thirty-seven days. It was the longest time he had ever spent on his own and when he arrived he was so garrulous he could hardly stop talking.

On a typical Caribbean winter's day in January 1989 a forty-foot yacht crewed by a middle-aged couple cut through a perfect blue ocean and arrived at the palm-tree-lined beaches of Prickly Bay in Grenada. Eine and Fergus van der Geest were enjoying their first year of retirement. Their children were grown up and off their hands and Fergus had a healthy pension from his former job as a pilot with the Dutch airline KLM; so the previous year they had decided to fulfil a long-time dream of sailing around the world in the *Corona Borealis*.

At first they paid little attention to the fair-haired young man on the boat moored next to them, but then Eine began to notice his daily fitness routine. First thing every morning he would pull on his goggles, leap off the boat and power his way through the water doing the butterfly stroke. He would swim right round the edge of the bay – not straight across it – and then far out to sea.

It was the exotic sounds of French calypso music from their cassette recorder that attracted him. The young man said he had seen the Gipsy Kings in concert in Paris only the previous year – could he borrow the cassette? The request was so politely made that Eine immediately agreed. The young man introduced himself, then something on the side of the *Corona Borealis* caught his eye: he stopped and stared. 'Javea? You come from Javea?' he said, pointing to the yacht club badge. 'I used to live there.' Sure enough, by coincidence Eine and Fergus's own holiday home in Spain was only a few minutes away from the Newalls' villa. Not only that: they were members of the same yacht club, and now they had turned up in the same bay more than 3000 miles away and were meeting for the first time! The three sailors got chatting and the van der Geests were soon won over by the young man's relaxed, easy-going manners. They invited him for a meal aboard their yacht and later that evening in the galley of the *Corona Borealis*, as the music of the Gipsy Kings roared from the cassette player, Fergus produced his speciality – an Indonesian fried rice dish called *nasi goreng*. Over several glasses of beer they exchanged their life stories. Rod spoke of his adventures at sea and in the army; how he had made his way across the Atlantic, had visited Barbados, Tobago and hoped to move onto Trinidad for the annual carnival. Both Eine and Fergus were completely charmed. In their year at sea they had met many single-hand sailors and they were a curious breed: some simply relished a challenge

but many had resorted to sailing as a form of escape –
often from themselves. By contrast Rod Newall seemed
remarkably level-headed and sane.

'Do your parents still live in Javea?' asked Eine as
they cleared away the dishes. Rod was still for a
moment, then the blue eyes stared straight into hers.
He looked like a lost little boy. Eine realized she had
intruded and had accidentally touched on a deep sadness. Eventually, later that same evening, Roderick
mumbled a few words about how his parents had mysteriously disappeared. From his demeanour the Dutch
couple understood that he did not want to discuss the
matter. Later, they wondered what could be troubling
Rod Newall, but Fergus thought they should not press
him. If he wished to talk about it he would, otherwise
they should not pry.

The van der Geests weren't the only people to be
taken with Newall. One night they left him chatting to
a pretty local girl by her boat and saw him emerge from
her cabin the next morning looking slightly bedraggled.
Eine had to thump her husband to stop him from shouting bawdy encouragement to the red-faced Roderick.
The boy reminded she so much of her own son and
when, finally, it was time to exchange farewells Eine
couldn't help but feel a pang of sadness. 'I promise I'll
look you up the next time I'm back,' Rod shouted as
he cast off then, with a wave and a brilliant smile, he
was gone.

Three years later Eine and Fergus found themselves
dining with another sailing couple in a tiny inlet on the
Pacific island of Bora Bora. When their guests revealed
that they came from Jersey Eine clapped her hands in
delight and asked them if they knew the story of the
couple who mysteriously disappeared. 'Except they
didn't disappear,' said the woman. 'Everyone on the

island knows that their two sons murdered them. It's just the police can't prove it.' Stunned, Eine looked at her husband in astonishment and horror.

From each point on Roderick's journey the postcards and letters flew. They went to his friends and relatives – to his grandmother in Scotland, to his colleagues from the army, and to old girlfriends. The next postcard received by Alex and Joan in Spain in January 1989 came from Caracas in Venezuela. Roderick wrote that he'd been crewing for a woman who owned a huge yacht. For such a voracious reader as Rod Newall it was only natural that it should have been a book that led to a drastic change of plan. The words of the intrepid French sailor Bernard Moitessier came to echo in his mind:

> For ever since the day of the shipwreck, Marie-Thérèse had come to haunt me nearly every night and crush my chest, as though demanding justice. I would wake up in a panic, drenched in perspiration and almost demented. I must turn the page for good, and without delay, otherwise the outcome would be tragic.

Moitessier was describing how the wreck of his vessel had brought him to the edge of suicidal despair, and how he had sought out and found redemption in a journey across the Pacific and then home via Cape Horn. It was a singular feat of navigation and, after reading *Cape Horn, the Logical Way*, Roderick abandoned his plans to sail down the South American coast. Instead he resolved to follow in Moitessier's wake.

Everywhere he went he read, and everywhere he went he made friends. From the Caribbean he travelled through the Panama Canal and on to Wreck Bay in the Galapagos Islands, where the beaches of fine white sand stretched away to the horizon. Porto Chico, the capital of the Galapagos, is a motley collection of small low houses made of corrugated iron, where only the lizards move in the heat of midday. The island is a freak thrown up by volcanic action; here the laws of nature have gone their own way. No one arrives at the Galapagos without feeling that they have stumbled across a lost world. Roderick would spend hours climbing the volcanic rock, seeking out the iguanas, the giant turtles and the lizards that rule the island. While moored in the bay the *Chanson du Lecq* found itself adopted by a local – a pelican which sat on the mainsail waiting for scraps to be thrown to it.

Then, in the steps of Captain James Cook, Roderick reached the Polynesian chain. The Marquesas are remote islands of giant palm-rimmed beaches and green lagoons of crystal-clear waters. Visitors are rare, but in the eighteenth century men who chanced upon the island convinced themselves that not only had they found a new country but a new world completely. Making his way along the Polynesian chain, Rod visited in turn the Tuamotu Islands, Tahiti, the Society Islands, the Cook Islands and, with Moitessier, felt 'The joy of weighing anchor . . . the joy of sailing on a limitless ocean . . . of feeling the blue speck of an island on the horizon being born and growing within oneself . . . of seeing the boat sailing for her anchorage at top speed . . . All that explains many things.'

In early 1989 the battered and bruised *Chanson du Lecq* rode gently into Bounty Bay on Pitcairn Island, a remote speck set in an infinity of ocean 3000 miles from the nearest land. Here, 200 years earlier, another fugitive from justice, Fletcher Christian, had arrived with his eight fellow mutineers from Captain Bligh's *Bounty*. They lived there with their nineteen-strong Polynesian harem for nearly eighteen years, but all but one died through illness, accident or murder by the natives. The legacy of the mutineers can still be found today in the surnames of the islanders and in the local patois of Pitcairnese – a mixture of native dialect and eighteenth-century English. To the islands' forty-nine inhabitants, the arrival of a visitor is a big event. Their only point of contact with the outside world is the weekly freighters which steam along the Great Circle Route from New Zealand to the Panama Canal, so even a lone sailor like Roderick became a minor celebrity. The moment he arrived the locals clamoured around the yacht, pleading to be taken out for a jaunt. Roderick, eager to please and make friends, was only too happy to oblige. But after a couple of weeks he had tired of the attention. 'Paradise Island', with its innocence and lushness, was not for him; always his wandering spirit drew him on.

Back in Spain, the final postcard received by the Riches announced Rod's intention of travelling to New Zealand. The news of his far-flung adventures was greeted triumphantly by Joan. She had never fully believed that the Newalls could be dead. Instead, she suspected that the hapless couple had got into some kind of financial mess and had simply done a bunk. 'There, I told you, Alex,' she said to her husband. 'This proves it. They've hopped off somewhere else and this is their son going to join them.'

By September 1988 Nan was growing deeply worried about Roderick. She had not seen or heard from him since bumping into him on the flight from Valencia more than two months before. Eventually the Clarks decided to drive north from the Casa Fidra to Javea and investigate.

The house had indeed been let but it was being badly neglected. The pot plants Elizabeth had tended so carefully were dead or knocked over and her beloved garden was overgrown. The swimming pool was filled only with twigs and leaves, the barbecue set had been scattered around the patio, the solar heating panels on the roof had been stolen, and the Newalls' car had been badly smashed up. As she stood on the patio and looked around, Nan for the first time felt overcome with emotion at the loss of her sister and brother-in-law. Elizabeth had imbued the villa with such hope for the future. She had splashed out on home improvements here as she had never done at the Crow's Nest. It was to be the place where she and Nick would spend the rest of their retirement.

A neighbour said that Roderick had left on 28 June for the Caribbean. Nan was taken aback; she thought Roderick had only planned to sail around the Spanish coast. But when she learned that Mark had been in Javea at the same time she was intrigued. The ever-calculating Mark, she decided, must have been given a fright by his brother's arrest and had realized that Roderick was a 'loose cannon' liable to give the game away at any time. Far healthier to have him out of harm's way. Not for the first time Nan found herself wondering what kind of control Mark had over his elder brother.

Mark stayed in touch. Nan would get phone calls from time to time but, although he seemed friendly, she doubted his motives and suspected he was once again trying to find out how much progress – if any – was being made by the police. He seemed to have a good intelligence system on the island. Every time she phoned the police station he would be on the phone two or three days later trying to find out what had been said. This fact did not strengthen her faith in the competence of the St Helier police, who were becoming less and less helpful.

On 27 September Chief Superintendent John Saunders of the Sussex Police arrived at the flat in Liberty Mews for dinner with Nan and Alaster. The news that a senior detective had been brought in from outside had filled her with hope, and she had invited him round specifically to hear about the progress of the investigation.

John Saunders was a breath of fresh air. He was confident, experienced, and he seemed to have a total grasp of all the facts; moreover, he was more than happy to discuss the case with them, and they went over the details again and again. As they talked, Nan got the distinct impression that he was as puzzled at the lack of progress as she was; when she expressed surprise that the boys had never been arrested he raised his eyebrows in agreement. 'This might surprise you, but I'm confident we'll get to the bottom of this somehow,' he said as he pulled on his coat to leave. 'In fact I would not be surprised if there were not arrests shortly.'

On 4 October 1988 Gay Newall phoned Nancy to ask for John Saunders's telephone number; the relatives in Scotland wanted to hear about the progress of the inquiry too.

As the months went by Mark became a much more elusive figure. At the beginning of October he cancelled a lunch appointment with his aunt and uncle, saying he had 'too much shopping' to do. But occasionally he would make an effort. Despite the growing distance between the boys and their close relatives, there was one family member to whom they were still apparently devoted: never a weekend went by without the boys' grandmother in North Berwick getting at least a telephone call. Often Mark would send her flowers, and she was the first close relative to learn of Roderick's whereabouts after he set sail: he had sent her a bouquet of flowers on 4 September and phoned her from Morocco on 12 September.

Almost a year after the Newalls had gone missing there was a small family gathering at the Clarks' flat: they were celebrating the birthday of Nan's mother, who had come down from Scotland. It was Mrs Nelson's eightieth birthday and the Clarks had been joined by an unexpected guest – Mark. There was a round of applause as Mrs Nelson cut her birthday cake. But although he tried to put a good face on it for the sake of family unity, Alaster could barely contain his anger at his nephew's barefaced cheek. He had long suspected that the attention the brothers paid to their grandmother had more to do with future legacies than any real affection.

At the end of the meal he stood up and addressed the family: 'Well, ladies and gentlemen, as I'm sure you won't need reminding, it is now nearly a year since we last heard from Nick and Elizabeth. I think we should have a three-minute silence.' As the seconds ticked by Alaster glanced at the bowed head beside him, but Mark's expression did not change.

On 9 October, the eve of the anniversary of the Newalls' fated dinner at the Sea Crest restaurant, Mark again met his aunt and uncle for lunch. As usual the conversation revolved around his work. He had sold La Falaise and bought a flat in London's Docklands and he had virtually severed all his links with Jersey. He also told them he was flying to Kenya shortly for a safari holiday. Nan remembered that Mark had enjoyed exotic holidays even when he was a teenager. 'I need the break, with all the pressure I've been under at work lately,' he told her. But something was bothering him: the upsurge of media interest in the case one year on.

As no apparent progress was being made on the case, the publicity had begun to die off. But the first anniversary of the disappearances brought a fresh resurgence. Although Nan Clark and Stephen Newall refused to talk to the press, Maureen Ellam was more obliging. An interview with her duly appeared in the *Jersey Evening Post* and another was shown on television. 'We've got to keep the public eye on this thing somehow,' she told Angela Barnes. 'We've got to use anything to keep the pressure on the police.'

On 5 October Nan and Angela had had a long telephone conversation about an article that had appeared in the *Evening Post*, hinting that the Newalls' family were not doing enough. It irritated Nan intensely: if the people responsible for the investigation had not bungled it so badly then the whole matter could have been cleared up long ago. What the heck were the police doing? And what on earth was she expected to do from London or Spain?

Now Mark was imploring Nan not to speak to the press. 'They'll only twist what you say – use it for their own purposes,' he told her. It seemed he was more worried about media coverage than anything else.

'And did you see any of the television coverage about your parents, Mark?' asked his aunt.

'Don't get much of a chance to watch TV these days,' he replied quickly, sipping his usual glass of orange.

Mark had other worries too – in particular he feared that newspapers would publish details of the will, which would show that his parents, and not he and Roderick, had been the beneficiaries of his uncle's Trust. 'People might read something into that,' he commented. Money problems were on his mind as well – especially the continuing failure of his father's Lloyd's syndicates. They had incurred losses of £60,000 and he had decided to pay the bills so that his father's name would not be posted as a defaulter. After all, it was the least he could do. It was an apparently generous gesture: he had no legal obligation to pay; but somehow Nan Clark doubted his motives. 'That's an awful lot of money you will have to find, Mark,' she had said to him.

'Not to worry,' he replied, 'I'll get it back when the estate is settled.'

So that was it, she thought. They are finally making a move on their parents' money. Ever since the Newalls' disappearance their relatives had been waiting for this. Nothing had happened for a whole year, but then, on 11 October Gay Newall phoned Nan in Spain to say that Mark had been in touch: he wanted to discuss the future of his parents' estate with his Uncle Stephen. Unfortunately he had a problem. Technically the Newalls were not dead but only missing. Before the boys could inherit the estate their parents would have to be formally declared dead in a court of law and that usually took at least seven years. Until then, in theory at least, the estate was to be frozen. If Mark gained control of the estate it would mean they had got away with it. The relatives were determined to thwart him and discussed how to do so.

It was Angela Barnes who came up with an idea. On 14 October she phoned Nan to say she had discovered that before her death Elizabeth has signed over power of attorney of her own estate to another advocate on Jersey. He could stop the movement of funds if Nan approached him. Nan phoned Stephen at the Creggan

Inn Hotel in Scotland; they discussed this possibility and decided to use it if all else failed.

Meanwhile Mark's career, now largely based in Paris, had caught the thermals and was soaring. When John Ginsbury's second wife Sandy, an American, moved to Paris she could not speak any French; being a sociable person, she liked to have people who spoke English around her. She took to Mark and soon he became almost a member of the family. Here Mark began to enjoy a much wider social life than he had in Jersey, and he was befriended by all the Ginsbury children. Régine's, the famous nightclub, and the Ritz health club were among his regular haunts. He had a steady girlfriend and for a while his flatmate was Elena Irrgang, Roderick's sometime girlfriend, who was also working in the Paris office.

With the world markets booming, Mark was spending more and more time chasing the sun as a passenger on Concorde. The global trading revolution meant that when the market shut down in London, dealers would merely turn to Hong Kong or New York or wherever was still open.

The police had been keeping track of Roderick's movements, but were having difficulty keeping tabs on Mark. His constant commuting between Paris, London and New York meant they were never sure where he was at any one moment. He had suddenly developed the habit of changing his plans at a moment's notice. In October he phoned Nan in Spain to say he had arrived in Paris, but in fact he'd had to return to London because a general strike had paralysed the city. Over the next few weeks he became more and more elusive. It was almost as if he were trying to avoid his family altogether. At the end of October Mrs Nelson was taken by her daughter Nan to the Intercontinental

Hotel in Paris. She was desperate to see her grandson, but again Mark cried off. Nan could hardly believe it: his grandmother had come all that way especially to see him.

Nan and Alaster Clark were trying to get on with living a normal life. On 1 November they attended an engagement dinner for their son William and his fiancée Amanda Younger at Wester Leckie. Amanda came from one of Scotland's oldest families. She was the daughter of Lord Younger of Leckie and the niece of George Younger, then Conservative Defence Secretary. It was a sparkling occasion, held in one of the oldest castles in Scotland, and it should have been one of the happiest moments in the Clarks' life. But their enjoyment was marred by the shadow that hung over Nan: the bodies of her sister and brother-in-law still lay undiscovered, and their murderers were free to go about their business – she felt her life had entered a kind of limbo.

Mark was not at the dinner, but he did, however, manage to make the wedding, which took place on 9 May 1989. The cream of Scottish society converged on a hotel in Callendar in Perthshire: it was one of the highlights of the social calendar, and Mark had flown to Scotland especially for the occasion. The proceedings were interrupted by one unfortunate incident: exception was taken by the bride to the presence in the wedding photographs of Priscilla Rawa, the glamorous Asian girlfriend of the Clarks' other son Kenneth. Priscilla retired sobbing to her room while the guests attended the reception. There was a knock at the door and she opened it to find Mark Newall there. He had heard there had been some unpleasantness and wanted to know what was going on. When she told him he exploded with anger and promptly announced that he was not going to attend the wedding dinner either, but would sit and comfort Priscilla instead. It was all the Clarks could do to paper over the incident.

Like Nan, Maureen Ellam could hardly contain her frustration with the police. One day, driven to exasperation by the apparent inactivity of the inquiry, Maureen had marched into reception at police headquarters and demanded to speak to the detectives. She made no attempt to hide her disgust and eventually tempers were lost and voices raised. Even Bob Le Breton appeared at the reception desk to try and calm things down. 'Surely you've missed something,' Maureen insisted. 'There must have been bloodstains on the ceiling. Did you check it for fingerprints?'

Yes, the detectives assured her, they had. In fact Roderick's prints had indeed been found there, but he had accounted for them by claiming that his mother had asked him to replace some of the ceiling tiles.

However, in late 1988 at the police headquarters at Rouge Bouillon, a group of men sat listening to Detective Inspector Nimmo argue the case for the Newall brothers to be arrested and charged. The gathering consisted of Nimmo, Detective Sergeant Jimmy Adamson and their boss Martyn Le Brocq. Round the other side of the table were the Attorney General, Philip Bailhache, the island's Director of Public Prosecution, and the Bailiff and Chief Prosecutor, Sir Cyril Whelan. The thrust of Nimmo's argument was that without the bodies the case could only ever be circumstantial but that, nevertheless, the amount of circumstantial evidence was so overwhelming that he was sure a jury would convict. Painstakingly he ran through more than forty crucial points that could form the backbone of the case.

When the Attorney General announced his decision

Elizabeth Nelson in her first year at New Park School, 1963, sitting two seats away from her future husband, Nick Newall.

Nick and Elizabeth, standing to the right, grape-picking with Bob Blayney and friends at La Mare vineyard, Jersey.

Grape-washing at La Mare. Roderick is the third child in from the right, Mark the second.

Children's party at the Blayney's, Roderick at the top of the table, Mark bottom right.

Roderick playing rugby in the army.

The *Chanson du Lecq* in Ibiza, summer 1986. Roderick is on board.

Roderick on holiday, summer 1986.

Nick Newall in Spain, Christmas 1986.

A dinner party with the Riches and the Matthews, Christmas 1986.

Roderick and Elizabeth, Christmas 1986.

Jersey detectives oversee the search of the garden at no. 9 Clos de L'Atlantique. Detective Inspector Graham Nimmo stands centre right.

The Newall's kitchen at no. 9.

Mark Newall answers journalists' questions weeks after his parents' disappearance.

Above: Roderick and Mark leave the church service after the death of their Uncle Kenneth in November 1988. Stephen Newall, their father's twin brother, is far left.

Left: Roderick after his court appearance on drugs charges, 2 March 1988.

Opposite above: Detective Inspector Nimmo displays one of the handsaws purchased along with tarpaulins and shovels at a hardware store on the last day that Elizabeth and Nick Newall were seen alive.

Above: David Le Quesne, the brothers' defence advocate.

Above right: Desmond de Silva, Crown QC, who led the case for the extradition of Roderick Newall from Gibralter.

Above: Port Stanley police inspector Mark Bullock and his wife Fran, who Roderick and Donna lodged with for several weeks.

6 November 1993, Roderick Newall returns to Jersey and justice, hand-cuffed to Detective Superintendant Martin Fitzgerald. Following is David Le Quesne.

The discovery of the bodies, wrapped in tarpaulin. In the grey overcoat is Assistant Chief Officer Paul Marks; to the right is Detective Superintendant Martin Fitzgerald; Detective Inspector Jimmy Adamson stands with his back to the camera and pathologist Dr Guyan Fernando is centre, in woollen hat.

The wooded glade of the Moulin de Lecq, burial site of Elizabeth and Nick Newall's bodies.

it left Nimmo shattered. Philip Bailhache had concluded that, as persuasive as the case was, it was just
too risky. It was a personal blow from which Nimmo
never recovered. He retired from the police on health
grounds in 1990: the strain of the Newall inquiry had
taken its toll.

So the biggest investigation ever undertaken on
Jersey had almost completely run out of steam. It had
taken up hundreds of man hours, and has cost tens of
thousands of pounds – a huge proportion of a tiny
force's energy and resources – and it was no nearer a
solution. Of the commitment of the two detectives at
the head of the inquiry, Nimmo and Adamson, Nan
Clark had no doubt. 'I tell you, Mrs Clark, I'll solve
this case if it's the last thing I do,' Nimmo would say
to her. But she suspected that his determination was
not shared at more senior levels, and when Nimmo
retired Nan was convinced the investigation would have
stopped altogether had it not been for Jimmy Adamson, who always kept in touch with her, always kept
her up to date and always returned her phone calls. He
stubbornly refused to be taken off the inquiry and had
constantly to fight for time and resources.

On television Sergeant Bergerac conveniently solved
his crimes in the course of the programme. But Jersey's
only real murder investigation of any size seemed to
be insoluble: it was deeply embarrassing to the Jersey
police.

CHAPTER 10

The request for help that came over the VHF radio was straightforward: a small single-handed yacht was drifting just outside the marina – its engine had packed up. Could anyone help? asked the owner in a well-bred English accent. Sure, said Ralph Williams, the superintendent of the marina, and minutes later his motor dinghy, *Birth Control*, was speeding out to lend a hand. There are always at least 600 yachts moored in Auckland's West Park Marina, but more than twice that number were crammed in during the busy summer season of 1989. Pulling alongside the becalmed yacht, Ralph was hailed by a bedraggled, smiling young man with his hair tied back in a pony-tail. Throwing the stranger a rope, he began pulling the yacht back into the harbour and as the two vessels piggy-backed in, Ralph suddenly gunned the engine and prepared to swing his dinghy sharply to one side to carry out his marina speciality. Ralph called it a 'split-arse turn': it was a manoeuvre he had executed thousands of times and could judge it to within a millimetre. Nevertheless, it was alarming if you hadn't seen it done before – especially if it was being done to you. There was a shout of alarm from the stranger when Ralph suddenly whipped the dinghy round, sending the yacht spinning backwards and coming to rest perfectly within a millimetre of the jetty.

It wasn't until later, over a few beers, that the young stranger confessed to Ralph that he had suddenly thought how ironic it would be to make his way halfway round the world only to meet his Maker at the hands of some silly old coot in a marina dinghy! Rocking on his stool with laughter, Ralph slapped his thighs and got in another couple of beers.

In the West Park Marina Ralph had seen them come and go, and he hadn't taken a liking to many of the poms who had washed up, but there was something about this one – a lack of stand-offishness perhaps, and an easy manner. Rod Newall explained that he was just planning to stop over for a couple of weeks until he could get his boat fixed up. His travels to date impressed Ralph, and unlike many, he wasn't all talk; he had actually had the guts to go and do it. And that wasn't all they had in common: Ralph was an ex-military man – he'd spent years flying Sunderland flying boats for the Royal New Zealand Air Force – and when the young Brit told him of his time with the Royal Green Jackets it seemed to cement the bond further. In fact Rod Newall reminded him of someone he once knew. Much later, he realized who it was: himself.

When the young man revealed that he planned to round Cape Horn, Ralph was intrigued. It had long been an unfulfilled ambition of his. Cape Horn sailor Sir Joshua Slocombe was a legend to sea-faring folk in his part of the world.

Rod was keen to continue his journey, but the *Chanson du Lecq* was a shadow of her former self, and had been well and truly battered by her 12,000-mile journey. She needed a complete re-fit. 'No problem,' said Ralph, and he fixed it for Rod to stay with his young friends and next-door neighbours Tony and Donna Westend and their other lodger Craig.

191

And that was how Rod became one of the West Park Crowd. After so many weeks alone at sea he had developed a real thirst for company and obviously relished being part of a group again. He fitted in well. One night, after a few drinks, Ralph and Rod were loudly imagining what it would be like to actually try and do a 360-degree turn in a yacht. In all his years Ralph had never done it. The New Zealander already noticed a marked reluctance in Rod to talk about his background. 'And your folks, Rod,' he had asked, 'what do they do?' He swilled the dregs of the beer at the bottom of his glass.

'It's a long story, but they disappeared – no one's ever found out what happened to them,' replied Rod. Ralph was taken back, but something told him not to press what was obviously a delicate matter.

Over the long weeks at sea Rod had become proud of his culinary skills – he could brighten up any meal with just a few spices. So when Ralph's partner Marina showed him how to make a traditional Maori dish of pork bones and watercress, he decided to show off. One evening shortly afterwards, he insisted they all get together next door to sample his version of the same dinner. The first attempt was not a great success, so he made a second batch. His new friends all nodded in approval as they tasted the result: it was definitely a creditable effort. They all raised their glasses and toasted his talents.

During the next few weeks Rod took the opportunity to explore New Zealand on the back of a motorcycle. Postcards home to friends were full of his bungee-jumping and white-water-rafting exploits. The boy had a zest for life and a taste for adventure that was totally missing in most of his generation, Ralph decided. He was born a hundred years too late.

On his visit to the Southern Island Roderick had, without warning, paid a visit to Ralph's Auntie Joy. Ralph had had his reservations about passing on the address: at the age of eighty, Joy was a formidable old bird who didn't take kindly to unexpected visitors. But Rod had insisted and, a week or so later, Ralph received a call from his aunt, half expecting to be bawled out for having given out her address. Rod had visited her, taken her out for tea, and sat talking to her for more than two hours. During their chat, he had revealed that he was going to take around the Horn with him one of Ralph's most prized books – a rare edition of an account by Joshua Slocombe of his seafaring travels. Joy had searched far and wide for years before finding the copy: she had presented it to Ralph proudly one Christmas – and now here was this young stranger planning to take it on one of the most dangerous journeys in the world. Carefully and tactfully – and trying to hide a smile – Rod explained that the safekeeping of the book was his top priority: he would swim ashore with it under one arm if necessary.

It was thoughtful of Rod to go out of his way to visit an old lady he did not know, thought Ralph. How many other twenty-six-year-olds would show such kindness? 'Ralph, I just did not want him to go,' he was later told by his Auntie Joy.

One night over a beer Ralph asked Rod, 'You know, I've often wondered why you do this.'

The blue eyes looked up and for a moment Rod seemed to be somewhere else. 'Escapism,' he said eventually. 'Pure escapism.'

Not long before he was due to sail again, Rod said to Donna Westend – completely out of the blue, 'Why don't you come with me?'

At first she laughed the suggestion off, but as she

gave it more thought she began to think, 'Why not?' At the age of twenty-six Donna felt that life was passing her by. Her marriage was dying from lack of interest. She had married Tony when she was seventeen and the couple had drifted into the kind of mutual cordiality common in those who marry too young. So, at an age when many others were about to settle down, she had only just begun to wonder what life was all about. Then into her life stepped Roderick Newall. She had never met anyone like him before. She listened in amazement to the tales of his travels. He seemed to be bursting with life, and he had already done so much and been to so many places. With his English public-school accent, self-confidence and charm, he seemed to come from another world entirely. He fascinated and intrigued her.

Donna felt she had been nowhere and done nothing. She had no children to tie her down, so why not? Her husband accepted her decision. He had realized for some time that they needed a break from each other to sort out their lives. But when she told her parents of her plans they were devastated, especially when they discovered that the *Chanson du Lecq* would be sailing without a radio transmitter. Rod had insisted that their fate should be entirely in their own hands. No one had asked them to go to sea and if they got into trouble then it was not fair to ask others to risk their lives to save them.

'Mum, I really trust the guy. I think he'll look after me – make sure I'm all right. I really do,' insisted Donna.

Despite their misgivings, Donna's parents recognized how determined their daughter was, so they decided to bite their tongues and give her as much backing as they could. In any case, they liked Rod and whatever worries they had about their daughter's safety, they were in no doubt that her life was in the hands of a very capable sailor as well as a trustworthy and likable man. Maybe it would be just as well to let her get it out of her system. It was her life, after all.

So on 18 December 1989, a windy summer's day, a small group gathered at the end of the jetty at West Park Marina. As Christmas presents were exchanged Donna hugged her parents and kissed Tony goodbye. Rod promised Tony he'd look after her and the two men shook hands awkwardly. Then the couple got into the boat and cast off. The *Chanson du Lecq* nosed into the sound and then out into the vastness of the Pacific.

Those first two weeks were full of excitement and interest for Donna. There was so much to learn, so much to do. Once when she was on watch a flock of gulls suddenly swirled into the air up ahead. Shouting for Rod, she soon saw the reason why: an enormous black shape emerged from the sea up ahead – a sperm whale accompanied by its calf. 'Quick, Rod,' shouted Donna, diving into the cabin to get her camera, 'see if we can get closer.'

'No way,' he shouted, heaving at the wheel. 'She'll smash the boat up if we got too close to the baby.'

But as time passed it became apparent that, barring storms or mid-sea collisions with whales or other vessels, fending off boredom was going to be one of the main challenges. Although they were slowly making their way through a vast open wilderness, Donna found that life on the boat could get incredibly claustrophobic. Rod may have been chatty onshore but he was much quieter now and would go for long periods without a word. She tried to winkle some information out of him about his past, and over the weeks, bit by bit, the picture became clearer. He and his brother had resented being sent away to boarding school at a very young age. He seemed to have been more fond of his mother than his father, of whom he hardly spoke at all. One night the two were in the cabin and Donna pointed at a picture of Rod's parents that hung on the cabin wall. She knew they had disappeared but had hesitated to broach what seemed to be a sensitive subject. 'Rod,' she said, 'what do you think happened to your parents?'

Rod looked up from his book and his gaze met hers. 'I really don't know,' he said. 'I've given it a lot of thought but I really don't know. It's hard to believe now but it could have been drugs. My parents were stupid and naive. It is possible they got mixed up in something without realizing how heavy it was.' He looked away. 'Whatever it was, I only hope it was quick. I only hope they didn't suffer.'

Donna knew she had probed too far and sensed he was not far away from tears, so she put her arm around his neck and switched off the light.

Despite his reluctance to go into his personal background in any detail, it soon became clear that there was one relationship Rod prized more than any other. 'You would love Mark,' he said enthusiastically one night, 'he is ace. He is the real talent and the brains of the family.' Though Mark was the younger by a year it seemed to Donna that Rod almost looked up to him. He painted a picture of a jet-setting financial whizz kid who spent most of his time on Concorde travelling across the Atlantic. Certainly Rod relied heavily on his brother for money. In New Zealand he had never hesitated to buy any CDs or expensive jeans he wanted with his gold American Express card, but it was obvious from the frequent calls he made to his brother in Paris that Mark controlled the purse strings. And there was another family member on whom Roderick used to dote: his Uncle Kenneth, who had made up in generosity of heart what he lacked in inches.

As Rod and Donna made their way slowly across the Pacific they settled into a dull routine and the mood aboard the *Chanson du Lecq* changed. It was soon obvious that the couple were unprepared for the strains of a long sea voyage cooped up with each other. Despite his sociable nature Rod seemed to be temperamentally attuned to solitude. For hours he would sit smoking dope or buried in the classic novels and New Age self-help philosophies that lined the shelves of his cabin. To stay fit he would put himself through a punishing regime of sit-ups, press-ups and, if the sea was calm enough, would dive off the boat for a swim.

Donna, however, was gregarious by nature and missed her friends and family badly. She would stare out at the open sea as if in a trance for hours on end. Her enthusiasm for learning the rudiments of sailing waned too, and she would often spend whole days in the cabin drinking or sleeping – anything to escape. She had prepared for the journey by taking aboard three crates of beer and as the days passed she came to rely on them to ease the boredom – much to Rod's irritation. The two began snapping at each other. While showing a casual disregard for his own safety, Rod was always very conscientious when it came to that of others and he would nag at Donna for going aloft without a sea harness. 'Listen, Donna, you're just not taking the sea seriously enough,' he shouted one day. 'I'm responsible for you, I promised your parents I'd look after you. You must take all the precautions.' Some days not a word would pass between them and they would sit in sullen silence, cautiously trying to stay out of each other's way – a difficult task on a thirty-three foot yacht.

For weeks the only break from the dull routine came every Thursday at 4 p.m. New Zealand time. That was when Ralph Williams turned on his powerful long-wave transmitter and kept them in touch with the news from home. Although Rod had refused to carry a transmitter, Ralph had persuaded them to take a receiver, and in the office at West Park Marina he ad-libbed furiously, trying to keep up a steady stream of chatter – although he didn't know whether anyone was listening or not. In fact, the fading and crackling dispatches from home provided a welcome weekly break for Donna and Rod.

It was during one of their rows that Donna pushed Roderick too far. Afterwards she was never even to remember what it was she had said that provoked him – all she knew was that he'd suddenly lashed with a fist and sent her flying across the boat.

She'd got back on to her feet in a flash and went at him with fists, knees and nails and the two grappled as the boat rocked violently underneath them. Then suddenly it was over. Roderick, who had seemed to loose control for a moment, suddenly regained his composure and the two sat in stunned silence. Both scared and furious, at that moment all Donna wanted to do was get as far away from Rod as possible.

They were both relieved as well as exhilarated when they sighted landfall on 27 January 1990, nearly six weeks after leaving New Zealand. The *Chanson du Lecq* sailed into harbour at Cape Horn for a brief stop-over, then set off for the Falklands on the final leg of the trip. Rod had spent weeks preparing the *Chanson du Lecq* for a stormy passage, but the actual rounding was a complete anticlimax: the sea was calm as a millpond. Months afterwards, Ralph Williams's valued book arrived safely back in New Zealand. In the flyleaf it contained a photograph of Rod and Donna standing triumphantly on Cape Horn, which the delighted Ralph presented to Auntie Joy.

Freed from the pressures of ocean sailing, Rod and Donna found those first few weeks on the Falklands idyllic. They sailed from island to island, making friends as they went and enjoying the warm hospitality of the hardy people who had chosen to live their lives in one of the world's most isolated and forbidding locations. One day they called in at Ajax Bay, where there is a memorial to the dead soldiers buried there. As Rod stood in silent contemplation before it, Donna could see he was clearly very moved. She had not realized how much his own time in the army had meant to him. He went out of his way to make friends amongst the large contingent of army officers.

In addition to the native kelpers and the armed services, there is a third community in the Falklands: the 'yachties' – the free-spirited travellers who ply the world's oceans. Often they would limp in out of the mist and spend the winter in Port Stanley before attempting to round the Horn. They were about as varied a crowd as you could find – some were young, hippy types; some were ex-servicemen; some had chosen to leave the drudgery of nine to five; some were escaping other, unnamed, things. Donna and Rod naturally gravitated towards these sailors and were accepted immediately. In the evenings groups of ten or twelve would gather together for vegetarian dinners followed by long, rambling discussions on the meaning of life.

Almost every night, it seemed, there was a meal on someone's yacht or a beach barbecue or a barn dance organized by the islanders. Rod and Donna soon had a wide circle of friends: among others there was Mark

Bullock, the local police inspector, and his wife Fran, who put the couple up when they first arrived; and Steve Beldham, an engineer from London who owned the *Black Pig*, a steamer liberated from the Argentinian invaders.

The *Compass Rose* was a yacht that plied the waters between Chile and the Falklands and took parties of tourists to the Magellan Islands. When Rod and Donna were asked to help crew her they readily agreed. On one of their trips to Chile they met up with two intrepid English girls who had cycled through North and South America from Alaska – Sandy Davies and her friend Josephine Hunter. Sandy met and fell for Francisco, a Chilean crew member of the *Compass Rose*. Later, six days before Christmas, 1991, they were married on the beach in the Falklands. It was a big affair – there were about a hundred in the congregation. Steve Beldham, Rod's engineer friend, was the best man, Roderick was an usher and Josephine was the bridesmaid. Sandy's mum had flown from England to give her away. There was a short interruption in the proceedings when a nearby barking seal decided to compete with the vicar for the congregation's attention, much to everyone's amusement. When the pair were pronounced man and wife and kissed, a loud cheer went up which sent the seal slithering along the rock and skimming through the water. The party moved to a hall for some food and drink. Steve, never one for words, declined to make a speech and passed the honour over to Rod. Rod immediately made a bawdy joke that had everyone laughing – he was in his element.

Every spring hundreds of islanders and visitors would converge on Pebble Island in West Falkland for the annual games – the island's sporting highlight. Patrick Watt, a local journalist, was organizing the mile-long run sponsored by his paper. When Rod Newall strolled up and said he wanted to take part Patrick thought he was joking: Rod didn't have any kit and planned to run with his trouser legs rolled up. He certainly stood out from the other runners in their expensive running gear. When the starting pistol went off, Patrick seriously doubted whether such a heavy smoker as Rod would finish. They rounded the shore twenty minutes later in a tightly bunched formation and Patrick was surprised to see that Rod appeared to be keeping up. Suddenly there was a burst of movement at the back and Rod, clearly visible with his turned-up trousers and red hair, bolted away from the rest. He won by a clear twenty yards.

As the boat rocked gently on the swell Roderick Newall, who had been quieter and more thoughtful than usual, turned to his friend Mark Bullock and said: 'Look, Mark. We're mates, but you are a policeman and to be fair to you there's something you ought to know about me.' And he told his friend everything about his parents' disappearance more than two years earlier – about the huge search, the police investigation and their undisguised suspicions.

At the end of his remarkable story Mark Bullock sat in stunned silence while far above them an albatross hung motionless in the air.

After fifteen years as a policeman in Gloucestershire, Mark had been in need of a change of scenery. It was his girlfriend Fran who saw the newspaper ad for police officers to serve on the Falklands. And three months later – after a brief holiday in the Seychelles, where they got married – Mark accepted the post of police inspector, Fran took a job as a customs officer and they set off.

In January 1988, as the Tri-Star banked and turned into the approach for Mount Pleasant airport at the end of an eight-hour flight, Mark stared out of the window at the bleak smudge of brown hillside set in the South Atlantic Ocean and felt a stab of apprehension. What the hell am I doing here? he wondered.

But his fears were groundless. He and Fran took to life in the Falklands almost immediately. It was a world without class-consciousness where you were accepted for what you were. It was as if the community's isolation broke down barriers between people in a way that would be completely unthinkable at home. In a strange way Mark felt more at home here than he had ever done back in the Cotswolds.

His tiny force looked after a population of 6000, divided into those three communities: the native Falkland islanders, the 3000-strong armed forces, and the seafaring travellers. There was very little crime beyond a few drunk and disorderly servicemen and the odd dispute between fishermen or farmers.

One thing Mark had not foreseen was getting involved in one of the strangest murder investigations of recent years. A fire had swept through the Port Stanley hospital in 1984, killing eight patients and nurses. At the time it was assumed to be an accident, but when it later transpired that the NCO who raised the alarm had also been found near the scene of half a dozen suspicious fires in other army bases, an investigation was mounted. Mark was placed in charge of reinvestigating the hospital fire. It was a job that would absorb most of his energies.

He was working on the investigation when one day, literally out of the blue, in stepped Rod Newall and Donna Westend. The first thing the two bedraggled sailors wanted after their 3000-mile journey was a bath and, as Mark and Fran had one of the island's few supplies of hot water, they were only too happy to oblige. The two couples had a lot in common and took to each other instantly. They were all young, easy-going outdoor types, looking for new experiences. Mark and Fran said they could stay as long as they wanted.

Mark had always had a secret hankering to sail and was delighted when Roderick offered to give him lessons on the *Chanson du Lecq*. Rod was a scrupulous teacher and they spent days going through emergency drills in Stanley Bay to prepare Mark for the open sea. In the short time they had known each other Rod Newall and Inspector Mark Bullock had become firm friends.

It was through Rod and Donna that Mark and Fran began to explore the natural wonders of the islands. Fran was delighted when, emerging from the cabin one bright morning, she found the *Chanson du Lecq* surrounded by a school of leaping dolphins. She would throw crusts into the water, causing a flock of penguins to dart after the boat. Everywhere there was wildlife: high above, petrels, skuas and albatrosses performed their graceful aerobatics, while bull seals and penguins crowded the island coastlines.

Early one morning the four of them had gone to visit a king penguin colony. They dropped anchor, heaved the Zodiac inflatable dinghy into the water and silently made their way to the island. Then, on all fours, they crawled through the tussock grass to within fifty yards of their target and, passing the binoculars to each other, watched in amazement. There were king penguins everywhere. From the shoreline to the bottom of the rock cliffs at the foot of the mountain it seemed as if every inch of ground was occupied by parents or fluffy brown chicks. On one rock a bird was squawking noisily and protectively around its small brown bundle as a couple of skuas made low, menacing passes.

While the days were taken up with sailing, the evenings were spent having long, drunken dinners. Always the philosopher, Rod would try and engage Mark in his more arcane philosophical theories about life after death. Mark would laugh and tell the younger man he was full of shit. But despite Rod's taste for oddball religions and philosophies, Mark was always won over by his charm. It seemed there was nothing that Rod wouldn't do. One night at a party on Goose Green, Rod suddenly tore off his clothes and went streaking through the sand, screaming at the top of his voice. Rod was, Mark decided, the last of the free spirits.

But the story Rod had told him that day at sea gnawed away and he resolved to find out more. His opportunity came in June 1990. On a visit to London, when he was investigating the arson case, he punched Newall's name into the computer at Scotland Yard. The message on the screen seemed to confirm Rod's story: he was 'of interest to the Jersey police . . . if sighted please report to them as soon as possible'.

Mark's innocent enquiry led to an immediate request from the Jersey Police for him to fly to the island. The next morning – 21 June 1990 – he caught the early flight from Heathrow and at the airport he was met by Detective Sergeant Jimmy Adamson and Superintendent Martyn Le Brocq. The moment the detectives heard that Newall had been befriended on the Falklands by the local police chief, no less, they realized that finally, after three years, there could be a breakthrough in the Newall case. The important thing was to get Bullock on-side: he had to believe in Newall's guilt as much as they did.

The briefing took a whole day and they showed him everything – the discrepancies in the boys' statements; the evidence of the friends and neighbours; the blown-up photographs of the minute bloodstains found in the bungalow; the history of threats and violence within the family.

They questioned him closely and he described the carefree, charming young man who had come from nowhere and been a big hit with the Falkland islanders. He seemed very close to his brother Mark, who had even got Mark Bullock to take Roderick back a hamper from Fortnum and Mason when he was over on a previous trip.

In the afternoon they took Bullock out to No. 9 Clos de l'Atlantique. They showed him the spot in front of the fireplace where they thought Nicholas Newall had been battered to death, and they showed him the master bedroom where they believed Elizabeth had lain after she had been murdered. Then they explained how they wanted Bullock to help them. If Roderick could be lulled into a false sense of security, then he might be persuaded to confess to his parents' murders. Would Bullock consider helping?

On the plane back to London that evening, Mark Bullock's mind was in turmoil. He stared at the copious notes he had been making on the back of his driving licence in disbelief. How could the man he had come to know and like so much be capable of such a thing? And how could he betray such a good friend, to whom he had extended hospitality and to whom he had entrusted his life at sea? Yet the evidence was compelling and his policeman's instincts were too deeply ingrained to ignore. If Roderick *was* guilty of such a hellish crime, then surely it was his duty to investigate further.

When he returned to the Falklands Mark discussed the matter with Fran: he planned to try and get Rod to talk and suggested going on a long sailing trip.

'Great,' came Rod's reply. 'That would be terrific.'

A week later the *Chanson du Lecq* sailed through the brilliant clear blue waters of Port Stanley sound. They had stocked up on the essentials – the forward part of the cabin was weighed down with necesssary provisions including crates of beer and whisky. As Port Stanley receded into the distance Mark began to question the wisdom of what he was going to do. If Roderick was guilty – and despite the evidence he could not conceive of it for a moment – then he was alone at sea with a double murderer, a man capable of instant psychotic rage. He was not encouraged by the fact that he was a few inches taller and was more heavily built – nor by the fact that he had never shyed away from a 'ruck' in his years with the police. The fact was the sea was Rod's environment; if anything went wrong his word would stand. 'Look,' Mark had promised a worried Fran before he left, 'I'll just get round to it softly, softly, try and draw it out. If he doesn't bite then I'm not going to press it.'

For the first two days Mark concentrated on the sailing. Not for the first time he appreciated what was one of the few great wilderness experiences. On the third day they took the *Chanson du Lecq* into a quiet cove on a remote island and weighed anchor. Two dolphins had been tracking them all day; now they followed them in and occasionally Mark would lean over and try and touch a snout. By dusk they had both had a few beers and Mark began describing his childhood in Gloucestershire, his school and his family life. Then he asked, 'So tell me about Jersey, Roderick. What was that like?'

Apart from that one previous occasion Roderick had volunteered nothing about his background and he seemed reluctant now. It was strange, thought Mark, because he was usually so garrulous. Gently he turned the conversation away.

Later, when the only light came from the cabin lamp, and the only sound from the waves lapping against the hull, Roderick lay stretched out on his bunk. Mark, sitting cross-legged, asked him, 'Do you miss your parents, Rod?'

For a second the boy hesitated and Mark thought he wasn't going to say anything. Then he began to speak. 'It's really sad my father disappeared. We were at odds for a long time but just before he went missing I felt we were getting a bit closer.' Then he turned over and went to sleep. And that was as close as Mark ever got.

Despite the easygoing pace on the Falklands, it wasn't long before the strains in Rod and Donna's relationship returned. In the tiny community of Port Stanley Donna noticed that Rod's good looks, charm and wit aroused fascination amongst the women – and irritation in the men. Although Donna was relaxed about this – after all, they had never been an 'item' – she noticed that it didn't cut both ways. Once, at a beach party, she responded to some bloke's overtures; she'd had a bit too much to drink and when Rod told her it was time to leave she lost her temper. 'Fuck off back yourself,' she screamed at him. A huge public shouting match ensued. The next morning the two had trouble looking each other in the eye. They made it up, but Donna couldn't help but wonder if she and Rod were beginning to outgrow each other. She liked him – if she was being honest with herself, at one time she had more than liked him – but maybe some things were not meant to be. And maybe this particular friendship had run its course. After some months on the Falklands Donna felt the old restlessness returning. She longed to see something of South America and, though the Falklands was enjoyable and the people were kind, it was all too much like the community she had left behind in New Zealand.

Rod and Donna's tour of Argentina proved to be the highlight of her travels. They arrived in Punta Arenas on 3 May 1990 for an extended tour of South America and bussed and planed around the country, seeing the pampas, the forests, and the huge waterfalls of southern Patagonia. Donna felt her intimacy with Rod returning. She was amazed at his resourcefulness during the trip. 'If you have Spanish and pidgin English you can get through anything,' he said one day.

The parting in Buenos Aires was quick: 'I hate goodbyes,' said Donna.

'I know, so do I,' said Rod. 'Look, I won't wait for the plane. And remember to give my love to everyone in New Zealand and tell them I'm coming back one day, soon, I hope.'

'Don't worry,' said Donna, giving him a last hug. 'Write. And you take care of yourself. And if ever you are looking for some more crew you know where to find me. And I promise I'll pay attention next time.'

And then suddenly he had gone. Just before he reached the door he turned round, waved and flashed a smile. She waved back, and after he had gone, made her way to the check-in desk. Only then did she allow the tears to flow.

CHAPTER 11

On the island at the end of the world temperatures can plunge to minus thirty-nine degrees in mid-winter, and fierce winds batter the treeless hillsides remorselessly. The nearest human settlement of any size is far away across the ocean, but for Jerome and Sally Poncet and their three children Beaver Island is home.

The couple arrived in 1982, after sailing their steel-hulled yacht *Damien* across the southern oceans for ten years. They never wanted to live on dry land and, had it not been for the birth of their second child in a hut on the Antarctic peninsula, they would probably still be roaming the Southern Ocean today. Since then they have survived by combining sheep-farming in winter and yacht-chartering during the brief polar summer. In the specialized field of Antarctic sailing there is no name more revered that that of Jerome Poncet. Every year for the last twenty he has sailed the polar seas and he probably knows them better than anyone alive. In the *Damien II*, which he built himself, he has earned himself an unrivalled reputation as a man who can go anywhere in the ice.

When Rod Newall appeared in the bay he was, to the Poncet's, just another of the many solo yachtsmen who called in from time to time. He needed somewhere to stay while he did some repairs on the boat; Jerome and Sally offered him accommodation in an empty building next to their home in return for help around the farm. Soon he was fencing, shearing, dipping and rounding up the sheep flock on a motorized tricycle. The bearded, pony-tailed young stranger was an immediate hit with the children, and it seemed to Sally that he relished just hanging around the house and being one of the family. Probably very healthy after all those months at sea, she thought.

Indeed the solitude had been getting too much for Rod. He had planned to sail the *Chanson du Lecq* to South Georgia but he did not want to go on his own and, besides, he wanted to learn how to handle a bigger boat. Jerome said he could come along and crew the *Damien II* on its next charter, and in mid-November 1990 they set sail with three scientists from the British Antarctica Survey.

The aim was to carry out a census of South Georgia's fur seal population which, after falling for decades, had begun to grow again. The team wanted to discover how fast their numbers were growing, how much krill they consumed and how it would affect fish supplies. It was a job that had to be done quickly during the breeding season – between mid-November and mid-December.

The *Damien II* arrived on the island on 1 December. It is a spectacular and remote place with unconquered snow-capped peaks, vast glaciers and deserted Norwegian whaling stations occupied only by a small British military contingent. In a tiny cemetery near the settlement of Grytviken lies the grave of Sir Ernest Shackleton, who died there in 1922. A lone albatross followed the ship from the Falklands – on nearby Bird Island, their nests cover the tussock grass and macaroni penguins scream from the hillside. Over the next few weeks Rod took turns, along with the rest of the crew, to sit in the crow's nest with binoculars trained on a shoreline carpeted with barking seal pups, laboriously ticking off their numbers on a clipboard.

During the trip Rod had demonstrated that he was a natural sailor, and his talent and stamina had impressed Jerome. He was also friendly and an excellent cook – no mean qualities on an arduous journey in cramped conditions. In the galley Rod would take great pride in showing off what he could do with just a bit of this and that.

That the two men got on at all was surprising: they could not have been more different. Rod was the archetypal drifter, a hippy of the sea, travelling wherever the fancy took him. Jerome was solid, practical and hard-headed. Rod's lifestyle and outlook were completely anathema to him, and he wasn't slow to let the younger man know it. From the beginning there was an edge to the relationship, but somehow they connected. Occasionally Rod would boast about his army or sailing exploits, only to be mercilessly slapped down by Jerome, who baited him about his military past. 'The army are robots, Rod,' he would say, winking at the BAS scientists. 'Have they turned you into a robot too?' But Rod would take it all in good heart. Beneath the bullshit and the verbal jousting a strong mutual respect grew between the two men. Rod was an eager and intelligent pupil, and in Jerome he had found someone who had achieved something in his life – someone to look up to and respect.

As the *Damien* creaked in the ice late at night Jerome and Rod, fuelled by a bottle of whisky, would embark on deep philosophical discussions. Jerome asked, 'Why are you showing off all the time, Rod? What on earth are you doing with your life?' He saw through a lot of the bravado; his teasing was meant to test the boy. Once, when Rod boasted of his sexual exploits at sea,

Jerome upbraided him. 'Don't you want to fall in love, Rod?' he asked. 'Don't you want just one special woman?'

Rod considered his words for a moment but said nothing.

Despite Rod's tendency to shoot off at the mouth sometimes, Jerome thought there was a man of substance in there. If he would stop his wandering and set himself a target he really might be able to make something of himself one day. And although Rod did not yet know it, he was already in training for his life's work; he had already found himself.

On the 800-mile journey back to the Falklands Jerome let Rod take the wheel for the first time. It was a tough trip: they covered a total of 11,000 nautical miles in thirty-five days against prevailing winds. Once they got into harbour the bedraggled sailors celebrated their feat with a huge dinner. Scientifically and physically, it was a major achievement for the BAS team, as well as Jerome and Rod.

Meanwhile, on the other side of the world, Mark was getting on with business. The letter that had arrived at police headquarters in St Helier early in 1990 was brief and to the point. The Newall brothers' advocate, David Le Quesne, was requesting the police's assistance. He planned to apply in court for a formal declaration of death to be made and wanted the police to give evidence, saying they believed the Newalls were dead. Normally the relatives of a missing person have to wait seven years before obtaining a legal declaration of death, but if there is other evidence then a court can make the declaration sooner.

The lack of a death certificate was proving a problem with Nick's Lloyd's syndicates. Lloyd's still had him down as a name and Mark was paying out increasingly large amounts to cover his losses. The granting of a formal declaration of death meant that the couple's wills would come into force and the boys would inherit.

As he looked at the financial records piled high on his desk Detective Constable Charles MacDowall wondered – was it as simple as that? As long as Nick Newall was alive, his Lloyds syndicates would have to pay out year after year to stem the losses that were accruing. And there was no sign of them ever coming good again. Only when he had been pronounced dead in court would the estate protection plan be triggered which said, in effect, that no more monies would have to be paid out.

Had the brothers realized that their birthright had been in great jeopardy? Had they simply and cold-bloodedly decided to do away with their parents so as to hang on to the money remaining? Certainly Mark Newall had the financial nous to see the trouble that lay ahead. And the dirty work was not beyond Roderick. Was this the thing that had drawn the boys together? Hatred and greed – could that be the motive?

This placed the police in an invidious position: they were being asked by the prime suspects in a murder inquiry to testify in court that a murder had taken place so that those suspects could get their victims' money. The move infuriated some of the detectives. Their first instinct was to tell the boys where to go, but they had no alternative: they were legally required to give evidence.

The application to have the Newalls declared dead was applied for on 3 September 1990, in an affidavit from Mark Newall lodged with the Royal Court of Jersey in which he said he had had neither contact nor news of his parents since 11 October 1987 and that he believed them to be dead. His purpose in asking the

213

court to presume the death of his parents was to enable him to inherit his share of their estate.

The hearing was held before the island's Bailiff, Sir Peter Crill, in the Royal Court in St Helier on a grey drizzly day at the beginning of January 1991. Mark Newall had flown back from the United States to attend and Nan and Alaster Clark had arrived and were staying with Angela Barnes. Roderick, the court was told, was working on a yacht in the South Atlantic and was uncontactable until late 1991. His place was taken by barrister Peter Barnes, Angela's son and a co-executor of the estate.

From the moment he entered the courtroom the tension in Mark Newall was obvious: his face was white and he sat with his fists clenched. The court was told that he had been trying to look after his parents' assets and properties and that he was faced with large claims against his father's estate because of his Lloyd's syndicate losses. Mark was the first of four witnesses to give evidence. He crossed the courtroom floor in silence and stood in the box to take his oath, his face impassive behind the spectacles. His appearance was brief and again he restated his claim that his parents were alive and well on Sunday, 11 October 1987.

Sitting in the public benches, Nan Clark was stunned and angered by the swiftness of Mark's cross-examination. She had hoped he would be given a stiff grilling and that some of the inconsistencies in his story would be thrown in his face. Instead, it was over in minutes. In a clear, low voice he gave a brief account of the final dinner he had had with his parents, then told the court he had seen his parents the next day before leaving the island, but had 'never seen them since'. 'I believe they are dead primarily for three reasons,' he said from the witness box. 'I have not seen or heard from them for more than three years. I have seen no evidence that they have used any of their financial assets in those three years; and also largely because of information given to me by the police. They have indicated to me they are investigating murder.'

Mark was followed into the witness stand by his barrister Peter Barnes, and then Detective Chief Inspector Martyn Le Brocq gave evidence. He said that bloodstains had been discovered which had not been apparent at the start of the inquiry because of a thorough cleaning of the property. Again Nan Clark couldn't believe what she was hearing. She had been there with Adamson and Nimmo when the bloodstain on the poker was found.

It was the testimony of forensic scientist David Northcott, a senior scientific officer from the Forensic Science Service at Aldermaston, that provided the first public inkling of what had happened in the Newalls' home. Maureen Ellam's eagle-eyed discovery of a strange stain in the doorway of the bedroom had not been immediately acted upon. It was not until long after the Jersey scene of crime officers had drawn a blank in their examination of the house that the bloodstains had been found. From his examination Northcott had deduced that blood had soaked through the carpet and underlay in the area in front of the fire. 'At some stage someone was lying on the carpet long enough to lose quite a large quantity of blood,' he said. The blood had been sprayed quite widely on the walls and up onto the ceiling. The blood in the lounge was the same group as Mr Newall's twin brother Stephen.

'Was the amount of blood sufficient to be consistent with death?' he was asked.

'More than sufficient,' he replied.

'And what were your conclusions?'

'From my examinations, given the substantial amounts of blood that appeared to have been lost in each case, I concluded that Mr Newall probably died in the lounge and his wife probably died in the bedroom.' He said that it was clear from his examination that 'an episode of sustained violence' had taken place in the house.

The bailiff made his decision without retiring. After a brief summing up he announced that the court had 'found that presumption (of death) is proved beyond reasonable doubt'.

As the court rose Maureen Ellam slid from her place on the public bench and went over to Mark. She patted him gently on the arm and leaned over to speak to him, but he stared back at her impassively. The result of the hearing was predictable but had a devastating effect on Maureen. She broke down outside the courtroom and rushed away in tears. She ducked into a nearby department store and, when a young sales assistant asked her what was wrong, she could hold it in no longer: 'It's those boys. They've murdered their parents and now they've got all their money too,' she blurted out.

After the declaration of death Mark left the courtroom in a hurry. He agreed to attend police headquarters and for the first time since the disappearances was formally cautioned and told he was a prime suspect. He took the news calmly. Pursued by press reporters and TV cameras, Mark, Nan and Alaster went straight out to St John and sought sanctuary with Angela Barnes. As reporters circled the house they discussed how best to go back to Clos de l'Atlantique without being seen. Angela and Nan had a glass of gin each, Mark only a glass of water. He wasn't saying much, but Angela could see he was in a state. He clutched his glass in both hands and was so pale she thought he was going to be sick all over the carpet. Eventually they set off for the bungalow to empty what was in the house into cardboard boxes and bin liners.

Nan decided that all she wanted to take was the portrait of Elizabeth and the rocking horse that had been hers when she was little. Mark, however, was very organized. He filled boxes with clothes and Elizabeth's bits of jewellery and decided he would take the furniture and some pictures. What happened to the prized Rockingham china tea service and Nick's collection of port Nan never discovered, but she assumed Mark had it auctioned off. The dozens of bottles of port had been a christening present intended for when the boys came of age. Typically Nick had clung onto them, and it was a sign of the couple's dire financial straits that he had sold some of them off a few years before.

Angela noticed that the solid gold necklace that Nicholas had given Elizabeth as an engagement present was missing from the valuables. As Mark sorted through the clothing on the bed and divided it into separate piles, Angela looked at him and a curious thought passed through her mind: did he take the necklace off his mother's dead body or did he simply lift it out of a drawer?

As Mark was getting ready to leave, Nan asked him to make sure he went to the police station and arranged to leave the blood sample they had requested for their records; yes, he assured her, he would do precisely that. But instead he made his way straight to the airport and flew back to London.

Rod's first meeting with Emma Hatfield had not been auspicious: she was a scientist with the Cambridge-based British Antarctica Survey, whose purpose was to map and measure the last great wilderness. One of their tasks was to measure the size of the potential harvest to be gathered from the South Atlantic Ocean by the stocks of fish and molluscs that flourished there. In practice this meant a trip of anything from two to six weeks on a trawler, plying through freezing waters to collect squid samples and look for larvae. It was a hard job – frequently dangerous and sometimes boring – but it was one she relished. There were two great passions in her life: wildlife and the great outdoors, and now, at the age of twenty-seven, she was at last able to indulge them.

At the end of a trip the scientists would head back to Stanley and join the rest of the disparate groups that mingled there. Everyone would eventually meet everyone else – usually in one of the local pubs: the Globe or the Rose or the Victory.

In the pub one night Emma was furious to find two men cramming her into the corner. One was an officer from Mount Pleasant, the other a red-haired 'yachtie' type, and they were loudly braying about their military exploits. Emma was a successful woman in what was largely a man's world, but she had not got there by playing men's games, and few things annoyed her more than little-boy stories.

After ten minutes of this, Emma decided to get up and go. Squeezing past the pair on her way to the door, she leaned over and said, 'Why don't you two grow up?'

The one in the uniform was slightly taken aback by the sudden hostility, but the other red-haired one with the public-school accent said, 'Look, stay, I'll get you another drink.'

'Don't bother,' she retorted, 'you make me sick with your kids' stories. Why don't you grow up and do something worthwhile?' And with that she stormed off. Before she slammed the door shut she glanced back at the red-haired man; he looked neither angry nor indignant; instead he was smiling at her.

But when she met him again at a party, Emma found herself talking to Rod Newall as if she had known him all her life – and it wasn't the drink. There was a relaxed, easy-going quality to the young man and, to her surprise and delight she discovered that, far from being some kind of armed forces nut, he was laid back and intelligent. They talked about their love of the sea and what had drawn them to this godforsaken part of the world. Emma was delighted at Rod's genuine interest in wildlife, and she was impressed when he revealed the extent of his epic single-handed voyage. Then suddenly, out of the blue, Rod asked her, 'Can you remember the single most important thing or event that changed your life?'

Without hesitation Emma found herself telling him about the time she had been attacked. It was something she had revealed to very few people but it seemed natural to tell Rod. The attack had been traumatic and had left her nearly suicidal. In turn she asked, 'And what about you, Rod?'

The young man took a deep swig from his beer can and looked up at her: 'I think it would have been when my parents disappeared . . . ' He talked steadily in a low voice for a few minutes without hesitating or stumbling. When he had finished he took another mouthful of beer and looked directly into Emma's eyes.

For a fleeting moment when he had begun his story Emma wondered if he was joking. She did not know how to react properly to such a revelation. The celebration wore on and despite the alcohol the pair were subdued but easy in each other's company. At the end

219

of the evening, as they said goodbye, Emma felt that a bond had been established between them.

A few days later, between Christmas and New Year 1990, Rod met Emma and asked her if she wanted to come on a sightseeing trip on his boat with his friend Josephine. 'Sure, why not?' she replied.

'Jason' is the name given to a group of islands to the north-west of the Falklands which are home to thousands of seals and birds. Also found there are bull elephant seals, which do not take kindly to being disturbed: in an instant they can change from a slumbering mass of grey blubber to two tons of roaring aggression. So when Rod suddenly announced he was going ashore to count them the girls thought he was mad. 'No, it will save you the time and effort of having to send a boat to do a census,' Rod told Emma. Undeterred by the girls' protests, he insisted he would be all right and lowered the little dinghy – an Avon with an outboard motor. Emma was to take him ashore in the dinghy and pick him up later while Jo tacked up and down the coast in the *Chanson du Lecq*.

Elephant seals packed the shoreline in heaving, steaming packs and Emma was full of misgivings as she carefully manoeuvred the boat through the kelp that matted the shoreline. As they got closer the bull seals became increasingly agitated. 'Rod, are you sure about this?' Emma asked nervously.

He turned back from the bow. 'Look, it's no problem. They are more scared of us than the other way around.'

For such huge animals, they had a surprising turn of speed on land and were very much faster in the water. Emma knew that if her little dinghy got into an argument with one of them, there was no doubt about who would win, and she was more than a little perturbed by Rod's carefree attitude towards the bulls. All her experience told her that they should be taken very seriously indeed.

Gently Emma let the dinghy bob into the shore. Rod turned to tell her, 'Wait for me to signal you before you come back. I won't be long.' And before she could reply he had leapt over the side, waded through the surf and scrambled onto a rock.

At that moment there was a loud noise to Emma's left and she turned round to see a bull seal roaring at her. For a moment her heart nearly stopped: it must have been 100 yards away, but seemed much closer. Then the animal lowered its nose and, with an enormous splash, plunged into the water. Emma realized it was not a place to hang around. Gripping the motor starting handle, she pulled as hard as she could: the engine spluttered for a second, then choked and was silent. She gripped the cord again and, as she did so, heard another roar directly behind her. Another two bull seals were dragging their great bulk towards the edge of a rock only yards away. There was no doubt about it now: they were taking a keen interest in her and the boat. Emma pulled the starting handle again and again the engine wheezed and died. Behind her there was another huge splash, which sent up a plume of water splashing onto the Avon and soaking her. The swell sent the dinghy rocking violently from side to side. Emma realized that she was on the verge of panic; she had to concentrate. With both hands she grabbed the handle and gave it a pull that sent her flying onto her back. The engine barked into life and moments later, with the Avon nosing its way back towards the yacht, she was thanking God for her good luck – and cursing the reckless fool who had got her into that position in the first place.

Back on the *Chanson du Lecq* Emma, still shivering
– with fright as much as her soaking – was complaining
bitterly. Where the hell had Rod got to? All they could
see was seals. Half an hour later there was still no sign
of him. As they sailed to and fro, they could hear what
they thought was the roar of a seal; it was Roderick.
He stood on a rocky outcrop, waving furiously.

Making doubly sure there were no bull seals in the
area, Emma set off again in the dinghy. When Rod
climbed aboard he was fuming. 'What the hell were
you playing at?' he roared. 'I've been shouting and
waving for ages.'

Emma was indignant. 'What do you mean? You
should have behaved responsibly and turned up when
you said you would. I've risked my bloody life to pick
you up.'

For a second the pair stood shouting insults at each
other; then both seemed to realize how absurd they
looked in amongst all the seals, and they both collapsed
with laughter.

Emma later decided that this was when she fell in
love with Rod Newall. In her heart she wanted more,
but she realized he was too much of a wanderer.

And indeed, Rod was soon off to explore the South
American coast in the *Chanson du Lecq*. Before he
left, he said goodbye to the Poncets: after hugging the
children, Rod kissed Sally and shook Jerome firmly by
the hand and then sailed into the horizon. He promised
he would come back, but Jerome sensed in Rod an
underlying unease and hoped the boy would find whatever it was he was looking for.

The first thought that struck Helena Pedot when the
scruffily dressed stranger walked into the bar was that
he looked a bit like a Viking. With his long, matted

hair and ginger beard, Roderick Newall was certainly an incongruous figure in the sophisticated Veleiros do Sol Yacht Club – a watering hole for the rich and famous in Porto Alegre.

It was July 1991 and, as a break from the rigours of the South Atlantic, Roderick had sailed the *Chanson du Lecq* up the South American coast and eventually arrived at the bustling town in southern Brazil.

Helena, who was with her friend Eloisa Endres, had been through a traumatic time. After thirteen years of marriage she had just divorced her husband. He had kept their three children and she was now a single girl again with a lot of living to catch up on. She was slim, with shoulder-length brown hair, and looked a lot younger than her thirty-two years. She was a popular girl in the local club scene and the Veleiros do Sol was a regular haunt for her and Eloisa. The club's car park was filled with Porsches, Ferraris and BMWs; inside it was wall-to-wall designer clothing and fancy cocktails: this guy didn't fit in at all.

Helena's curiosity was aroused when she heard him order a drink. She had taught English and spoke the language fluently, so she immediately recognized his accent and quizzed the good-looking stranger on his origins. The three fell into conversation and after a few drinks Eloisa asked the young man if he would like to come to her birthday party.

Why not? Roderick Newall didn't know anyone else in town. As he left the bar he smiled at Helena.

The next night at the same clubhouse Eloisa's party was in full swing, with music blaring and drink flowing. But at a corner table a couple were deep in conversation, oblivious to everything around them. Rod Newall had been smitten with Helena from the moment they met and the attraction was mutual. She was beautiful and intelligent and totally beguiled by his conversation and his experiences. By the end of the night, with more than a few drinks inside him, Roderick was telling her repeatedly how beautiful she was and how she would love the South Atlantic. During his years of travelling there had been many casual sexual encounters, but Helena was nothing like the others.

Within a few days Roderick had decided he was in love for the first time, and Helena chatted excitedly about the guy who had walked in from the sea and was going to change her life. Eloisa smiled: she had heard it all before – Helena was always falling in love.

But not everyone was beguiled by the Newall charm. Eloisa's boyfriend had spoken to him for only a few minutes and then moved away. 'That guy's trouble,' he whispered to his girlfriend.

But Helena and Roderick had no doubts. As far as Roderick was concerned Helena was a genuine soul-mate, someone he could open up to and communicate with. As the months passed the relationship grew more intense. Roderick rented a flat in Porto Alegre, got to know Helena's family and for the first time in years began to think of his future.

One night in November Roderick turned up at Helena's flat in great excitement and said they were going out for an expensive meal. She quizzed him all the way, but it was only after pouring the champagne that he revealed the reason for his happiness. 'Today,' he said, lifting his glass, 'is the day I become a million-aire.' His inheritance had come through.

Roderick clearly yearned for somewhere he could call home and someone he could love, and Helena pro-vided all that. But Brazil was advantageous for other reasons. Like Ronnie Biggs, if Rod married a local woman, he would effectively be beyond the reach of Britain's extradition laws.

As the relationship progressed, however, other aspects to Roderick emerged that Helena found less attractive. His sudden mood switches began to alarm her: the most trivial dispute would soon flare into a major row. She sometimes felt scared of him.

Then Roderick announced he was going back down to the ice to crew on the ice-breaker; he would only be gone a few months and when he returned they would be able to start planning a proper future together.

Jerome Poncet was surprised when the sails of the *Chanson du Lecq* appeared in the sound off Beaver Island again. Rod Newall was back, and he could hardly contain his excitement about Helena. From Rod's animated description Jerome and Sally were left in no doubt. He was going back to see her father after his next voyage with Jerome: this was the big one.

From December through to March the blanket of ice that cloaks the Antarctic peninsula shrinks back far enough to permit exploration. On New Year's Day 1992, at the height of the Antarctic summer, the *Damien II* set off with Roderick Newall crewing again. This time the passengers were a film crew from the BBC's Natural History Unit in Bristol, who were making a major documentary series on Antarctic wildlife – *Life in the Freezer*, presented by David Attenborough. For most of the year Antarctica is a barren white desert, but for two months during the polar summer it blossoms into a land teeming with wildlife: albatrosses and petrels fill the sky and the air echoes to the clacking of penguins and the roar of elephant seals. The *Damien II*'s job was to ferry the production team around some of the bays and islands, putting ashore and supplying the four land-based camera teams with food, tents, medical kit and radios. The trip was filled with the most unforgettable natural wonders, and it was to mark a turning point in Rod's life in more ways than one.

Even at the height of summer the waters of the Southern Ocean are battered continually by winds such as the notorious 'roaring forties', and are the most dangerous anywhere. And it is not just the winds that pose a hazard to seafarers. When the temperature suddenly dropped to mark the passing of the Polar Front – the wall of cold air that rings the continent – lots of small dots began to appear on the *Damien II*'s radar. Though apparently harmless, the small icebergs grew steadily in number and were a constant threat, especially at night. Navigation was slow, tiring and extremely dangerous. Even with a steel-hulled boat like the *Damien II*, the risks are just as great now as they were when Shackleton's ship the *Endurance* was crushed by ice in 1916. Successful navigation calls for an eagle eye in reading the 'lines', the tiny frissures that indicate a possible way forward. A nose for danger is also helpful and on several occasions Jerome noticed the wind had changed so imperceptibly it had not even registered on the ship's instruments. He was able to take the boat out of trouble before the ice began to close in.

In the water the heads of Weddell seals would suddenly emerge and occasionally a sinister-looking killer whale accompanied by scavenging petrels would glide by. Eventually, as they approached the peninsula, the air filled with seabirds: skuas, petrels and albatrosses wheeling and diving around the ship. From time to time the sea would suddenly turn bright pink with giant shoals of krill that provided food for so much of the sea life. Taking advantage of the perpetual summer daylight, the *Damien II* spent ten days following hump-backed whales. Two of them went round and round the ship, hoovering up the krill, diving and resurfacing.

It was not until the middle of February, after five weeks at sea, that the *Damien II* nosed her way between two ice floes and came within sight of the white continent first glimpsed by Captain Cook in his polar explorer the *Resolution* on 16 January 1776.

As on the last trip, Jerome and Rod would sit through the night and argue and talk while the rest were asleep. 'Why all the bullshit, Rod?' Jerome would say with a provocative grin. 'What do you think it proves?' He would be merciless about Rod's enthusiasm for offbeat American self-improvement philosophies. 'Why do you bother with all this crap, Rod?' he would say, grabbing a paperback from Rod's hands and throwing it to the other side of the cabin. In other circumstances it was an act that might have drawn a very different reaction from Roderick; as it was, he smiled, picked up his book and went back to reading.

Rod's duties aboard the *Damien* were varied. He would take his turn at the wheel and keep watch and, once again, his abilities as a cook made him very popular with the television team. Jerome would never have admitted it to Rod, but secretly he was delighted with the progress his young protégé had been making. He showed a real understanding of the ice. Over the two seasons they had spent together, he had become a much steadier individual – less inclined to talk rubbish as well.

During those long, drunken nights on the Antarctic ice Roderick began thinking long and hard about his future. He often spoke of how fed up he was with wandering aimlessly and a thought seemed to crystallize and grow in his mind. The days of the Antarctic

227

pioneers such as Shackleton, Amundsen and Scott had gone for ever, but their place had been taken by a new kind of invader: Goretex-clad tourists anxious to discover the last wilderness on earth. The continent was opening up as a major tourist attraction and cruise ships regularly plied the waters between Chile, South Georgia and the ice. If Jerome could do it, why couldn't he? After finally inheriting his parents' estate, money was no problem. All he needed was a suitable boat.

The end of the BBC expedition was celebrated with a dinner at the Malvina Hotel. More than fifteen people crammed into the small lounge and huge quantities of food and drink were consumed. At the end of a long table Rod entertained Jerome's three children. That night, with his arm around Jerome's neck, Rod suddenly outlined the plan that had been taking shape in his mind during their second journey together. He wanted to start up his own chartering business once he had bought a boat. He would travel to America to look for a suitable vessel because they were half the price they were elsewhere.

Far from being put out at having trained a potential rival, Jerome was delighted. He could envisage a good, mutually supportive working relationship with Rod – one where they could both reap the benefits of the coming tourist harvest. They charged their glasses and drank to a bright future together.

Later Rod mapped out his route. He planned to fly to Brazil and take Helena to Miami, where he thought he would be able to find the kind of vessel at the right price. Steve Beldham had agreed to crew for him and, once Rod had found the right boat, he was going to send for him. Together they would sail it down to the South Atlantic.

The day before he left Rod went round and said

goodbye to all his friends in Port Stanley. They were startled by the change in his appearance. Gone was the bearded and pony-tailed figure in the oil-stained boiler suit; he had cut his hair and shaved and was wearing a smart blue blazer. It was the first time he had worn it since marching out of the depot at Winchester four years previously.

In Miami in March 1992 Roderick and Helena went to see the film *Cape Fear*, a gripping thriller about a man pursued by his past. Afterwards Roderick was quieter than usual. He said to Helena, 'Sometimes it is good to live in fear.'

The fights and rows between the couple continued and were not helped by the fact that Roderick was having no success in finding a yacht. Eventually he did find a suitable candidate: a sixty-six-foot former Canadian coastguard ice-breaker; ironically enough, she was in England on the river Thames.

CHAPTER 12

Emma-Jane Lonsdale couldn't tell if the guy across the table was bullshitting her or not. 'No, seriously,' he said, casually breaking off another slice of pizza. 'It's all quite true.' He was a friend of a friend and she'd only met him an hour before. Over dinner he'd regaled her with his stories of his last four years on the ocean wave; then he'd hit her with this amazing tale of his missing parents and how they'd been bumped off by drug dealers.

'Of course the cops all thought I'd had something to do with it,' he said with a shrug and flashed a smile at her. 'Still do. In fact they'll probably come and see you to find out if I've told you anything.'

Earlier that day Emma had received a phone call from an old friend, Charlie Shaw, who was back in London after a few years in the States. He hadn't changed – same evil smile, twinkling eyes and fatal charm, and he'd introduced her to this casually dressed blond-haired guy with the impeccable manners. 'I'm very pleased to meet you,' he'd said. 'The name's Rod.' Even if she hadn't known he was at Radley his self-confidence would have betrayed his public school background.

They had all gone out to a restaurant in Fulham and Rod had told them he was in town to buy a yacht for his new business. Emma was fascinated by the idea of

230

a yacht in Antarctica and had only been half joking when she asked if she could crew for him.

'Maybe.' He'd smiled at her. 'Who can tell?' And then he'd come out with this weird story about his parents. She didn't know whether to take him seriously or not, but it certainly added to the air of intrigue surrounding him.

A few weeks later, on 10 June 1992 Rod phoned her out of the blue. 'I've done it,' he said, his voice trembling with excitement.

'Done what?' she asked.

'I've bought the bloody boat!' he said, and Emma-Jane remembered their conversation. She was impressed: he wasn't a bullshitter after all. But he needed a favour. He had nowhere to stay – could he 'crash' over at her place for the night?

'Sure,' she said.

That night, over a rapidly emptying bottle of whisky in Emma-Jane's Fulham house, the two got talking and Rod, still on a high, began waxing philosophical. He spoke of the changes taking place in his life, of his current relationship with Helena and how he planned to settle down with her. But there were problems. When two people get together, he said, there is an initial infatuation, then a period of chaos as two strangers get to know each other, then stability. He and Helena had been through a bad patch but were coming out the other side.

On 26 June Rod took Emma-Jane and a couple of her friends out to dinner at Blake's – a discreet exclusive hotel in South Kensington with one of the best and most expensive restaurants in London. They were joined by a smartly dressed young man in a suit and glasses. Roderick sprang out of his seat, gave the young man a hug, and introduced his brother Mark, who was

231

staying in the hotel briefly while on a business trip.

To Emma-Jane the dark-haired, serious-looking young man seemed much older than Roderick; so she was surprised to learn he was a year younger. At the end of the evening she noticed that it was Mark – not Rod – who picked up the bill for everyone.

Roderick Newall's search for a yacht had ended in May at St Katherine's Dock on the Thames. She was no beauty and had obviously seen better days. Her paintwork was flaked, the main mast woodwork was cracked and broken, but the moment Rod saw her he knew she was the one for him. She was a sixty-six-foot steel-hulled schooner, built for toughness rather than elegance or speed. She could berth six and was owned by a doctor who had found the cost of getting her afloat again prohibitive. Mark put up the bulk of the purchase price, but there was still a £150,000 mortgage to pay off. Rod renamed her *Austral Soma*.

When not working on the purchase of a boat Roderick could be found hunched over a kitchen table in a large house in Lymington, struggling over the advertising blurb for a brochure on the *Austral Soma* which would entice would-be Antarctic visitors. The house belonged to Charlie Shaw's mother. She was used to young visitors, but Roderick occupied a special place in her thoughts: from the age of thirteen, when Charlie had first brought him home, Roderick had seemed like a member of the family. He had always taken great pains to keep in touch – rarely a month went by without a letter or postcard. Now here he was, planning his first business in her kitchen.

The *Austral Soma*, he wrote, would offer an unforgettable journey, 'Sailed by an experienced crew with a comprehensive knowledge of Antarctica and the spectacular waters of the South Atlantic, this steel-hulled

schooner offers a never-to-be-forgotten experience.'
Austral Soma Yacht Charters would offer a choice of
two cruises: 'one from Argentina to South Georgia in
January, and the following month from Argentina to
Cape Horn and Antarctica, both at a cost of $3880 per
person'. The brochure also gave a brief description of
'the Captain, Rod Newall, aged twenty-eight, born in
Glasgow', followed by a resumé of his army and travelling experience to date.

When the purchase was completed, Rod had the *Austral Soma* transferred to a dry dock in Dover and began
stripping her down and getting her ready for the long
voyage ahead. He was working against the clock: he
had to get the boat down to the ice and ready for the
beginning of the new season. In Dover he was reunited
with someone who had once been his closest friend. He
had taken a break from the yacht to have a drink in a
pub when he bumped into a young rifleman from his old
platoon who told him that Patrick Sanders was based in
Dover.

When Rod phoned and explained that he was spending two weeks in town working on his boat, Patrick had
no hesitation in inviting Rod to stay with him and his
wife Fiona for the duration. Four years had passed since
they last met and the young man who strode into the
regimental mess seemed much changed to Patrick's
eyes. Rod seemed steadier, more in control – a more
substantial individual altogether. The impetuousness
had been curbed and replaced with a seriousness totally
lacking in his army days. One of the most abiding tenets
to a British army officer is loyalty to one's comrades
and friends. When the whispering about Rod's parents
had started Patrick made an early decision to stand by
his friend. He did not believe Rod could possibly be
guilty of such a crime and he had never wavered from

this belief. Throughout the long dark days after the disappearances Patrick had been one of Rod's staunchest supporters in the battalion.

After Rod left the army, however, it had been difficult to stay in touch. Rod had sailed away over the horizon and out of Patrick's life. Occasionally there had been a postcard from some exotic port of call, but these became less and less frequent. Meanwhile Patrick, always much more serious about the army, had settled into the life of a career soldier. He had married and now Captain Sanders was the battalion adjutant at the Green Jackets Connaught Barracks high above the town beside Dover Castle.

As Roderick flicked through a regimental scrap book that was left lying about in the mess he came across glimpses of himself from another world. Here he was preparing to go to a Bruce Springsteen concert; here in sunglasses, setting off for a party. Near the end was a formal portrait of the young Lieutenant Newall in full dress uniform, smiling proudly beside some fellow officers. Looking over his shoulder, Patrick found it hard to believe they were the same person.

Four years had passed but the rapport between the two men was as strong as ever. Over dinner that night Rod outlined his plans. Patrick caught the glint of excitement in his eyes as he talked, and remembered how his old friend could so easily be caught up with the most unlikely enthusiasms. Rod had once read a book by Bernard Levin in which *The Times* columnist lists his top ten greatest experiences of all time. One of these was apparently listening to Wagner while looking at Rembrandt's 'The Night Watch'. So one afternoon a bemused but indulgent Patrick found himself sitting on a bench with Rod in the Rijksmuseum in Amsterdam as classical music boomed into his ears through a pair of Sony Walkman headphones. For an intelligent man, Patrick thought, Rod could be almost childish in his oddball ideas – but that was all part of his charm. And now, despite his new-found maturity, Rod had not entirely left his old self behind. One evening Patrick asked him about a strangely shaped pendant that hung around his neck.

'Do you like it? I designed it myself and had it made,' Rod told him. It was made out of platinum. Patrick mumbled a polite, 'Er, yes, Rod . . . it's . . . very interesting.'

But Rod was a man with a dream now, and it was clear it was one that consumed him. As he showed his old friend over the boat, he demonstrated his formidable technical know-how and was able to explain in tortuous detail the workings of the engine. Patrick was amazed at the change that had come over him. Five years earlier he and Rod had both been not much more than novices when they sailed in the Med. Rod was now an experienced sailor who had rounded Cape Horn and taken the helm in some of the most dangerous waters in the world. Patrick listened to his friend's stories of tropical South Sea islands and adventures in the Antarctic pack ice with wonder and not a little envy. It all seemed far removed from the mundane day-to-day regimental life.

One evening Patrick and Fiona decided to hold a dinner party for Rod. A few old friends were rustled up from the old days at Celle, and a relaxed and drunken evening ensued.

But mostly Rod would work. Over the next few weeks the dry dock was the scene of frantic activity as he displayed a determination that had been all too lacking during his army days. He would usually be up and out of the house by six thirty and would take advantage of the long summer nights to work on until late. There was so much to be done if the boat was to be ready for the long journey ahead and a lifetime of ploughing through the iceberg-strewn waters of Antarctica. Speed was of the essence: if his business was to be viable, then Rod had to be back in Port Stanley and ready to take his first charter by January – the beginning of the South Atlantic summer. He was very short of money and when the Dover Yacht Company quoted him over £1000 to scrape the paint off the bottom of the boat and take it back to the steel, he decided to do it himself. He explained to Patrick that although Mark had helped with the purchase he still had a substantial mortgage to pay off, so the money would have to start coming in before the end of the year. It was a heck of a commitment to take on.

One hot June night Patrick and Rod were enjoying a pint in the Griffin's Head and having a laugh about the old days. Rod had just finished another gruelling session on the *Soma* and was covered with blue dust from the anti-fouling material he was using to coat the hull. The talk drifted to the events of five years before. Rod's arrest for possession of hash on Jersey had cast a shadow over his departure from the Green Jackets. His features grew animated as he recounted the story: 'The bastards were out to frame me, Pat. It was a set-up. The moment I stepped off the plane the drugs squad were there in the fucking lobby with police dogs. I was the only passenger taken to one side. It was a complete fucking set-up.' On the mainland possession of hash might merit no more than a caution these days – and then only if the police could be bothered – but on Jersey it was viewed in a very different light. Rod went on excitedly; two other men in jail with him had been leaned on, he said. They had been told to implicate him in drug-smuggling, jewel robbery – anything; they were even told to say he had confessed to killing his parents.

Patrick decided it was a suitable time to broach the subject: 'Rod, what do you think happened to your parents?'

'Oh, I have my theories . . . ' he said darkly. He did not seem remotely thrown by the question but was uncharacteristically reticent about elaborating – strange in someone who was usually so willing to talk. Patrick was sympathetic and interested; he realized immediately that five years had not lessened the pain.

When the boat was ready to be sailed from Dover to Brighton, where it was to be stocked, Rod's old girlfriend from the Falklands, Emma Hatfield, turned up to lend moral support and travel with the yacht. She was back with the British Antarctica Survey in Cambridge after having successfully gained her Ph.D. And Rod was off to a good start: he had already been promised one charter by the BAS, who wanted a team of scientists taken down to the ice.

Some of Rod's other Falkland friends were also in the UK. Sandy Davies and her husband Francisco stopped by in Dover to check over the boat and lend encouragement; Steve Beldham also turned up. He had agreed to help Rod sail the *Austral Soma* back down to the South Atlantic. The two men were diametrically opposite in character: Rod was sociable and extrovert; Steve was taciturn and undemonstrative. In spite – or perhaps because – of that, everyone agreed they made a perfect crewing combination.

During the final few days Roderick had to see someone about advertising his business and the yacht had to be stocked and finished. Then, one afternoon, when it was all nearly completed, Rod mentioned he had a couple of relatives he wanted to visit before he set sail for the South Atlantic.

On 2 July he phoned his Aunt Nan in the flat she had moved to in Hurlingham Square, Fulham. She was taken completely by surprise. She had no idea Roderick was back in the country. She had long given up her desire to see her nephews brought to justice. The memory of her dreadful nightmare on the night of her sister's murder still lingered and she felt sure it was her sister's last wish to let matters rest. Whatever happened, there was no bringing Nick and Elizabeth back, and God knows what effect two life sentences would have on the boys' grandmother, let alone the rest of the family. One day Roderick and Mark would have to answer for their crimes, but Nan was happy to leave that to a higher court. Until then, despite what her nephews had done, she felt she still had a duty to them.

Nan's invitation to come round for dinner that night was accepted and when she opened the door to Roderick, she was mainly surprised at the lack of change in him. He was a bit sturdier, maybe – he had filled out; and, after a few minutes' casual chat, she thought he seemed quieter and more grown-up than before.

Alaster was deeply reluctant to have Roderick in the house, but he shook hands stiffly and, after pouring drinks, they sat down and listened as Rod told them about his adventures on the high seas, about his newly purchased yacht, and his long-term plans to set up a chartering business based in Port Stanley. Roderick was relaxed and at ease up until the moment Nan placed his meal in front of him. It was lobster, the same dish the Newalls had eaten at the Sea Crest. He looked slightly awkward and said, 'I haven't had this for some time . . .'

When the Clarks mentioned they were planning to spend a lot more time in Spain Rod became enthusiastic. 'You've just got to go and do the things you want to do,' he told Alaster. 'You've only got one life, you know.' He seemed to think it important they appreciate this.

Then there was a phone call summoning Alaster to Brixton police station, where he was the duty GP. Alaster was relieved to escape from an awkward atmosphere, but he felt apprehensive about leaving Nan alone – although a glance from her told him she would be all right.

As Nan and Rod talked the conversation turned to philosophy. Even when he was a little boy, Nan remembered, Rod couldn't bear any criticism of his weird ideas. Now he told her about the German philosophers he had read at sea and how their views on life had influenced him. When he asked his aunt if she believed in life after death, Nan replied that she did. Roderick was quiet for a second, then asked if she had ever seen or heard from his mother.

'Yes, the night she died,' said Nan.

'What did she say?'

'She said, "I told you he meant it and I told you it would happen. But let the matter rest."' A silence hung over the room for a few moments and Roderick sipped his coffee. Then Nan said that despite everything she still wanted to know what had happened that night.

By now there was no sign of any defensiveness or anger in Roderick – it was as if he were spent. Then he looked straight at Nan and for a moment she thought she saw a strange light in his eyes. 'Even if you knew what happened you still would not understand,' he said.

'Why would I not understand, Roderick?' she asked.

'I do not understand myself,' came the reply.

At that moment the front door slammed shut: Alaster was back. It was as if a spell had been broken and Nan had lost a chance to find out what had happened five years previously. Later, as Roderick said goodbye, she felt she should give him some word of encouragement. 'Well, goodbye, Roderick,' she said as they stood at the door. 'I hope you do find whatever it is you are looking for.'

'Thank you, Auntie Nan,' he said, kissing her on the cheek.

It was only when he had gone that Nan realized what the strange look in his eyes had been: that of a soul in torment.

Before his departure, Rod also wanted to say goodbye to his relatives in Scotland – his grandmother in North Berwick and his Uncle Stephen and Aunt Gay. Emma-Jane Lonsdale had lent him her Golf GTI for a few days while she was abroad and the next day he sped north, taking his usual liberties with the speed limits en route. In the early afternoon the car pulled up in front of the large comfortable stone house overlooking the seafront in North Borwick, where Roderick and Mark had played in the sand as children. The sight of her grandson for the first time in four years delighted Mrs Nelson. Like everyone else, she sat in wonderment as he described his adventures on the high seas. That afternoon Rod took his grandmother to visit his cousin, William Clark. Since their wedding William and Amanda had moved into a fine old farmhouse, South Caldoch, between the Campsie Hills and the Ochill Hills near Stirling. William was the managing director of the Nelson family firm in Glasgow, and Amanda had produced two sons, Harry and Rhuairidh, in quick succession. As he cradled baby Harry in his arms, Roderick was obviously delighted to be there. His solitary travels had made him appreciate what he was missing without a family and now for the first time in years he felt as if he belonged.

At midday on 14 July Roderick, dressed casually in jeans and tartan shirt and sporting his usual Ray Bans, made his way through crowds of tourists along to the east end of Princes Street in Edinburgh, turned right and pressed a doorbell. His godmother Vanessa Prosser had been surprised at his sudden reappearance after so many years at the ends of the earth, and she was curious about what prompted it. She had agreed to meet and the two went for a pub lunch near her home.

Rod told her he was a changed man and that his drug-taking was all in the past. He was going to devote himself to his work. But despite his cheerful optimism, Vanessa could tell there was something gnawing at him. In the middle of an anecdote he broke off and asked her, 'What do you think happened to my parents?'

Vanessa could hardly believe what she was hearing. There was a moment's silence then, as he made to speak again, she raised her hand. 'Stop there, Roderick. I don't want you to tell me any more.' They finished their meal stiffly and walked back to where Roderick had parked his car. As she watched him drive away, Vanessa thought she had detected within her godson a strong need to unburden himself. Whatever else he had found on his travels, peace of mind was obviously not among them.

The unexpected call from her cousin had thrown Amanda Newall into a bit of a fluster. Like the rest of the family, she had no idea Roderick was in the country – she had never expected to see him again. Like Roderick, Amanda had changed over the years. After university she had worked briefly in marketing but had given up her job to marry a salmon farmer, Henry

Barge, and live in a house near Loch Fyne in the wilds of Argyllshire. She devoted her days to a cake-baking business and looking after her baby and she could not imagine ever being happier.

Roderick congratulated her belatedly on her wedding and apologized for not being able to be there. Could he travel to the West Highlands to see her? It would be a good chance to catch up. Amanda had to say no – she felt unable to handle it. They chatted for a bit and Roderick said that one day she would have to come down to Antarctica for a trip on the *Austral Soma*. Yes, Roderick, she said. Perhaps. Maybe one day. Before he rang off she gave him the name of the Perthshire hotel where her parents were spending the weekend. Roderick was glad to track them down – he'd been on the verge of giving up when there was no answer from the house in Rhu.

For her sixtieth birthday Gay Newall had decided she wanted the minimum of fuss: she declined all her children's efforts to organize any kind of celebration – even a small, intimate supper party. Instead she wanted a few quiet days with her husband – preferably somewhere not far from home. She decided on the Dunkeld House Hotel.

Later in the afternoon of 14 July the Golf GTI sped over the Forth Road Bridge past Perth and then onto the A9 dual carriageway – the main artery leading into the Highlands. It was the height of the tourist season and caravans had slowed the traffic to a crawl. The Golf weaved in and out of the traffic, overtaking recklessly. After twelve miles the rolling Perthshire farmland began to give way to hills and forests. Roderick drove through Dunkeld and then turned sharp left through a large imposing stone archway flanked by lodges. When it was built by the Duke of Atholl, Dunkeld House was the family seat, but today it is a luxury hotel, offering a swimming pool, a gymnasium and shooting and stalking. Roderick was led upstairs by a kilted porter who showed him into his uncle and aunt's suite – the Atholl Lounge.

From the window of room 138 it was possible to see the fallow deer darting in and out of the bushes and the sunlight playing on the surface of the river Tay which ran through the hotel grounds. Stephen and Gay Newall greeted Roderick; his aunt kissed him and his uncle poured coffee. They had not met since Uncle Kenneth's funeral nearly five years before. They were not to meet again.

Later the two men stood at the door. They did not shake hands. Stephen Newall spoke first: 'And you will give me your assurance, won't you, never to contact me, my wife, my daughter or any of the rest of your cousins again?'

Roderick looked back into the eyes and face of his father. His tone was respectful and affectionate. 'There's no need to worry, Uncle Stephen. I won't be coming back.' He shifted awkwardly. 'But I can't speak for my brother.' His uncle nodded in understanding.

For nearly four hours they had talked of secrets – of guilt and absolution, of the power of remorse, of dreams and hauntings; of other things too: of plastic sheeting and ropes, of night-time assignations and hurried burials in the dark and, finally, of a terrible vow made by two small boys.

And all the time Roderick was speaking, two revolving spools turned, bearing silent witness.

'Well, it was good to see both of you. Thank you for seeing me, Uncle Stephen, goodbye.'

Stephen Newall watched as Roderick climbed into the car and sped off, scattering some deer that had been grazing nearby. He continued staring long after it had disappeared behind the trees.

Two men emerged from the hotel behind him and came over. The overweight one pumped his hand vigorously, saying, 'Congratulations . . . we've got him. It's all there.'

In the hotel room Gay Newall, drained and exhausted, sank her head into her hands and began quietly sobbing.

The news that Roderick Newall was back in Britain had taken the detectives by surprise. It was Angela Barnes who had raised the alarm and contacted the police. A distraught Nan Clark had told her of Roderick's visit.

Adamson was amazed that none of the relatives or even the port police had informed them, but immediately passed the news on to his boss, Detective Chief Superintendant Paul Marks, the new head of the CID at Rouge Bouillon. Marks instantly realized that here was an opportunity to get something on Newall. Admittedly it was a chance in a thousand but it was one worth trying.

In more than twenty-five years with the police he had spent much of his time with the Special Branch, so was especially familiar with the covert side of police work. He made up his mind on the spot to try and carry out a secret tape recording of Newall's meeting with his uncle and aunt. There was no time to lose.

Obtaining Stephen Newall's agreement to the operation was easier said than done. They couldn't find him anywhere. He wasn't at his house in Rhu or on the family island of Shuna. Where on earth was he? After a frantic round of phone calls they eventually traced him to the hotel in Perthshire. Reluctantly Mr Newall agreed to co-operate though he didn't think the plan had much chance of success.

The next thing Marks did was obtain the permission for the operation from the various chief constables on whose patch he would be operating and enlist the aid of the Scottish Crime Squad's technical support unit to carry out the nuts and bolts of the operation. Whatever happened he was determined there would be no repeat of the previous covert tape-recording operations which had ended in fiasco – this time the job would be professionally done.

Eventually the chief constables of Lothian and Borders and Tayside police forces agreed to co-operate and lend the assistance of their officers. The Scottish police would make their way straight to the hotel and carry out the preliminary setting-up while Adamson and Marks flew to Scotland to meet them.

The two Jersey detectives flew to Glasgow airport via London then drove at speed to Perth where they had arranged to rendezvous with the local police at a large roundabout on the outskirts of the town. Yet another of the farcical incidents that had dogged the inquiry from day one occurred. They had just parked their car near a distillery when the security guards, suspicious of the two large men, called the local police themselves. After a few loud words the situation was finally sorted out.

It was just after 3.00 on the afternoon of Tuesday 14 July when they arrived at the hotel and once again narrowly avoided disaster when they nearly bumped into Newall getting out his car in the car park. As it was, they were able to sneak in the back door just as he was making his way in the front.

Roderick was shown upstairs to the Atholl Lounge, room 138, where his aunt and uncle were waiting for him. Minutes later Marks and Adamson tiptoed past the door of the suite to a nearby room where the Scottish police had set up their tape recorders.

The first problem faced by Inspector Ian Wark of the Scottish Crime Squad had been where to place the microphones. This had been solved for him immediately when he learnt that the relatives were meeting up after some years. There could be emotional embraces, so that ruled out the use of personal microphones on Stephen and Gay Newall themselves. Instead, he placed a microphone in the settee and one under the bed. A solid state recorder was also placed under the bed by way of back up.

That first meeting between the uncle, aunt and nephew was cordial enough though it was hardly the return of the prodigal child. At the end of the first hour it looked as if Marks and Adamson would be out of luck. Over coffee and biscuits the conversation centred on Newall's travels and his adventures on the high seas. Then the three went out for a walk in the extensive hotel grounds and, as detectives hiding behind trees kept them shadowed, Inspector Wark took the opportunity of changing the tape on the recorder in the room.

By the time the three returned from their walk Marks and Adamson were in downcast mood and were beginning to think the exercise was a complete waste of time. Then, gently and carefully, Stephen Newall began to steer the chat back to the past. He had sensed that underneath the affable exterior Roderick was fragile and that he needed to talk about the events of five years previously. Gently, with a few cajoling words, Mr Newall began to persuade Roderick to unburden himself.

And then it came. The confession of Roderick Newall. As they sat with their headphones on the detectives were stunned and could hardly believe their luck. Newall had apparently broken down.

After three hours Roderick said an emotional farewell to his uncle and aunt and just after 7 p.m. in the evening he jumped into his car and set off on the long journey south.

As Newall settled into the drive he remembered how, long ago, he had said that the Highlands were so beautiful they almost made him cry. Now, with his eyes stinging from the tears, he realized he would probably never see these hills again. His confession to his uncle and aunt had been intended as a purging of the soul, an attempt to lay old ghosts and to call an end to a chapter in his life. But in fact it was just the beginning.

Later that evening Rod stopped off at a motorway service station on the M6 from where he rang his Aunt Nan in Fulham. He sounded very agitated. 'Aunt Nan,' he said, 'I've met Uncle Stephen and he doesn't want to let matters rest where they are.' Roderick asked if he could come and see her again to discuss what he should do and she agreed. But something else was bothering him. A car had been keeping pace with him for the entire journey south and now it too had stopped off at the service station. 'Do you know anything about it, Auntie Nan? Do you think it's the police?'

Even before Newall had left Dunkeld the massive operation that was to end in his arrest had swung into action. Marks had phoned the Attorney General on Jersey to say that it had been a success and to request permission for a warrant to arrest Roderick Newall. Ever cautious, Philip Bailhache decided he wanted to hear the tape for himself, and arranged to fly to the UK.

As the surveillance cars from the Scottish Crime Squad tracked Newall on the road south, Newall was driving like a demon and ignoring all speed limits. Eventually the police decided that keeping up with him was not worth the risk to life and limb and just after midnight on the M6 they broke off the chase.

Emma-Jane Lonsdale had returned to her flat to find the wing of her car dented and a note of apology from Roderick to say that he had had a slight accident but that the lorry driver responsible had handed over the £160 in cash, which he hoped would cover the cost of the repair. By the time the police got there the Golf was parked outside, but it was too late – the bird had already flown.

After seeing that he was being tailed Roderick had lost no time in travelling straight over to France. At 2.30 p.m on Wednesday 15 July, Roderick phoned his aunt again saying he would be unable to visit her after all, that he was sure he had been followed and had gone straight to Boulogne where his crewmate Steve Beldham had taken the boat.

At exactly the same time Rod was speaking to Nan, in the offices of the Special Branch at Heathrow Airport Philip Bailhache, together with Marks and Adamson, was listening intently to the tape. He gave the go-ahead for the arrest.

Two days later, on 17 July, the warrant was issued and a full-scale operation, dubbed 'Operation Snowbird', swung into action to find and arrest Roderick Newall. Detailed descriptions of him and his vessel were flashed to Interpol, the Royal Navy and the police in France, Spain and Portugal, but despite extensive searches they came up with nothing. By this time the *Austral Soma* had already left France and was heading south into the Bay of Biscay.

Then on 30 July, while monitoring the credit card purchases of Mark Newall in France, the police discovered he had bought an air ticket to fly from London to Paris and then on to Tangiers via Madrid. Immediately the detectives suspected that the younger brother was passing on the registration papers for the *Austral Soma* that Roderick would need and the next day, sure enough, confirmation was obtained that the *Austral Soma* was in Tangier.

Detective Sergeant Charles MacDowall had already made his way to Gibraltar to liaise with the local police to help in the arrest operation and by the time that the *Austral Soma* sailed from Tangier at 6.30 p.m. on 4 August, permission had been given for the Royal Navy to lend assistance by the Secretary of State for Defence Tom King.

One morning, about a week after Rod had left, Patrick was putting recruits through their paces at HMS *Dolphin*, a training establishment in Portsmouth. He was about to take some of them out in a dinghy when a rating handed him a routine signal. It had been sent out to all military shipping and was marked 'classified and restricted'. The message gave Patrick such a shock that he had to sit down; it said. 'Wanted by police. Roderick Innes Nelson Newall. Believed to be at sea aboard yacht *Austral Soma*. Possibly dangerous. If spotted do not approach. Immediately inform shore base.'

As he read and re-read the telex Patrick wondered if there was any way he could get a warning to his old friend. But it was already too late for that.

It was, the admiral admitted, a rather unusual operation. Certainly he had never known the Gibraltar Squadron – or any other Royal Navy establishment, come to that – to be called upon to do such a thing.

Through the Admiralty in London the squadron had received a request from the government of the States of Jersey for help in carrying out the arrest of a civilian on the high seas. The fugitive was a twenty-seven-year-old former army officer wanted for murder. He was now the master of a sixty-six-foot yacht thought to be heading south past Gibraltar en route to the South Atlantic. The admiral had been asked to carry out the arrest and, under the navy's 'military aid to civil powers obligations' policy, it had been decided that such help would be given.

At least one of the men in the room was deeply intrigued. Lieutenant Commander Tim Appleyard was a navy veteran of more than ten years' standing; he had been commanding his own vessel for several years but he had never undertaken a mission like this. His launch, HMS *Ranger*, a high-speed inshore search and rescue craft, was to lead the operation, locating and tracking the target vessel, a yacht called the *Austral Soma*, while the actual arrest was to be carried out by the much larger frigate HMS *Argonaut*.

It was not an easy task. Unlike a regular search and rescue there would be no distress flares or radio signals to guide him, and he had not the slightest idea where the *Austral Soma* could be. Moreover, he had to locate and follow the yacht without the captain suspecting anything untoward and keep it in sight until the frigate caught up to make the arrest. But there was no guarantee the *Argonaut* would actually sail: she had docked at Gibraltar to undergo urgent repairs, so Appleyard was faced with the possibility of having to make the arrest himself. For that reason the *Ranger* would be carrying some heavily armed additional crew members: police officers from Gibraltar and one from Jersey – Detective Sergeant Charles MacDowall.

After the tasking conference was over Appleyard and his crew were placed on immediate standby. The 999 signal on his bleeper giving the order to scramble came through at 8.15 that evening, 4 August. By 8.36 the *Ranger* was gunning its engines and reversing away from the jetty; then it whipped round and surged towards the southern mouth of Gibraltar harbour.

Once out in the open sea, Appleyard mapped a course of 230 degrees. Dusk was already descending as he pointed the nose of the launch towards the winking lighthouse at the tip of Cape Espartel in southern Spain. With only an hour of daylight left Appleyard realized he had to close the gap between himself and the fugitive as quickly a possible, so the throttle was opened up and soon the boat was punching its way through the waves into the Straits of Gibraltar at its top speed of 21 knots.

It was a beautiful balmy summer's evening with calm seas and good visibility. Thank God for small mercies, thought Appleyard, for he had his work cut out: he would be sailing far beyond his usual range and was looking for a sixty-six-foot yacht in one of the world's busiest seaways.

Appleyard quizzed MacDowall about the fugitive and the reasons behind the whole curious chase. The replies were not reassuring. Yes, he was dangerous, and there was another problem: the police didn't know if he was armed or not. Commander Appleyard looked down at his passengers loading their Hoeckler and Koch machine guns and decided to concentrate on the radar and cross other bridges when he came to them. As darkness fell Appleyard and MacDowall studied the charts.

Although Appleyard was unaware of it, the problems did not end with the logistics of interception. The vexed subject of the arrest of a civilian at sea by a naval vessel had already been the subject of a series of long, agonizing communiqués between the offices of the Attorneys-General in London and St Helier, and the Admiralty and Gibraltar. Legally speaking, the whole matter lay in uncharted waters. Such an operation had never been carried out before so there were no precedents to fall back on. International regulations required the *Argonaut* to stay out of other nations' territorial waters, so they would have to wait until their quarry was well clear of Morocco before they could make a move. Beyond that no one really seemed to know what to do.

Appleyard knew the yacht wasn't going east, but heading west would take him straight out into the Atlantic, which didn't make any sense. The most obvious route seemed to be south towards the Canary Islands. He calculated that the yacht couldn't be more than 100 miles ahead so, having blocked off an area on the map, the launch identified and eliminated one by one the rest of the ocean-going traffic. In daylight it was easy, but after nightfall they had to rely completely on the radar and nightsights. Peering at the screen, they discounted the blips which seemed to be going in the wrong direction and at the wrong speed, and eventually narrowed the field down to about a dozen. The high-speed craft weaved across the night seas, buzzing first one vessel, then another. For the majority, identification was reasonably easy: a sixty-six-foot yacht doesn't have much in common with a 10,000-tonne tanker. After the *Ranger* had cleared the shipping lanes the number of blips on the radar fell drastically until there were just a few solitary signals.

By 11.45 p.m. the *Ranger* was 150 miles south-east of Gibraltar – far beyond its normal operating range. Appleyard had just ordered the switch to reserve fuel tanks when the second lieutenant called him back to the radar. They had picked up a signal that seemed to fit the bill: its size, speed and heading were right. But it was still in Moroccan waters and they had to wait until it was clear before they could approach. As the *Ranger* closed, Appleyard peered through the night-sights and handed them to MacDowall. It was the best one yet, they agreed – there was certainly a strong resemblance between the silhouette and the pictures the policeman carried of the *Austral Soma*.

Still, they could not be sure. It was just too dark to make out the name on the side of the boat. There was no alternative but to move closer, but Appleyard didn't want to get too near. The steel-hulled yacht would make short work of the fibre-glass launch. He ordered everyone to pull on their bulletproof jackets. By now the crew of the launch had fallen completely silent and the tension was palpable. Dropping its speed to reduce swell and engine noise, the *Ranger* chugged past the yacht at a distance of less than 1000 yards while Appleyard peered through the nightsights. Suddenly there was a blinding flash of light from the yacht. 'Everyone get down,' he yelled, momentarily sightless, waiting for the first sounds of gunfire. Agonizing seconds passed but none came. The searchlight from the yacht had swept over the cruiser, dazzling everyone aboard and effectively knocking out the infra-red nightsight.

The *Ranger*, feigning indifference, cruised straight past out of searchlight range and, to allay any suspicion, swept closely by a couple of other yachts near by before disappearing over the horizon. MacDowall and Appleyard were about as sure of the yacht as they could possibly be in the darkness. Now all they had to do was to stick with it until the *Argonaut* caught up. Anxiously

Appleyard checked the radar to make sure the *Austral Soma* didn't try and make a dash for the safety of Moroccan territorial waters, but it stayed on course. *Ranger* reduced speed and shadowed it at a range of four miles until the *Argonaut* arrived.

By the time Captain Bob Stephens of the anti-submarine frigate HMS *Argonaut* got word to sail it was almost midnight. Within the hour the ship was heading through the Straits at its top speed of twenty-six knots. After several hours the frigate was able to tuck itself in behind the *Ranger*, while keeping the yacht on its long-range radar. Then Appleyard ordered a burst of speed and the *Ranger* dashed into position between the yacht and Moroccan waters, thereby cutting off one avenue of escape. At first light the *Ranger* pulled alongside the *Argonaut* for urgent refuelling.

MacDowall and the Gibraltar police officers were now transferred onto the frigate. They discussed how they were going to grab Newall. If he could be lured onto the frigate, then there would be no problem. But if there had to be a forced arrest things could get messy. There was a suggestion he might have an anti-tank weapon of some sort. It was highly unlikely, but Captain Stephens, concerned about his men's safety, was determined to take absolutely no risks: the boarding party and weapons crews were told they would have to prepare for a worst case scenario.

At a conference in the captain's cabin the officers tried to cover all the angles. The arrest had to be carried out within the constraints of international law, and it was crucial to establish that the yacht was flying a white ensign. It was agreed that a helicopter should make one overflight soon. A timetable was agreed, the pilot was briefed, and the Sea Lynx was raised from the ship's bowels and placed in readiness on the helipad. It made one low swoop over the yacht and returned. There seemed no doubt the yacht was the *Austral Soma* – and it was flying the British ensign. The helicopter was stowed away out of danger as quickly as possible in case there was any shooting.

The *Austral Soma* was sailing in blazing hot tropical sun in clear sea 150 miles south-west of Gibraltar when the *Argonaut* closed in. Again Captain Stephens was taking no chances: he was going to keep the frigate out of the range of any weapons Newall might have aboard. Lieutenant Mike Wardle of the *Argonaut* hailed Newall on Channel 16 of the VHS and asked to check the vessel's papers. Initially Newall was reluctant to co-operate but after a few minutes he was persuaded it was just a routine matter. He agreed to row over in his dinghy. Looking across the water, Lieutenant Charles MacDowall caught the flash of red hair and knew beyond a shadow of a doubt that he had the right man.

Roderick's last moments of freedom were captured by an amateur cameraman from the crew of the *Argonaut* who filmed the red t-shirted figure rowing himself the few hundred yards over to the frigate. After he tied up a friendly hand from a rating is seen helping him aboard.

Lieutenant Wardle greeted Newall with a big smile and led him to the centre of the flight deck where he turned, smiled again and said to the guest: 'Boy, have I got a surprise for you.' At that moment the armed Gibraltar Special Weapons Team appeared with Charles MacDowall alongside and pointed their weapons at Roderick.

Astonished and indignant, he initially refused to obey and at a pre-arranged signal one of the policemen went behind him and took his legs out from under him. Roderick crashed onto the deck and was restrained with plasticuffs around his wrists. He was then shown the warrant for his arrest for the murder of his parents and conveyed into the ship's storeroom where he was tied to some grills.

Charles MacDowall stood over Newall for the rest of the journey back in. He seemed to have accepted what had happened and was almost reflective, but there was still that element of chippiness. He identified one of the police guns and said that he reckoned it would have taken four rounds to stop him if he had made a break for it. 'If I'd realized what was going to happen I think I'd have rammed you,' he said.

CHAPTER 13

The HMS *Argonaut* glided into harbour at Gibraltar on Wednesday 5 August 1992. The States of Jersey authorities were elated – 'Operation Snowbird' had been a complete success and the interception and arrest had been a textbook operation carried out without injury or damage. Roderick had been held under guard, manacled to pipes in the ship's naval stores, during the journey back to Gibraltar. As the ship docked the arrest immediately made the news. The video of Newall rowing himself over to the *Argonaut* had been released to the media and that, combined with the lurid nature of the accusation against him, ensured front-page headlines and national TV exposure.

Justice seemed a foregone conclusion. But only twenty-four hours later the euphoria disappeared when the authorities realized they had made another massive blunder. Although a Crown colony, Gibraltar – like Jersey – has it's own constitution, its own legal system and its own laws. For any fugitive to be successfully extradited, a local court had to be satisfied that evidence against him had been properly gathered. A long, expensive and risky extradition battle that could easily have been avoided if Newall had been taken straight back to the Channel Islands or arrested before he left Britain.

On the night of Thursday 6 August advocate David

Le Quesne was struggling to get his new-born baby off to sleep when the phone rang. Picking up the receiver, he heard a voice he had not heard in four years – that of Roderick Newall. Frantically Roderick explained what had happened. He was in custody in Gibraltar and had been allowed the customary phone call. He didn't know why they should have picked him up but he needed Le Quesne's help desperately.

As he put the phone down Le Quesne's mind raced. He was astonished that the case should have returned to haunt him after five years and he could not imagine what had happened to reactivate it. Why the sudden drama on the high seas? Why the arrest? What the hell was going on?

The next day, as Rod Newall was conveyed from the Gibraltar police station and then taken to the Moorish stone prison high up on the Rock, Le Quesne frantically tried to find out. Although an advocate, he was only qualified to practise law on Jersey, not on Gibraltar, and his first priority was to find local representation for his client. He needed the best criminal lawyer available and, after a few enquiries, the same name kept resurfacing. 'Put it like this,' said a local journalist, 'if I was guilty then he's the man I'd want.'

'Looks like he's the one for me then,' replied Le Quesne.

Christopher Finch, has frequently said that if there was one thing he didn't like it was losing. It was not something that happened very often. With his gold bracelets, expensive watches and finely tailored suits, Finch could be the successful partner of a prominent law firm anywhere from New York to London. Only the slight hint of a working-class London accent gives an indication of his background. He first arrived in Gibraltar when he was an aircraft technician in the RAF in the early sixties. After national service he returned to the Rock and became a policeman with the tiny local force. He worked his way through night school and then left to read law at university in England. After gaining his degree he returned to Gibraltar to work as a lawyer for the Attorney General.

But Christopher Finch's ambition stretched far beyond the Attorney General's office. Although Gibraltar occupied only two square miles on the very edge of Europe, he could see that it was a Rock of opportunity. For hundreds of years the colony has retained a firm British identity, clinging proudly to its maritime history. But although a Royal Navy Squadron is still maintained there the strategic importance of the Rock has declined sharply in the course of this century. Despite this, the inhabitants have managed to find more lucrative business. For behind its 'end of empire' feel – the ubiquitous portraits of the Queen, the Union Jacks and the pubs named after Nelson and Trafalgar – Gibraltar has the atmosphere of a Wild West frontier town. Like Jersey, it had developed a thriving international offshore finance industry and local lawyers concentrate mainly on the lucrative and plentiful corporate and tax work provided by the companies based there.

Christopher Finch's experience in the police and the Attorney General's office had, however, equipped him perfectly for a very different speciality – criminal law. He knew from the inside how to undermine the prosecution by highlighting weaknesses in police evidence and procedure. And there was no shortage of business. The Rock's strategic position made it a natural haven for the smugglers operating between Morocco and Spain. Nearly every night speedboats laden with contraband would skim across the Gibraltar Straits, hotly

pursued by police and navy launches. Many successfully make the crossing, but many are caught and there
is a regular procession of tobacco- and drug-smugglers
through Gibraltar's tiny courthouse.

The formidable combination of a razor-sharp mind
and a confident courtroom delivery soon established
Finch as the foremost criminal lawyer on the Rock. His
thorough understanding of basic constitutional rights
and the fundamentals of law has been the cornerstone
for many of his successful defences.

Today Finch is one of the best-known and most successful figures on Gibraltar. Years of trouncing his
courtroom opponents have provided him with all the
trappings of success. His thriving legal practice has its
offices in the town's Marine Parade; the stained-glass
panels to his door spell out his name in large letters.
He owns a Jaguar XJ6, several other large cars and a
luxurious yacht; he partially owns a restaurant and is
said to be on first-name terms with several of the 'Costa'
criminals. At major art exhibitions on Gibraltar Finch
invariably buys up a few pieces. The blazers and ties
are, some feel, an affectation, as are his pronunciation
of R's, which become W's.

But unlike many local lawyers he has never been
afraid to take on the establishment and has successfully
defended many controversial defendants. Confirmation
of Finch's formidable courtroom skills came in the late
1980s when he represented the families of three IRA
terrorists shot dead by the SAS in broad daylight on
a quiet Gibraltar street. Finch seriously embarrassed
the British government and came close to proving the
terrorists had been unlawfully killed. He also successfully sued on behalf of Carmen Proetta, who witnessed
the shootings and was then pilloried by right-wing
British newspapers. The cases created headlines across

the world and gave him an international reputation.

After a brief chat with Le Quesne Finch agreed to take the case and the two men talked through a strategy. Their main problem was that they did not know what the new evidence against Newall was, so they decided to question the legality of the operation at sea and the harsh treatment of Newall himself. Until they could find out more, they just had to play it by ear.

If the defence was having problems, so was the prosecution. After lengthy discussions with his Gibraltar counterpart the Jersey Attorney General, Philip Bailhache, realized with dismay the scale of the battle that lay ahead. The situation was unique. There was no relationship, law or treaty that could be enacted between the two Crown possessions to allow a quick and easy extradition. It would have been easier to extradite someone from France or Germany. In public Bailhache tried to put a brave face on it, but there was no hiding his embarrassment. 'One would have hoped that between two Crown dependencies there would be a simplified procedure,' he told one reporter. 'Apparently there is not.'

So why wasn't the *Argonaut* told to take Newall straight back to Jersey?

'I expect that was not an option because of operational reasons,' he replied weakly.

The legal complexities were formidable. An extradition from Gibraltar to Jersey had never been attempted before. Because both had unique relationships with the UK, all official communications between Gibraltar and Jersey had to take a circuitous route. The request for extradition was passed from Bailhache to the island's senior official, the Bailiff, who in turn sent it on to the Lieutenant Governor, who represented the Crown on the island. Then it was forwarded to the

Home Office in London with the request that it be passed to the Foreign Office, and from there it would finally be relayed to the Governor of Gibraltar. When it reached Gibraltar it was to be placed before a local court.

It was, on the face of it, a straightforward question: if the offence had taken place on Gibraltar, was there enough evidence to issue a warrant there? Under the colony's Fugitive Offenders Act extradition proceedings were not to be used to establish guilt or innocence. The prosecution merely had to establish the defendant had a case to answer.

But there were a number of weak points the defence could exploit. Apart from the questionable arrest at sea there was the manner in which the evidence had been gathered. The taped confession, though damning, was obtained under circumstances that were in total breach of the UK Police and Criminal Evidence Act. The introduction of PACE meant that the police had to be much more rigorous in the collecting of evidence, and this applied to confessions in particular. The suspect had to be cautioned and given the opportunity to have a lawyer present. The Newall tape had obviously not been obtained in the proper way. Roderick could fight his case all the way to the Privy Council of the House of Lords if he wanted, and there was no guarantee he would fail. Either way it could take many months.

Despite these huge problems, Bailhache maintained that the case would reach a successful conclusion, no matter how long it took. 'I am confident that Roderick Newall will be returned to Jersey,' he told reporters.

On 12 August, while Le Quesne was visiting Rod for the first time in prison, Bailhache arrived in Gibraltar, accompanied by the head of the Jersey CID, Detective Superintendent Paul Marks, and detectives Adamson and MacDowall. Speaking to the press, Philip Bailhache said the Crown case would be led by Gibraltar's Attorney General John Gittings, who would 'be appearing for the British government who are acting for the Jersey authorities in this matter, and he will be opposing any bail application.'

Finch and the new Attorney General had little in common either in background or approach. John Gittings, a fifty-nine-year-old former London barrister, had only been Attorney General for a few days when Newall was arrested. The post had been offered to him out of the blue and he had leapt at the chance to swop the London drizzle for a life on the edge of the Mediterranean. He had remarried and, with his attractive young wife Gail, was just beginning to adjust to the relaxed local round of cocktail parties and receptions. Then the Newall case exploded in his lap.

Gittings dismissed the concern over the arrest as a quibble: 'It does not matter under what circumstances a wanted person is returned to the jurisdiction,' he said.

What lawyers say to each other in court is very different from what they say outside. In front of a magistrate or judge the abuse and mud-slinging may get vicious, but most take the view that it's not personal. Nevertheless, from the beginning of the Newall extradition hearings the exchanges between Christopher Finch and John Gittings were marked by such obviously ill-tempered clashes that some observers felt there was no love lost between the two men.

Finch argued for reporting restrictions in case proceedings prejudiced his client's chance of a fair trial later on. It was a move resisted by the Attorney General, who argued against what he called 'justice behind closed doors'. 'No one else at this stage knows that there is any evidence against him,' he said. 'He could be as innocent as the driven snow.'

At a court hearing a week later Finch rebutted the suggestion that Newall had absconded from Jersey – an allegation made in the arrest warrant. 'He did no such thing,' he said, pointing out that at no time did his client try to conceal his whereabouts. And then he played a strong card: he claimed the arrest was improper because a warrant should only be issued when a person was in the colony or on the way there. The manner of Newall's arrest, he said, 'was the closest to modern piracy that one can imagine . . . are we to become the extradition box of the world?'

Despite the British connection, there is a strong streak of independence amongst Gibraltarians, who have in the past resented being used by the UK as a port of convenience. That the Rock might have been taken advantage of to effect a dubious arrest struck a deep chord of indignation with many locals.

Meanwhile, behind the battlements of Gibraltar's prison Roderick Newall's moods were alternating between panic and despair. He was being kept in virtual solitary confinement and that, together with the worry about what new evidence the authorities had, was taking its toll. For hours he would pace around his cell and he was ill-tempered and abusive to the prison warders. He desperately wanted to find out what was happening to the yacht – to get in touch with anyone; but the authorities refused to allow him his filofax and he couldn't even write. The few telephone conversations he had had with his brother Mark were stilted because the line was obviously being monitored, and when he met Christopher Finch the warders had sat so close they were not able to have a proper conversation.

In protest against the way he was being treated, at the end of August he began refusing solid food.

Five days later, still on hunger strike, the gaunt Newall was led into court to hear for the first time the nature of the evidence against him. Attorney General Gittings outlined Newall's movements in Britain two months earlier: 'During a three- to four-hour conversation with Stephen Newall and Auntie Gay he made statements amounting to a confession that he killed his father and mother,' said the Attorney General. 'This is the most serious crime in the calendar. If allowed to go free he will abscond.' He went on to refer to the police surveillance operation: 'He knew he was being followed and he lost them.' He also read out the letter Newall had left to be posted to Emma-Jane Lonsdale after his departure: 'See you in Brazil – but only time will tell.'

Finch completely failed to see why these few words should be taken as incriminating. 'What on earth is that supposed to mean?' he snapped, whipping round angrily in his seat.

'Precisely the same as what it meant for Mr Biggs,' replied the Attorney General, referring to the fugitive train robber, 'that he would be difficult to get hold of.'

Gittings claimed that Rod Newall was a 'dangerous man . . . trained in anti-surveillance and weaponry'. If released on bail he would try and get his hands on the family fortune and use it to escape. And he even suggested that the lives of crucial witnesses – namely his uncles and aunts – might be in danger if he were set free. Finally he drew attention to a curious remark Roderick had made to the Gibraltar Police after he was arrested – that he had calculated on being hit by four bullets before being able to grab a rifle. 'It was a strange thing to say in that situation,' commented the Attorney

General. The picture painted of Newall was of a solitary, desperate though intrepid man. 'He is a man who is happy to sail the world alone; the seas of the South Atlantic hold no fears for him.'

All this was meant to swing the Magistrate against granting bail, but Finch argued that the warrant, as issued on Jersey, was invalid and again he attacked the prosecution for suggesting that his client had absconded. Newall had lived openly on another British possession, the Falklands, for four years. He also criticized the 'unnecessary brutality' of Newall's arrest. The action on the high seas was 'illegal', he said; why could his client not have been picked up while he stopped off in France, Tangier or Spain?

The Attorney General argued that the manner of Newall's arrest was not relevant to the bail application: 'We all learnt on our mother's knee that there are only three issues which have to be addressed: if he will turn up; if he will interfere with the witnesses; and if he will commit further offence.' Bail should be refused to Newall, he said, because of the magnitude of the allegations against him. The nature of the crime and the length of the anticipated sentence would provide a strong inducement to abscond: 'Someone accused of such a double murder would face life imprisonment, probably with a recommendation that he not be released for between twenty and twenty-five years . . .'

Roderick Newall sat looking straight ahead, his face expressionless; he seemed barely aware of the Attorney General's voice. He wore his smart blue blazer and was carrying a book to alleviate the boredom of courtroom proceedings. Only inches behind him in the packed press and public benches dozens of fascinated people had crowded in to listen. But Rod's mind was elsewhere: only two months earlier he'd hardly been able to contain his excitement at the impending voyage and the beginning of the realization of his dream. Now the *Austral Soma* languished in the nearby Royal Naval Dockyard, its boxes of vegetables rotting in the hold.

The Crown case was tendentious. At no stage could Newall's wanderings have been described as a 'flight from justice': he had never tried to hide. The account of the 'police surveillance' operation also omitted to mention the embarrassing fact that, driving back from Scotland, Roderick had briefly been taken into police custody for speeding.

But however insubstantial the argument, it seemed to sway the Magistrate, Felix Pizzarello. 'If Newall knew he was being followed, it does put a certain complexion on things,' he said, refusing bail again. However, he did order an investigation into the conditions of Newall's detention, and Roderick called off his hunger strike.

The news that his uncle and aunt had told the police about the Dunkeld meeting devastated Roderick. For several days he lay motionless on his bed, staring at the ceiling and refusing to speak to the warders. Some of them felt he was on the verge of a nervous breakdown. For the first time he began to consider that it really was all over. On 10 September, a warder glanced through the peep hole in the cell door to see Newall slumped unconscious on the floor in a pool of blood, a razor blade at his side. He was only minutes from death and, by the time they got him to the Rock's St Bernard Hospital intensive care unit, he had lost several pints of blood.

On hearing of her nephew's suicide attempt Nancy Clark rushed to his bedside. She and Alaster had been in Spain when they learned of the arrest. They had no idea of the police operation or the tape recording; it had come as a bolt from the blue. Within hours their villa was under siege from reporters. One – a *Daily Express* man – asked whether it was possible their phones had been bugged; the *Daily Mail* asked whether Roderick had been arrested in connection with the horrific murder of a girl called Rachel Nickell on Wimbledon Common some time previously. But Nan and Alaster were completely in the dark.

When Nan arrived at the hospital the doctor quietly drew her to one side. 'We nearly lost him, Mrs Clark,' he said. Roderick had cut deep into his wrists and groin with a blade that had been smuggled into him. Now he was conscious and sitting upright in a packed public ward, with three Gibraltar policemen at his bedside and a doctor tending his heavily bandaged arms. He seemed glad to see his aunt, but his face was as white as marble, his eyes sunken. Without even a screen to separate them from the rest of the ward conversation was difficult. Nan had just started to speak when someone appeared at the foot of the bed: it was Christopher Finch.

Curtly Roderick dismissed him: 'Can you leave us for the moment, Mr Finch?' he said. 'I need to speak to my aunt.' Nan thought the lawyer looked distinctly indignant but he reluctantly turned and strode away. Newall glared after him suspiciously. Turning to his aunt, he said, 'Can you check him out for me, Auntie Nan? I'm not sure if I trust him. Can you go and see him and tell me what you think?'

'Roderick,' whispered Nan, leaning over to speak, 'you are doing yourself no good here. You will have far more options if you just return to Jersey.' After a long discussion Nan got the impression that Roderick was agreeing with her. She walked away from the prison with Detective Sergeant Charles MacDowall, convinced her nephew was ready to give up the fight.

Later that day she visited Christopher Finch at his offices. He was urbane and smooth – a bit too smooth, she thought. He was smartly dressed except for the fact that he was not wearing any shoes. 'Mr Finch,' Nan said to him, 'I really think Roderick should return to Jersey. His situation is only going to get worse here and if he can get hold of a blade once he can certainly do it twice. I think it would be much better if he returned.'

Christopher Finch was polite but firm. The laws on Gibraltar were different from those on Jersey. His client had been illegally arrested and he thought he had every chance of beating the extradition.

That evening Nan did not return to the hospital. Instead she sent Roderick an anguished letter in which she repeated her plea for him to give up his fight. She explained she thought it was the only way he would ever be able to find true freedom within himself. That night, as he lay propped up in bed, Roderick read and re-read his aunt's letter.

No sooner was Nan back at her house in Spain than Mark Newall phoned her. He seemed angry and worried. Relations between Nan and Mark had deteriorated sharply and she got the impression he suspected her of being involved in the arrest. On a number of occasions she felt he was attempting to intimidate her: he had hinted darkly at his ability to find out what was happening on Jersey; the police there, he said, were not as 'incorruptible' as she obviously thought they were. Again he tried to squeeze information from her.

Nan explained she had tried to persuade Roderick to give up, but Mark exploded angrily. 'Auntie Nan,' he snapped, 'please stop trying to interfere.' Then the line went dead. It was the last conversation she ever had with Mark; it convinced her that Mark maintained his hold on his brother even in prison.

With the real danger that the only solid evidence against Newall – the taped confession – could be thrown out, the Jersey detectives were under pressure to find out if he had told anyone else of his guilt. So on 12 September Detective Inspector Martin Fitzgerald and Detective Constable Charles Cobham flew to Port Stanley. The plan was to interview anyone in whom Newall might have confided. But this was no easy task, for the normally chatty and outgoing kelpers were proving remarkably reluctant to talk. Rod had been a popular figure in Port Stanley and some of the islanders quickly became irritated at the detectives' brash tones. The one man the police wanted to interview more than anyone else was proving unco-operative. Jerome Poncet was adamant: No, he said, speaking on the phone from Beaver Island, Roderick had never talked of his parents. No, he had nothing to tell them. And no, he would not allow them to visit him. If they flew to the island he would refuse their aircraft permission to land.

Before Roderick's arrest, Donna Westend had also been interviewed by the Auckland police. She had gone along to the police station without a clue what it was about. The last thing she'd expected was a third-degree grilling over her relationship with Roderick Newall.

'How many times do I have to tell you I don't know anything?' No matter how many times she repeated it the police officers made it plain they didn't believe her.

She told them where they had been, who they had seen; but when she mentioned that they had had a fight on the *Chanson du Lecq* the eyes of the policemen had brightened with interest. But they remained insistent: he must have told her that he murdered his parents.

'Look, he just never mentioned anything about it and

I didn't ask, so let it drop, okay?' she told them. At the end of the interview she lost her temper completely and refused point blank to sign the statement they'd made out.

'Doesn't matter anyway,' she was told. 'We are sending it off. You could end up a witness in court in the UK.'

Donna felt intimidated and harassed. She had some wonderful memories of her trip with Roderick and wanted to keep it that way. Was it really possible that he had killed his parents?

A week after his attempted suicide Roderick, looking thin and pale, appeared in court for the usual remand hearing.

In mid-October the Crown finally supplied the defence with transcripts of the tape-recorded conversation. As Le Quesne and Finch flicked through it they were devastated. The tapes were wholly incriminating: Newall had talked about the burial of bodies and how they had been camouflaged in tarpaulin; he was not sorry about what had happened, he would not apologise when he met them on the 'other side', and he and his brother were fifty-fifty responsible. In one spine-chilling phrase Roderick had said, 'From the age of eleven and ten we knew this was going to happen.'

As the legal battle ground relentlessly on there was a major security alert in three countries. It all began with a phone call: an unidentified well-wisher was speaking to Roderick one day when she let slip a remark that was open to a variety of interpretations – it could have been a simple gesture of good will, but the detectives chose to read something far more sinister into it: they took it to be a signal that an escape attempt was imminent. The police and the prosecution were already deeply worried about Mark's part in the case;

they did not put it past him to interfere. The defence stoutly denied the remarks in question were any more than an innocent inquiry after Newall's well-being.

Whatever the truth, even though they ran the risk of seeming hysterical, the police decided they were taking no chances. A massive security operation was launched to protect the Newall relatives. In Nan Clark's flat in London the locks were changed and panic buttons fitted by members of the anti-terrorist squad; a police helicopter probed the roof to ensure there was no possible access for intruders. Nan was told not to open her door to anyone who did not give the correct password at the entryphone. Scottish Highland armed police descended on a farmhouse in Argyllshire. Amanda Newall, heavily pregnant with her second baby, was astonished when the large team of policemen arrived. Again a panic button was installed; she was told a helicopter would be with her within minutes if it was pressed.

In Gibraltar the number of warders on duty was doubled and armed policemen were despatched to the prison. On 22 October the police van again made its way down the steep winding streets from the Moorish prison to the courtyard behind the Gibraltar Magistrate's Court. Roderick Newall was led in surrounded by members of the Royal Gibraltar Police firearms squad brandishing sub-machine guns. The pictures made front pages across Britain. Just after ten that morning the court rose as Magistrate Pizzarello took his seat. Newall, as usual, wore his blue blazer and carried a book – *Heroes* by John Pilger.

During the next hour the Attorney General released more details of the case against Roderick Newall. Again Finch pressed for bail and again Gittings was set firmly against it, telling the court, 'Here we have a highly intelligent graduate of Sandhurst, trained in evasion camouflage and weaponry.' At this remark there was some muffled laughter in the court – one of the rare occasions when Newall's voice was heard. 'He is a loner – the classic example of someone who does not have family ties. The description "footloose and fancy free" fits him perfectly. He can disappear off the face of the earth. He already did. Six months after Mr and Mrs Newall disappeared, this young man leaves the army and almost disappears from the face of the earth.' Then, for good measure, the Attorney General questioned Newall's funding for his chartering venture: 'The money had to come from somewhere – maybe the uncle who coincidentally died four weeks after Mr and Mrs Newall.'

His reference to Nan's visitation by her dead sister, however, produced a contemptuous snort from Christopher Finch. 'I hope you produce the spirit to give evidence,' he sneered.

Ignoring the sarcasm, Gittings then recounted the exchange between Roderick and his aunt. 'Has Elizabeth ever appeared to you?' Roderick was said to have asked. 'Yes, the night she died,' came the alleged reply. Then, with Finch shaking his head in exasperation only feet away, Gittings pointed out that Roderick had not asked when that was – the clear inference was that he already knew when his mother had died. Newall had then travelled to Scotland and had made 'submissions amounting to a confession that he had killed his parents'. Gittings argued that, if released, Newall might have reason to interfere with his relatives. 'It would be easy to put pressure on these persons,' he said and, besides, the fact that Newall had already tried to take his own life meant he might use freedom to take that route to escape justice. Again the family opposed the bail application.

By this time Christopher Finch was outraged. Again he rose to criticize the atmosphere that he felt was deliberately being created. 'Sensationalism is a poor foil for justice,' he said. 'History shows people can be tried on rumour and not necessarily factual evidence.' He pointed out that Newall had not tried to take his life during five years of liberty, but since imprisonment had watched as his business plan collapsed and as a result had sunk into 'humiliation and despair'. Taking a swipe at the massive show of weaponry that was displayed every time the accused was moved between prison and court, he said, 'This high level of exposure can only do more damage to his case. If he is extradited, what possible chance of a fair trial can he have?'

Finch had spent hours reading the tape transcripts and the more he read the clearer one thing became: despite the innuendo and halting hints there was not one phrase or sentence that amounted to a clean confession that Newall murdered his parents. They were damaging but fell short of a straightforward admission. It was one small ray of hope. 'I ask you to listen very carefully (to Newall's tape-recorded confession),' he told the court. 'See if you can detect one word where he says what he is alleged to have said.'

Meanwhile, in the book-lined study of the Attorney General's library on Gibraltar, another man was listening to the tapes. He had taken off his shoes and lay with his head back, eyes closed and his stocking feet on the table, as if asleep. But he was very much awake. After nearly four hours Desmond de Silva took off his headphones, still stunned by what he had just heard.

When the Jersey Attorney General had approached him and asked if he would represent the Crown he was intrigued. The case was challenging: the manner of the arrest at sea; the constitutional position between Jersey and Gibraltar – not to mention the awful nature of the alleged crime. The principles of extradition do not constitute an exact science, but Desmond de Silva, QC, had a more profound understanding of the subject than most. One of the problems with the case was that the arrest took place in international waters. There have been executive kidnappings, such as that of Eichmann from Brazil by Israel, but the law in general disapproves of 'forcible extraditions'. It was de Silva's involvement in one in particular that led to his being chosen. It involved a British national wanted by the police who was put on a plane in Rhodesia and forcibly sent back; de Silva had helped win a spectacular victory in his favour.

Desmond de Silva's languid patrician tones and his height – he is well over six feet tall – belied his roots in the Anglo-Indian community. After leaving Dulwich College he read law at Trinity College in Ceylon. He returned to London and was called to the bar in 1964. He quickly gained a reputation as a powerful criminal advocate and much of his work took him abroad – it is a matter of some personal pride that in various Commonwealth countries he has saved more than thirty-five people from execution, in court or in appeals to the Privy Council. He has handled many cases involving the security services and was a neighbour and close friend of Sir Maurice Oldfield, the former head of MI6 – indeed both of them narrowly avoided death at the hands of the IRA in 1975 when a bomb was defused in a restaurant underneath their adjacent homes. His chambers in the Middle Temple have expanded rapidly and defended many prominent fraud cases.

De Silva moves in some of the highest circles in the land. He is a friend of Denis Thatcher, a prominent member of the Conservative Party and some years ago he married into royalty: his wife is HRH Princess Katerina of Yugoslavia – a direct descendant of Queen Victoria. They live in style in Kensington.

His first task was to give an opinion on whether the recording was admissible as evidence or not. It had been gathered without the suspect's knowledge. How could it have been done any other way? Although Newall did stop short of directly confessing, the implication of his words was as clear as day. There was no way a jury could come to any other conclusion than that he was responsible for his parents' murder. Yes, he told both Attorneys General: he had no doubts. The tape was admissible as evidence.

While the prosecution had determined that the tapes were admissible, the defence still felt this was the Crown's weakest point. Christopher Finch wanted to prove that the tape recording of Roderick's confession was obtained unfairly. If the court accepted that then, as it was only the evidence against Newall, the entire extradition case would collapse.

By 19 November, when a hearing was to decide whether the tape was admissible, the Newall case had become much more than a standard criminal matter. It was now a political hot potato, with many a reputation both on Jersey and Gibraltar resting on the outcome.

The Crown pulled out its big guns for the hearing. Behind Desmond de Silva sat the Attorney General. Behind them sat Assistant Chief Officer Paul Marks and the other detectives and, finally, the Jersey Police's own legal adviser, Ian Christmas.

The defence had won a small victory before going in: Finch's complaint that Newall would be denied a fair trial if proceedings were reported had been accepted and the case was held in camera. There followed, as Desmond de Silva later admitted, five hours of some of the toughest litigation he had ever undergone. The admissibility of the tape was the issue that would decide the outcome of the whole case, for it was the only new evidence the Crown had. If the court ruled it could not be used, then they would be back to where they were five years previously and Newall would be released.

The tape, argued Finch, had been obtained covertly and without Newall's knowledge. He had not been cautioned beforehand and was not given the chance of legal advice. It was, he said, a confession that would be totally disallowed under the new PACE laws – now enforced in the UK – and the Judge's Rules governing use of evidence.

In reply Desmond de Silva argued strongly that despite the circumstances Newall had spoken of his own free will. He had gone to meet his uncle and aunt voluntarily and no coercion had been involved. He emphasized that no future advantage of lenient treatment had been held out to him and no attempt was made to oppress him in any way. He denied there was a breach of the Judge's Rules and highlighted the police's difficulties: before the confession they did not even have enough evidence with which to caution the defendant. It did not make any difference, said de Silva, that the defendant did not know of the tape and that his uncle and aunt did; they acted as 'extensions' to the police, but they were not in any position of authority.

In an emotional rebuttal of all de Silva's points, Christopher Finch claimed his client had been taken advantage of and lied to. If the police wished to question him they should have arranged an interview and cautioned him in the normal manner. The contents of the tape were open to a variety of interpretations, and

'In any case,' he argued, 'the admissions made do not point to his being the murderer but they were consistent with him attempting to cover up for another.' It was the first time that the defence had admitted in court that the confession *did* indicate guilt – not that of Roderick, but of his brother.

'After the matter of his parents' death had been raised by his uncle, Roderick had broken down. The questioning by the uncle,' said Finch, 'however delicate, sapped his free will. Hope and advantage were held out to him when they talked of a brief period of imprisonment and the uncle's wish to put a full stop on this.' The words of Roderick's uncle, said Finch, were 'despicable' in that they were deliberately calculated to lead to an unwary admission. Much of what was said by the uncle and aunt was lies, and it was all part of 'a fraud, a conspiracy' by the police and Stephen Newall to get what they could not get if Newall's right to silence had been honoured.

Throughout the long hearing the atmosphere had been charged and some of the exchanges heated. The Crown representatives had walked into court confident of victory. The extent of that overconfidence can be judged by a crack made by de Silva. Finch had offered to outline his skeleton argument; de Silva replied, 'Don't talk to me about skeletons, talk to your client.' It was a glib – if witty – remark for which he was mildly slapped down from the bench.

The Crown certainly did not expect to see their case in ruins and Newall on the verge of walking free by the end of the week. After two days of argument Magistrate Felix Pizzarello delivered his devastating verdict – the tapes were inadmissible. In his judgement he set out his reasons: 'When I heard the tapes three things struck me: one, the defendant made no admissions to murder; two, the defendant had disposed of or aided and abetted in the disposal of the bodies; three, both parties, in the words of Mr de Silva, engaged in a verbal ballet . . .

'I must say that when I heard the tapes it seemed to me that the uncle and aunt were genuinely concerned about: a) what happened to the defendant's father and mother; b) where the bodies were; c) to give such support as they could to the defendant; and d) to give help to the police.

'None of these concerns are exclusive . . . and it is my view their preponderant motive was in helping the police which, after all, is what any member of the public is enjoined to do. Mr Finch railed at the unfairness of the police, how the whole affair was stage managed with lies and deceit against the defendant. I would pause to point out that if the police suspicions were correct they were dealing with a murderer against whom there was no hard evidence. I think in their investigative process they are surely entitled to use as many stratagems as they can in order to secure evidence.

'As for the uncle and aunt, while treachery, lies and deceit may be the perception of the defendant and those advising him, another view of the matter is that they were very brave people to have – in the belief they were dealing with a murderer – been in his company in the room at the hotel and gone for a walk, albeit the police were close by.

'In my view the tape is put forward as a confession or at any rate statements prejudicial to the defendant which amounts to a confession . . . It seems to me at first blush that the conversation first entered into by the defendant and his uncle and aunt was quite voluntary. If there was a trap he was quite unaware of it, and the fact of entrapment does not go to the root of voluntariness.

'However, not until the interview was over could the police be said to have had sufficient evidence – and I think this is very important – because any connection with the defendant to the murders is only a matter of inference from the conversation. The defendant does not admit the murder, (instead) he gives information which may be detrimental to his position.

'I am of the view that this tape recording has to be treated as a confession. It is prima facie receivable in evidence but in the exercise of my discretion and in the circumstances of the case it is unfair and I disallow it. It is unfair to the defendant. It was brought into being by the calculated act of the police through the agency of persons who could lull the defendant into a false sense of security. I do not believe the police acted improperly in the investigative sense but it is clearly improper in the forensic sense, for they used an avenue "in a sneaky way" of circumventing the code of silence.'

For a second Desmond de Silva and the rest of the Crown team seemed scarcely able to believe what they were hearing. The entire drift of the judgement had seemed to be going their way. Then, right at the end, the Magistrate had changed tack and kicked the tapes out. For the prosecution the judgement represented nothing less than complete and total disaster.

CHAPTER 14

Silently, their minds reeling, the lawyers and detectives filed from the courthouse to the hotel. If the Crown lawyers were to pull anything out of the fire they had only forty-eight hours in which to do it. For if Newall was granted bail the following week and absconded, they would have lost him for ever.

Throughout the weekend a steady stream of coffee and sandwiches were brought to the Trafalgar Suite of the Holiday Inn, where the prosecution team wrestled to understand the Magistrate's ruling. Neither de Silva nor Gittings could follow Pizzarello's reasoning. He had agreed that the tapes were prima facie receivable in evidence; he accepted they had been made voluntarily, that there had been no breach of rules surrounding the 'cautioning' of suspects, that the police did not act improperly in the investigative sense. His sole objection was on the grounds that they had been obtained in a 'sneaky' way. So what the hell did that mean? Surely the admissibility of the tape recording was a matter for a trial judge to decide, not an extradition court. Taking the judgement apart line by line, they agreed the only thing they could do was apply for a stay of proceedings while they tried to get a higher court to overturn the Magistrate's decision.

Desperately the Crown lawyers tried to come up with ideas that could keep Newall behind bars even if he was granted bail. 'You say he's only been out of the army five years,' said de Silva. 'Well, under Queen's regulations he is still obliged to serve as a reservist if called. Couldn't we ask the Governor to call him up to the colours?'

Bail could be refused if de Silva could tell the court he had more evidence. The problem was there wasn't any. The entire Crown case rested on the tape. As he sifted his way through the papers de Silva suddenly remembered the filofax seized from Newall's yacht. It was full of phone numbers of the people he had met on his travels. Late on Saturday night as they sat round the table in their shirtsleeves exploring the possibilities, he turned to Paul Marks and asked, 'Are you sure you've tracked down all the people he has met?'

As he strode out of the courtroom, smiling from ear to ear, Christopher Finch seemed to smell victory. He immediately asked his juniors to make preparations for a press conference following the expected release of his client on bail the following week.

At the end of the court hearing a jubilant Roderick had turned and waved at a tall man with close-cropped hair sitting in the public benches – his old friend from Port Stanley, Mark Bullock. Mark had remained loyal; he had never truly believed Roderick to be capable of such a crime and had approached David Le Quesne, offering to give any help he could. With Newall's release imminent, Le Quesne had a new headache. He feared that Roderick would be harassed by the press; he might even go on a bender and get into more trouble. What was needed, Le Quesne decided, was a 'minder' to look after him while they decided what to do. Mark Bullock, who had left the police and was now working as a private detective, agreed to help and flew to the Rock. He had already signed a statement for Le Quesne describing the Jersey detectives' amateurish and irregular attempts to 'bug' the brothers, which the police had injudiciously told him about and which he thought might help the defence.

The Crown's actions over the next few days generated bitter accusations between the two sides. After two sleepless nights poring over depositions, considering argument and counter argument, on Monday morning the Crown went before the senior judge, Lord Chief Justice Alister Kneller, and applied for a stay of all proceedings pending a judicial review of Pizzarello's decision. A stay was granted but, if the decision came as a relief to the prosecution, it was a shock for Christopher Finch. He only found out about the stay of proceedings after the event. Quite fortuitously – the Crown team would maintain – Finch had been off the Rock and uncontactable the previous day. In court the following morning, his voice trembling with rage, Finch accused the Crown of going behind the defence's back and behaving like 'thieves in the night'; everyone had been informed except the most interested parties. 'The interests of justice would have been better served if the defence had been present even if they had no right of address. The world's press was there and the public and it could not be said that Mr Newall is anything other than the most interested party. It is a sad episode in a litany of sad episodes surrounding the case.'

But the prosecution was not out of the wood yet for, although he put a stay on the release, the Lord Chief Justice said that did not stop the Magistrate from considering bail for Newall in the meantime. Would the Magistrate allow onto the streets of Gibraltar someone accused of a double murder? And if he did, would Newall's brother help him to jump bail? Following another fraught twenty-four hours, on 27 November Roderick was again refused bail and the Crown team were again able to heave a sigh of relief.

At sea Newall had made many friends and meticulously recorded names, addresses and phone numbers in his address book. Detective Inspector Jimmy Adamson was convinced Newall must have told someone during his travels that he had murdered his parents. The police desperately needed verification of any kind so Adamson was laboriously working his way through the filofax. When he came to the letter P he came across the name Pedot, Helena, and a Brazilian telephone number. He began dialling more in hope than in expectation – and the answer he received was better than anything in his wildest dreams.

Yes, said the female voice speaking in perfect English four thousand miles away. Yes, she and Roderick had fallen deeply in love and, yes, Roderick had indeed confessed to murdering his parents. She readily admitted it. Adamson was dumbfounded. Ever since, Helena said, she had been torn apart by her conscience and had not known what to do or even if anyone would believe her. She agreed to meet the Jersey detectives and give a statement if they came to Brazil. Adamson, together with Detective Superintendent Marks, lost no time in making travel arrangements. This time they decided everything would be done formally and they agreed to meet the local honorary consul in Sao Paulo. Standing at over six feet tall and dressed in a white suit, he seemed to have stepped straight out from the pages of a Graham Green novel. Helpfully, he gave the two detectives a crash course on the best methods of approaching Brazilian women.

Paul Marks would have been the first to admit he

was not the most experienced policeman when it came to operating in tropical climates. Almost the first thing he had done when he realized he was travelling to Brazil was to buy himself an anti-mosquito tent which he duly erected around his hotel bed in São Paulo to the great amusement of the hotel staff. Tactfully they told him there were no mosquitos for several hundred miles.

But that was the least of his worries. When Helena Pedot failed to appear at the agreed rendezvous, for one stomach-churning afternoon they thought they had lost their last hope of redeeming the Newall inquiry. Eventually the two policemen decided to fly down to Puerto Alegre and managed to locate her. Gently, she was persuaded to tell her story.

One evening Roderick had been scouring her bookshelves and had come across *The Glass Bead Game* (*Magister Ludi*) by the Nobel Prize-winning writer Hermann Hesse. 'This has meant so much to me,' he said, flicking through the pages. Later that month they were sitting by the fire and Rod was snorting cocaine, which he found an aid to his 'inner exploration', when he asked her to read a passage in English from the book. There was something she had to know, he said.

Helena was puzzled but did as he asked. The passage was about a killer's remorse. Roderick became very upset and Helena realized that it was not just the drugs that were affecting him. When she had finished reading he cast the book aside and gripped her by the shoulders, shouting, 'I'm a murderer, I'm a murderer.'

When Roderick told her what he had done she at first had to stop herself from laughing. People say funny things on coke and he had a strong streak of the melodramatic about him. But later that night, after he had gone to sleep in her arms, Helena's mind was in turmoil. Surely he didn't mean what he said about murdering his parents. He had spoken of a tortured childhood: his parents had been horrible to him and his brother and had sent him away from home to boarding school at an early age.

When she realized it was all true, however, Helena, a devout Catholic, was devastated: things could never be the same between them again, and it was the beginning of the end of their relationship.

Scarcely able to contain his excitement, Adamson asked if she would accompany him back to the UK to make a statement. Helena was troubled and asked her father, a lawyer, what to do. He advised against it, but when she consulted her own lawyer she was told to follow her conscience. The next day she agreed to accompany Adamson and Marks to St Helier. There she signed an affidavit in front of the bailiff, Sir Peter Crill, to the effect that Roderick Newall had confessed to the murder of his parents.

Just as Newall was on the verge of walking free, the commital was saved. The police were paranoid about the safety of their new witness she was 'placed under police protection' and installed in a room in the Tower Hotel in London.

The next round in the battle over the tapes' admissibility took place on 15 December before Gibraltar's Supreme Court. To square up to Desmond de Silva the defence appointed their own legal big gun from London. In 1971 Brian Leary, QC, had been a senior prosecuting counsel for the Crown and first gained publicity in the notorious *Oz* magazine obscenity trial. At the time he was described in the national press as 'pale, elegant and softly voiced; he uses his hands effectively and expressively'. Now a high-flying criminal barrister,

Leary sailed into Gibraltar on his own luxury yacht. At £3000 a day, he did not come cheap.

On the second day of the hearing de Silva argued for the reinclusion of the tapes, but also triumphantly dropped a hint of the coming bombshell. Rising to address the court, he told of a 'significant new matter which has arisen which implicates Mr Newall'. Roderick's head suddenly snapped up from his book.

After lengthy deliberations the Magistrate's decision was finally overruled by Lord Chief Justice Kneller – to de Silva's immense relief. Magistrate Pizzarello, he said, was exercising discretion he did not have in disallowing admissible evidence. The next day de Silva played his trump card: he named Helena Pedot as the source of the new evidence. Huge sighs of relief were breathed in police headquarters and the Attorney General's offices in Jersey and Gibraltar; the committal was back on the rails.

Desmond de Silva was determined that Helena should not be allowed back to Brazil 'where life is cheap' – and certainly nowhere near the defence. A request from Christopher Finch to interview her was rejected out of hand: 'In the light of the information given by Miss Pedot it seems an extraordinary request and one which will be refused as far as I'm concerned,' replied Philip Bailhache.

The discovery that Helena was the new witness hit Roderick Newall hard. He was devastated. Only months before they had been planning a future together. She was one of the few people he had loved – the only woman he could ever open his heart to. It felt like a final betrayal.

Two days before Christmas Roderick was found in a coma in his cell and once again was rushed to the

287

casualty ward in St Bernard's Hospital. Desperate attempts were made to revive him: it was discovered that he had overdosed on horded sleeping pills supplied by the prison. He lay unconscious for nearly three days and doctors had decided they could do no more – they were on the verge of having him flown to London for brain scans. It was a move which would have brought an end to the whole extradition battle as he could then simply be flown to Jersey for trial. But late on Christmas Day Roderick pulled around.

With a seemingly endless supply of energy – if not resources – the defence kept up their stubborn resistance and the tit-for-tat legal battle continued throughout early 1993. One day at the beginning of March Desmond de Silva was intrigued to receive a visit from Christopher Finch in London. In the convivial surroundings of the Carlton Club they sat, Finch with his chablis, de Silva with his usual glass of Irish whiskey, and discussed the timetable for the case. The two contrasted markedly – one a consummate insider and a metropolitan establishment man; the other the maverick outsider from the colonies.

In response to the Crown victory the defence planned to take the matter to a higher court still – the Court of Appeal. 'If it continues like this we could end up in the House of Lords,' said de Silva to Philip Bailhache at one point.

The prosecution suspected that the defence was being guided by a hidden hand: Roderick's legal costs were being met by Mark and his sole weekly telephone call was invariably made to his brother. Still working as a highly paid employee of his bank, and commuting regularly between homes in New York and Paris, Mark was mobile, energetic and probably had unlimited resources. While Mark Newall was still free, the case was under threat.

The police were determined to get not one, but both brothers for the murders, but, by the beginning of 1993, they were worried. They suspected that Mark was secretly planning to bolt to America – where he lived for much of the time anyway – and settle there. If he did so, he would become virtually unextraditable, but Philip Bailhache proved reluctant to move on him and had already turned down a police request for an arrest warrant. He felt that the evidence was not strong enough to sustain a case against Mark.

But Desmond de Silva had already spotted connections no one had noticed before. A pair of spectacle lenses discovered in the remains of the bonfire were never identified as either Nicholas's or Elizabeth's. At de Silva's urging the detectives managed to trace the lenses back to an optician in Spain, who thought it likely they did in fact belong to Nicholas.

However, de Silva was sure Mark could be tied in. In their statements the boys had said they stayed at Mark's house on the night of 10 October and went back to the bungalow at eight the next morning. 'Well, whatever happened, they were together,' said de Silva. 'If one is lying, the other is lying, if that is the case, then why?' A neighbour had told police that she saw two young men handing each other parcels and loading them into a van outside Mark's house at six o'clock that same morning. Later, two young men in a van had asked for advice on a suitable place to burn rubbish.

'Taken all together,' de Silva argued, 'we can prove both the boys were lying; it follows as night follows day that together they had a hand in their parents' demise. I tell you, Philip, it's a very strong circumstantial case.'

But even after he had accepted de Silva's point

Bailhache was still not convinced. How was it possible to spring a surprise arrest on someone who regularly commuted between Paris, London and New York? Mark's jet-setting had already posed great problems for the police keeping tabs on him but over the years Adamson had found a way. Every month Mark Newall sent flowers to his grandmother in North Berwick and, courtesy of the local florist, the detectives had always been able to track the bills' destination. 'Interflora are better than Interpol at tracking that bugger,' Adamson joked. But determining his movements with a view to arresting him needed much greater precision. 'How will we find him, Desmond?' moaned Bailhache.

'Leave it to me, Philip,' he was told.

On 12 March a warrant for the arrest of Mark Newall was issued by the Attorney General. The operation to arrest him was planned in the incident room at Rouge Bouillon and it was de Silva who solved the problem of tracking him. He suggested the police request the assistance of his credit card company to monitor his purchases. The break came in February, when Mark bought a British Airways ticket from the USA to Paris.

The police had twenty-four hours to set up the operation. Early in the morning of Wednesday 17 March Mark was in his flat at 33 rue Paul Valéry, situated in the exclusive 16ème Arrondissement, when the doorbell rang. The concierge said he had a telegram. Mark opened the door and immediately members of the Paris police equivalent of the CID – pushed in and arrested him. As he was led to the police van outside and taken to the police cells the Jersey detectives began to go through his possessions.

It was a stylish apartment with good furniture and some rather odd pieces of sculpture. At the foot of a spiral staircase there was a curious five-foot-high metal sculpture of a tree painted gold. Another was in the sitting room, where one wall was covered in mirrors. Both the bedroom and the kitchen looked barely used and there was a curious lack of any personal touches.

As they picked their way through a filing cabinet, they made an astonishing discovery: a small, faded piece of printed paper – a restaurant receipt for a dinner for four people. It was from the Sea Crest restaurant and was dated 10 October six years previously.

The Newall relatives had also been concerned about Mark: they were worried that he might be able to use his financial acumen to hide or dispose of the estate. Stephen Newall eventually persuaded Nancy Clark to embark on legal action. In Jersey's Royal Court they applied to replace the boys as beneficiaries of Nicholas's and Elizabeth's estate. They also moved to replace the brothers in taking control of trusts left behind by Kenneth Newall.

The defence immediately protested. Such an action, said Le Quesne, was 'greedy and distasteful . . . at a time when Roderick and Mark are vulnerable and isolated and in need of support from family and friends this action is a callous and cruel blow.' An interim injunction was already in place which prevented the sons from selling the bungalow.

A week after Mark's arrest the Court of Appeal met in Gibraltar to consider the latest development in the legal battle. Roderick Newall had appealed against the Supreme Court's decision and de Silva arrived to mount the case for the Crown. He was delighted when he discovered that Brian Leary would not after all be representing Newall. 'I told you, John,' he said to the Attorney General. 'The money's beginning to run out.'

The defence was instead to be argued by Christopher

291

Finch himself. He was a lethal solicitor, but advocacy on a pure point of law was not his strong point, and as he outlined his argument he seemed halting and unsure. At one point Sir Alan Higgins, the senior of the three judges, asked him if he would like a brief adjournment so that he could read up his legal notes again. At lunchtime the detectives and press were agreed: he was losing badly. 'The problem is that Finch has got just a few tricks and they work for him continually,' said one reporter. 'He's out of his depth here.'

Predictably the court gave the decision to the Crown. The Supreme Court had been right to overrule Pizzarello's decision.

The defence now embarked on a long and complicated round of appeals and counter-appeals. With the arrest of Mark, Roderick's last real link with freedom and the outside world had disappeared and with it so did his morale. Early in April 1993 he was again rushed to hospital. He had somehow got hold of a pen knife and had apparently once again attempted suicide. After he recovered he wrote an open letter, saying that he was going to refuse food and did not want to be force-fed or receive any medical attention.

Meanwhile, in Paris Mark was getting his first taste of prison. He shared a cell with three others in the city's main remand institution, Le Santé. His Paris lawyer, Anthony Van Hagen, said that the police may have been guilty of overkill in their sudden swoop on the flat. He made a statement to point out that Mark had never been a fugitive and had always responded to police requests for help. 'Mr Newall has made numerous visits to Jersey and the UK since the disappearance of his parents and, following his brother's arrest, the Jersey police categorically informed him they had no intention of questioning him any further.

'As Mr Newall always voluntarily kept the police informed of his whereabouts in the event that his assistance might be required, he was shocked and distressed to be arrested on an extradition request made by authorities to whom he has always given past co-operation.'

Getting Mark to Jersey was to be a great deal easier than prising his brother off Gibraltar. Extradition between Jersey and France is straightforward: all the Jersey police had to do was satisfy the French police that the person named on the warrant was the one arrested, that the offence he was accused of existed in French law, and that the penalty would not exceed that handed down by a French court. Even if Mark had chosen to fight, it would have been a foregone conclusion; as it was, he went quietly.

On Friday 30 April a specially chartered jet took off from Le Bourget airport near Paris with Mark Newall aboard, handcuffed to Detective Superintendent Martin Fitzgerald. Mark was then taken to police headquarters at Rouge Bouillon. Mark closed his eyes on taking off from Paris and did not open them again until touching down in Jersey. At 6.13 p.m. he was formally charged on two separate counts of murder by the St Brelade Centenier Barry Walsh and, after spending the night in the police cells, was remanded to La Moye prison.

On 4 May a crowd of reporters, photographers, TV crews and curious onlookers stood outside the police court as Mark was led inside. He was smartly dressed in his dark-grey suit, blue tie and gold-rimmed spectacles. The charges of murder were read to him again by Barry Walsh and a plea of not guilty was entered.

The final round in the battle had begun and, as ever, it was Desmond de Silva who figured out the prosecution strategy. The case against Mark alone was much weaker than against Roderick who, through his confession, had implicated himself. 'I'll tell you what their game plan is, Philip,' de Silva said to the Jersey Attorney General on the phone one afternoon. 'He will push for a committal as soon as possible, knowing he's got a better chance of getting off. Then, once he's off the hook, Roderick can argue he can never get a fair trial.'

By June Mark had settled in at La Moye. He worked in the kitchen, but otherwise kept himself to himself. There were no suicide attempts or hunger strikes.

At the beginning of his incarceration in Gibraltar Roderick had been allowed to mix freely with other prisoners, but that all changed dramatically after his first suicide attempt. From then on the prison authorities, with an eye to the potential bad publicity, were taking no chances. He was kept in virtual solitary confinement and searched several times a day. By the end of December 1992, only three days after his second suicide attempt, he was complaining of 'freezing to death' and of not being given proper clothing. Gradually, though, conditions improved. He struck up a good relationship with a number of the prison officers and was allowed access to the TV and newspapers. He was, of course, never short of books and had a few computer games. In mid-March 1993 he was taken to hospital again, but was released after a few hours. This time he denied attempting suicide but admitted using the heroin substitute methadone, smuggled to him in a syringe placed in an orange.

Despite the conditions and his state of mind the old Rod Newall bravado emerged from time to time. Once he boasted to a guard he could smuggle in anything he wanted – and then produced a razor blade from the spine of a book. He handed it over with a smile.

At the beginning of June Captain Patrick Sanders of the Royal Green Jackets was led through the dark stone hallways of the Moorish prison to an open courtyard, where he was allowed to meet his old friend. Roderick seemed in good spirits. He had apparently accepted his fate and wanted to go back to Jersey 'to get things over with'. 'It's pretty grim in here,' he told Patrick, 'but they do their best considering it's such a dump . . . I don't even see any proper sunlight – only the fluorescent striplight.' He had to undergo body searches several times a day and was shaved once a week, though his main complaint was that he was not allowed out into the exercise yard for long enough. And he was only permitted one call a week – usually to his brother Mark. The conditions had improved somewhat and he was now allowed limited access to other prisoners. Otherwise each day was a monotonous struggle, but Sky TV, a radio and a library had helped pass the time. Reading was a great consolation. He had enjoyed *Crime and Punishment* because 'long depressing books make me realize I'm still much better off than many other people.' He managed a wan smile and thanked Patrick for his three books.

There was one other consolation: at last, after months of practice, he was able to defeat his computer chess game. 'That lot are okay,' he said, nodding over to where two prison officers sat chatting, far out of earshot. Occasionally they would play chess or scrabble with him.

After about forty minutes the guards signalled the visit was over and Roderick gathered up his books and said goodbye to his old friend. As he turned to walk back Patrick could just make out the scars on the inside of his right wrist, the legacies of his suicide attempts.

* * *

By the summer of 1993 there were definite signs of strain within the defence camp. In July a press story claimed that there might be a short hearing and that Roderick Newall was about to throw in the towel. It came as a complete shock to David Le Quesne. He was finding it more and more difficult to find out what was happening on Gibraltar – he couldn't even raise Finch on the telephone for a policy meeting.

But it was still not over. In July an unexpected decision in the House of Lords led to another twist in the legal battle. Following the precedent of a case in which English police had inveigled a suspect home from a country which did not have extradition agreements with the UK, the House of Lords ruled that a court *did* have powers to query the legality of an arrest. This at least held out the possibility of further breathing space – if not a chance to fight the arrest. As a result, Roderick Newall's lawyers hoped to obtain a stay on extradition proceedings while they took the new precedent to Gibraltar's Supreme Court.

At the beginning of July David Le Quesne told the police court in St Helier that the fight was continuing in Gibraltar and that 'as a result it was unlikely that Roderick Newall would be returned this year, if at all', and he strongly urged the Magistrate to press ahead with committal proceedings against Mark. It was a shrewd move. Despite the Crown's claim that they had a prima facie case against the younger brother, David Le Quesne was sure they were bluffing. If he could get his client into court as soon as possible – and as long as he wasn't sharing the dock with his brother – there was a good chance of a result. In mid-July, however, the chances of Mark going on trial were dashed when a Jersey magistrate dismissed an application for separate hearings.

It was a decision which infuriated David Le Quesne, who on 13 August publicly accused the court of behaving like a Third World dictatorship. His angry words were a measure of the bad relations that had developed between him and the local legal authorities. He accused the Attorney General of dragging his feet so that the prosecution could keep Mark behind bars.

Meanwhile on Gibraltar the legal dance continued. The Crown tried to press ahead with the extradition while, in yet another hearing, the Supreme Court was to consider an application for a writ of habeas corpus based on the claim that the sea arrest was illegal.

On the Wednesday preceding the hearing the Crown team gathered in the Holiday Inn around a table stacked with papers. In the suite was the Jersey police legal adviser Ian Christmas, Detective Sergeant Malcolm Aubert and Desmond de Silva. De Silva had just begun to discuss court tactics when something protruding from above a large picture on the wall entitled 'The Battle of Trafalgar' caught his eye. He stared in silence for a second, then walked round the table to look at it more closely. It seemed to be a wire, but it wasn't part of the picture frame. By this time the others had gathered around. Then, carefully lifting the picture off its hook, they laid it face down on the table. The wire disappeared inside the backing canvas. The three men cut open the canvas and lifted it off to reveal a small black box. It was later established that the box itself was a battery-operated radio transmitter; the protruding wire was a microphone. Who could have placed it there and who had been receiving signals was never established.

The case was already enmeshed in intrigue and dirty dealings, and the listening device merely confirmed what de Silva had suspected: that Roderick Newall's brother would stop at nothing to get the extradition proceedings halted. At least one of Roderick's alleged 'suicide attempts' struck him as a ploy to get back into hospital. From St Bernard's to the Spanish border was less than five minutes on the back of a motorcycle. So the news that Roderick had made a request to be admitted to hospital to get a wart removed brought a snort of derision from de Silva. 'He's lived with it for this long,' he said. 'He can live with it for a few more weeks.'

On Friday 20 August the Supreme Court threw out the application for a habea corpus defence and, at the end of September 1993, the local justiciary finally ran out of patience: three Appeal Court judges said that extradition proceedings should 'proceed with all dispatch'. The court awarded costs against Newall and with a broad grin, Desmond de Silva, QC, commented, 'No one who can instruct Mr Finch can have anything other than a deep pocket.' Turning to his adversary, de Silva smiled and said, 'Only teasing.' But his quip appeared to have hit the mark: the next day a bankrupted Roderick Newall applied for legal aid. Mark had turned off the financial tap.

On 8 October 1993 time ran out for Roderick Newall. On the day of the extradition hearing Christopher Finch applied for a judicial review. He wanted the Supreme Court to look at the legality of the arrest, but the application had been thrown out by the Lord Chief Justice, who had described it as 'hopeless in law'.

Newall suffered another setback when de Silva successfully won an application for costs to be awarded against the defence. Finch tried to halt it, saying his client had a legal aid application pending, but de Silva, casting a mischievous smile at the glaring defendant, rejected the whole notion that 'Newall was a poor orphan who had squandered his patrimony'.

The extradition hearing took place before the biggest crowd of press and public ever seen in Gibraltar's tiny courthouse. Dozens of reporters had flown in for the occasion and court clerks struggled to keep people out. When Roderick stepped out of the police van he seemed in good spirits and laughed and joked with the accompanying prison officers; but his choice of reading matter for the hearing was to prove prophetic: it was *The Glass Bead Game* by Hermann Hesse.

The strategy agreed on by de Silva and Gittings was to throw in the whole weight of the case against Newall so that any lingering doubts about his guilt would be completely removed. The prosecution case took more than two hours to unfold, and from start to finish it held the courtroom spellbound.

As he rose to his feet de Silva's voice boomed around the walls. He said he intended to show to the court that Newall was 'an assasin to his parents on or about 10 October 1987'. During the secretly tape-recorded conversation in which he revealed his guilt, 'the accused gazed into the face of his father's identical twin and there spurted from his lips the pent-up guilt he had held for so long that finally broke its banks in a series of admissions that point inescapably to the conclusion that he was responsible for patricide and matricide.'

De Silva claimed that the Crown would show, with the aid of scientific evidence, that this was a carefully planned and brutally carried out double murder. Having arranged to have a meal with his mother and father, Newall took them home and cold-bloodedly killed them. He outlined how they had shared two bottles of champagne at the bungalow before heading for the restaurant, where they all downed a third bottle

299

and a bottle of wine. 'This was the last the world was to see of Mr and Mrs Newall.'

Earlier that day Nicholas Newall had been induced to hire a red van, supposedly to help Roderick transport mattresses to his brother's house and he did so not knowing that he was 'hiring his own hearse'. Newall went to his parents' home in the van that evening – a vehicle 'ideal in all respects' for the transfer of bodies. 'It is the Crown's case that they were done to death in their own home that night. The only clothes that have never been found are the clothes that Mr and Mrs Newall wore to the Sea Crest restaurant that night – leading to the inevitable conclusion that they went to their final resting place before they went to bed.'

The next day de Silva continued to outline the evidence for the Crown. Police dog-handlers, he said, had found lenses of glasses belonging to Nicholas Newall near the bonfire seven months later.

Forensic evidence concluded that 'sustained violence' had been suffered in the bungalow's sitting room by someone of Nicholas Newall's blood group and in the bedroom by someone of Elizabeth's.

Outlining Maureen Ellam's visit the following day, and her suggestion that Roderick place the flowers on her pillow so that when she woke up 'she will think she has died and gone to heaven', Mr de Silva said, 'It is the Crown's case that Mrs Newall's eyes never opened to the beauty of flowers or anything else.' On moving around the house later with Roderick, Mr Ellam 'noticed with a sharp eye the fluff that had come away in an effort to clean the carpet'.

Then de Silva moved on to Roderick Newall's meeting with his aunt and uncle in Scotland. Newall had been trapped, he said, because he was unaware that his chilling revelations were being recorded. His parents' bodies were apparently wrapped in plastic and camouflaged. He carried the blame for the crime and if the police moved in he had a suicide plan; he told his uncle he was looking forward to meeting them again 'on the other side' but he would not say sorry to them when he did. He said there were no mitigating circumstances but that he had to live with his guilt. He said that if he were a Catholic he would be seeking absolution, but that it was not going to help him by sitting in a prison for twenty-five years and that in any case it would finish off his grandmother.

When his uncle suggested to Roderick that after this period of time there was nothing of any practical use to anybody on the bodies, Roderick referred to his parents' clothes and said, 'Yes, but that pins it down to a night.'

'The crucial significance of this is that if the Crown are right and Mr and Mrs Newall met violent deaths that night,' argued de Silva, 'then a signed statement made by Roderick Newall to the police on 20 October sets out a false alibi for himself. In that statement the accused speaks of leaving his parents' home in the small hours of the morning of 11 October, with his parents returning to bed, and returning to his brother's home, La Falaise. Newall's statement on the tapes were an utter admission of "I did it myself."

'The Crown says that by dawn on 11 October not only had the killing of his parents been accomplished, but that the disposal had begun of the articles used in the killing and items of his parents' possessions which this accused could not have afforded to have lying about the house.'

He then turned to the evidence of Mark Newall's next-door neighbour, Mrs Sheila Cruickshank, who was woken at 6 a.m. on Sunday 11 October to see the red van with its doors open and the white Toyota with its boot open and two men passing articles to each other.

'These matters taken individually or together amount to the clearest confession to being involved in a murder that a person could make, short of the use of the phrase, "Yes, I did it."'

The only movement in the court was the frantic writing of the reporters. Newall stared at de Silva as if mesmerized. Then de Silva moved on to the statement the police had obtained from Helena Pedot. According to her, he had admitted he murdered his parents and then, 'with tears running down his face he shook her shoulders and said, "I'm a murderer, I'm a murderer".'

At the end of two hours de Silva sat down, emotionally drained, and the judge adjourned the case until Monday. As they walked from the court, de Silva and Gittings were confident. 'That's it, John,' said de Silva. 'The battle of Gibraltar's nearly over.' Newall, white and clearly shaking, was led through the side door to the police van. Just before he got in the back of the van it had been searched. A three-inch scalpel blade, still wrapped in polythene, had been placed there.

The chilling courtroom revelations filled the British newspapers the next day. When the case reopened on Monday de Silva piled on the pressure. Dissecting the forensic evidence of David Northcott, he pointed out that fragments of J-cloth found at the bonfire site near the Crow's Nest had matched fibres found on the chimney ledge and indicated a major cleaning operation. The Crown could prove that the house had not been cleaned by the maid: she did not use J-cloths.

Then de Silva elaborated on the evidence of the 'Brazilian beauty', Miss Pedot. He described how, on a cold day in July 1991, Newall had asked her to get him a book called *The Glass Bead Game*. She had opened it and begun to read:

> 'Oh, he thought in grief and horror, now I am guilty of his death. And only now when there was no need to save his pride or offer resistance, he felt in shock and horror, how dear this man had already become to him. He felt responsible for the master's death and there came over him with a premonitory shudder of awe, a sense that this guilt would utterly change him and his life and demand much greater things of him that he could never demand of himself.'

As de Silva spoke, almost imperceptibly Roderick Newall's bowed head began to move. As the passage came to an end he was clearly nodding.

De Silva went on to describe how Newall had said that only then had he realized how much his parents had loved each other. He spoke in terms of regret. He said he had only opened his heart to her because of their relationship.

In August 1992 in Miami Newall had taken Helena to see the film *Cape Fear*. The Crown maintained he said he did not like the film but thought that it was good to live in fear. Helena had asked him if he was not afraid of going back to Britain to see his family and he had said he was only afraid of meeting his father's identical twin and not being able to keep his silence. Helena had wanted him to see a psychiatrist but he had insisted that she would help him come to terms with his guilt.

Then de Silva described Newall's conversation with his Aunt Nancy in July 1992; her dream of his mother saying, 'I told you he meant it and I told you it would happen, but let the matter rest.'

Finally de Silva provided a motive for the murders: 'On 3 September 1990 this accused filed an affidavit in the Royal Court of Jersey, saying that he had neither contact with nor news of his parents since 11 October 1987 and that he believed his parents to be dead. The purpose was to ask the court to presume the death of his parents so that he could inherit his share of the estate.'

That Monday evening the three adversaries, Desmond de Silva, David Le Quesne and Christopher Finch, met for lunch at a restaurant owned by Mr Finch. During the long nights at the Holiday Inn Desmond de Silva had already impressed journalists with his formidable capacity for alcohol. Several glasses later the three went their separate ways, but Mr Finch had no sooner stepped onto the pavement than he was hit by a child on a skateboard. The impact sent him crashing to the ground, breaking his leg in two places. 'There you go, folks,' said de Silva triumphantly to the press when he heard the news. 'I always told you Finch never had a leg to stand on.'

The previous night the phone had rung in de Silva's suite in the Holiday Inn Hotel: the horse-trading had already begun in earnest; a deal was being hammered out. And a week later, during a ten-minute hearing in Gibraltar's Magistrate's Court, Christopher Finch, seated in a wheelchair with his leg in plaster, announced that Newall would not be contesting the extradition hearing. 'I am committing you now to be taken to Jersey,' said the magistrate, Pizzarello. After fourteen months of litigation costing hundreds of thousands of pounds, it was over; the deal had been struck.

David Le Quesne had already spent hours going

through his 'shopping list' of requirements. Essentially Roderick Newall would give up his fight and agree to return to Jersey and plead guilty to murder on the condition that his brother got a reduced sentence for aiding and abetting. That way an expensive trial, with no guarantee of a murder conviction against Mark, could be avoided and honour satisfied all round.

In the closing minutes of the last Gibraltar hearing Le Quesne had submitted more requests. Christmas shouted across to him, 'You have got a deal.' As far as Le Quesne was concerned it was an agreement, not an understanding. But the deal was soon to be the source of further trouble.

CHAPTER 15

Roderick Newall's battle to avoid extradition to Jersey ended on the stroke of midnight on Thursday 4 November 1993, when the time limit to lodge a last appeal against the court's sentence expired. Two days later the Governor of Gibraltar, Field Marshal Sir John Chapple, signed the extradition paper and at 6 a.m. the following day, Roderick shook hands with the duty prison warders, climbed into the police van and passed through the gates of the ancient prison for the last time.

At the airport he was handed into the custody of the Jersey police. 'Is there anything you want to know before you leave?' Detective Superintendent Martin Fitzgerald asked him.

'No, thank you,' replied Roderick, taking copies of his arrest warrant in his uncuffed hand.

Roderick and David Le Quesne sat together behind the detectives on the chartered jet. At 7.30 a.m. the plane was taxiing along the runway and Roderick asked if he could have a pen and some paper. Just over an hour later Le Quesne moved down the aisle, tapped Detective Superintendent Paul Marks on the shoulder, and handed him the sheets of paper on which Newall had written his confession, and then a map of Jersey with a dot indicating a location on the north-west coast of the island. Marks studied it for a moment, consulted

his colleagues, then handed him in return a larger-scale
Ordnance Survey map, which was returned with dots
on two fields on a wooded hillside marked 390 and 391.
For the rest of the flight Roderick was relaxed and
chatted with the officers.

At 10.07 the plane landed at Jersey airport to be met
by a huge contingent of photographers and TV crews.
Roderick, handcuffed, walked the twenty yards to a
police van, which took him straight to police headquarters in St Helier.

Just after 3 p.m. a long line of police cars moved
away from police headquarters and made their way to
the north-western corner of the island. Dusk was
already gathering by the time they arrived at the Grève
de Lecq and the vehicles' headlamps cast their beams
far into the crisp autumn evening air. At that time of
year, after the throngs of tourists have left, the place
is at its most beautiful, its woodlands peaceful and
deserted. Just before reaching the bay the cars pulled
up on the verge along some fields in the small valley
known as the Moulin de Lecq. A narrow stream ran
parallel to the road and into a pond. On the far side of
the fields the ground rose sharply into a steep slope
covered with trees and bushes.

Handcuffed to a police officer, Newall stepped over
the fence and, after hopping over the stream, began
walking across the field towards the bank. If he seemed
familiar with the ground it was because he had known
it all his life. The Moulin de Lecq had once been his
own secret place – a magical valley of dens, tunnels,
the haunt of fairies, monsters, cowboys and indians,
and pirates seeking buried treasure. Once it had given
refuge to a scared little boy. Twenty years later,
Roderick Newall had come home.

From his childhood home the Crow's Nest, high up

on the hillside not more than 500 yards to the north, a couple were watching with a growing sense of foreboding. Like everyone else on the island, Maureen and David Ellam had followed the live TV coverage of the extradition and had seen the activity below. Maureen thought back to her friends' disappearance and to the blue-eyed lad who would come loping into her house in the days that followed. At the time she had thought Roderick was just lonely and was returning to the scene of so many childhood memories. But now she grasped the significance of those visits with feelings of horror and rage. The bodies of her friends had lain virtually under her nose for four years. At that moment all the sympathy Maureen had felt for the brothers drained away, to be replaced by an intense and burning hatred.

After an hour and a quarter, as preparations were being made for the excavation, Roderick was taken back to the police station, and there, just before 6 p.m. he was charged by the Centenier with the murder of his parents on or about 10 October 1987. He was later placed in the remand wing of La Moye prison – only a mile from the scene of the murder. Asked by the Governor if he wanted to be kept separate from his brother, Roderick said no, he would be happy to see him.

Meanwhile at the Grève de Lecq, after an unsuccessful couple of hours the light had faded completely and digging work was called off for the day. At eight the next morning, Sunday 7 November, work began again. By midday the hillside was covered with police officers in blue search overalls either shovelling soil or combing the ground looking for disturbance. They were helped by a specialist team of search officers from the Devon and Cornwall Police.

On the morning of Monday 8 November a police van carrying Roderick Newall pulled up outside the police court in Seal Street in St Helier. A vast crowd of reporters had gathered for Roderick's first court appearance in Jersey. The street was cordoned off but when Newall, flanked by officers, stepped out the cameras clicked and whirred. As usual he was dressed in his blue blazer; as usual he was holding a book.

The charges were read out by the Centenier: 'That the said Roderick Innes Nelson Newall, with having, on or about the tenth day of October 1987, with Mark Stephen Innes Nelson Newall on the island of Jersey, murdered Nicholas Stephen Park Newall.

'That the said Roderick Innes Nelson Newall, with having, on or about the tenth day of October 1987, with Mark Stephen Innes Nelson Newall, murdered Elizabeth Newall née Nelson.'

Advocate David Le Quesne rose to say, 'I am instructed by my client to plead guilty to both charges.'

Roderick had remained silent throughout. The hearing lasted two minutes.

As the search at the Grève de Lecq entered its third day the police had widened their area of digging but still had no success. The field had changed dramatically since 1987 because the local water company had built a pumping station near by and had extensively re-landscaped the area. These changes were hampering the search so in the afternoon Roderick was taken back to the Moulin de Lecq and spent two hours with the detectives trying to work out the position of the bodies. He appeared to be making a genuine attempt to find the spot. Police asked nearby householders to switch on their lights so that he could try and picture the site as it was six years previously.

He described how he had driven the hired van with his parents' bodies in the back down the Grève de Lecq, rounded a bend and, on seeing house lights further ahead, realized he had gone too far and reversed back up a hill. He and his brother had then removed the two heavy, tightly bound bundles and tossed them over the fence. Roderick parked the van further down the road and walked back to help Mark. Together they dragged the bodies across an open field and up onto a bushy slope and began digging.

After Newall's second visit the search concentrated on a site about 100 yards from the roadside, where a footpath stretches the length of the valley just below the treeline.

On the morning of Tuesday 9 November Mark Newall stood in the dock at the police court and repeated his not guilty plea to the charge of murdering his parents. Outside the court Le Quesne said that Roderick Newall and he alone would be pleading guilty to the murders, 'and the important phrase here is "he alone"'.

By now the strains of the last months were beginning to tell. Le Quesne had already been conducting a running battle with the Attorney General about the propriety of him representing the alleged murderers of two of his former clients. But there was friction with his clients as well – especially Mark. In an impromptu statement to the assembled press Le Quesne said, 'I can represent either one – or, more likely, neither of the two brothers.'

Gradually the scene of the excavation became the focus of ghoulish interest as more and more sightseers turned up to watch. The Moulin de Lecq pub was allowed to stay open to cater for the scores of journalists and TV crews. It was eventually to be used as a makeshift press bureau.

At midday on Tuesday, 200 yards north of the Moulin de Lecq pub, a hush settled over the excavation.

Minutes went by as officers peered intently into the hole. Then a cry went up from the site and the expressions on the faces of the police said it all: it was over. After six years the bodies of Nick and Elizabeth Newall had been found.

Jimmy Adamson had been examining the trench dug by the JCB when he saw a piece of black polythene half hidden in the soil. Lifting it back, he saw the remains of a man's shoe. After scraping away more soil he found two large bundles, wrapped in separate green and blue tarpaulins. After a cursory examination, the Home Office pathologist, Dr Guyan Fernando, who had flown over from England, confirmed the discovery of human remains and the exhumation began. As he moved in to supervise the careful removal, screens were erected around the site. Just before the bundles were lifted out the arc lights, which had been illuminating the scene, were switched off and Dr Fernando doffed his woollen hat as a sign of respect. The remains were taken to the Jersey General Hospital, where Fernando began his examination.

The evidence of the bludgeoning was clear and gruesome. In the case of the female skull there were a series of lacerations – seven in all – which ranged in length from 1.5cm to 5.5cm. The male skull bore two lacerations at the front part of the head and six at the back. These ranged in length from 3cm to 8cm. The bodies had been so tightly packaged that one doctor described them as 'vacu-packed'; an entymologist said that if one fly egg had been laid inside the tarpaulins there would have been nothing but bones. Injuries on both bodies were consistent with being struck by 'rice flails' – a lethal Chinese martial arts weapon – but the more serious injury to the back of Nicholas Newall's head was thought to have been caused by a sharp-edged weapon such as would be consistent with the pick-axe bought on the day of the murders. Red refuse sacks were also found covering the bodies, again the same as those bought from the hardware shop. The bodies were both dressed in clothing identical to what they had been wearing at the Sea Crest Hotel on 10 October 1987. And the scientists made an even more terrible discovery: the presence of phenobarbitones in the stomach and liver of Nicholas Newall. Here, it seemed, was the evidence that the murder had been premeditated. The drug in question was normally used for the treatment of epilepsy, which neither Elizabeth nor Nicholas suffered from. Side-effects include drowsiness and sedation, which are especially dangerous when taken with alcohol.

The findings would be closely contested by the defence who would claim the testing was inconclusive, but as far as the police were concerned, here was the clearest evidence yet that the murders had been premeditated.

The police had never believed that Mark Newall had nothing to do with his parents' murder, and they were determined to show that he had at least known of his brother's intentions. There were even officers who believed that he had played an equal part with his brother in the planning, if not in the execution; and that Roderick was shielding him to expiate his own guilt.

Without a confession the evidence against Mark was thin, but the discovery of the barbiturates changed everything. They certainly had him bang to rights on everything short of murder. He helped dispose of the bodies, helped clean up the scene of the crime, perjured himself on oath in the Royal Court in 1990, when his parents were declared dead, and had provided an alibi for the murderer. It fell short of directly tying him into the killings or the planning, but the police were going to have a try. They hoped there would be enough in the pathologist's report to make a charge against him stick.

The Crown were in a dilemma. As deeply as the police felt about Mark's involvement, the fact was the evidence against him was still purely circumstantial. With Roderick taking the rap for the murders alone, placing his brother on trial for murder was a high risk course that could easily end up with Mark walking free.

After much soul-searching and legal argument it was decided not to pursue the murder charges against Mark. On Tuesday, 9 November 1993, Mark appeared at the Magistrates Court and was charged with two additional charges of assisting Roderick after the commission of the murders. The murder charges against the younger brother were quietly dropped in a subsequent hearing on 23 February 1994. Faced with the potential embarrassment and expense of an unsuccessful trial, it was a course in which the prosecution felt it had no choice. Nevertheless, it was galling for most of the police and the Newall relatives. They were to maintain that justice was only partially done.

After the full examination of the bodies Roderick was interviewed again at La Moye prison on Monday 7 February 1994. He denied purchasing the tarpaulins, the red refuse sacks and all the other items bought at the builders' merchant the day before the murder. He also denied the murders were premeditated and that he used phenobarbitone dissolved in whisky to drug his father before killing him. He agreed that an iron bar found near the remains of the fire discovered near the Crow's Nest at the Grève de Lecq could have been part of the set of rice flails' that he owned which might have been used to kill his parents, but he was not specific about it.

On 14 March 1994, three days before the committal – the next stage of the formal legal process – Detective Superintendent Martin Fitzgerald travelled to La Moye prison where, in the company of Le Quesne, Mark Newall finally made his own confession – but only to helping his brother conceal the bodies and cleaning up the scene of the crime.

Only a few months before the Newall committal two young Liverpool boys accused of abducting toddler James Bulger from a shopping mall and murdering him were placed on trial. The case gripped the nation for a week. In court both boys blamed each other and the harrowing testimony and cross examinations were reported in detail. But in the Newall case the public was to be denied a similar spectacle. In lengthy pre-trial discussions between prosecution and defence it was arranged that, in accordance with the deal, evidence made public would be kept to a bare minimum and the hearing would be as short as possible. No mention would be made of the drugs found in the bodies.

At 11.15 a.m. on 17 March 1994 flashbulbs popped and cameras whirred again as the brothers stepped out of a police van parked close to the door of the police court and were led into a tense courtroom, where more than thirty newspaper and television reporters from national newspapers and television packed the press benches. Instead of his familiar blazer and jeans Roderick was dressed in a grey suit, blue shirt, and the shuttlecock-patterned tie he had won on the Cresta run six years previously. But Mark's appearance was alarming. Dressed in an ill-fitting suit, he looked thin and drawn with long, unkempt hair reaching down to his stooped shoulders. As they stood listening to the charges read out by the St Brelade Centenier, they looked straight ahead.

Guilty pleas were entered by the boys' advocate David Le Quesne; then the Crown Prosecutor, Sir Cyril Whelan, proceeded to question the four witnesses arraigned to give evidence, which was, in each case, brief. Odontologist David Lewin, who had identified the remains after the excavation, was called to the stand. He gave a detailed resumé of his past experience and then described how, using X-rays, dental records and bite marks, he was able to identify the remains as being positively those of Elizabeth and Nicholas Newall. Next to give evidence was Dr Guyan Fernando, who described in detail the extent of the injuries to the bodies. In both cases, he said, there were extensive fractures to the skull.

Sir Cyril Whelan asked, 'Is it your opinion that the injuries were caused by blows to the head from some other person?'

'Yes,' replied the doctor.

'What do you give as cause of death?'

'In both cases the cause of death was multiple injuries to the head,' came the answer.

Seated next to each other only a dozen feet away, the brothers remained expressionless. The only unplanned moment came when Detective Chief Superintendent Martin Fitzgerald read out the confession Roderick had written on the plane from Gibraltar. He was nervous and stumbled over a few words at the beginning:

'Briefly the circumstances were that, after Mark left, my parents and I were alone in the house and continued talking and drinking in the sitting room of their home.

'A heated argument developed in which many

old wounds were re-opened. It came to a head with my father and I standing face to face. I told him what I thought of him saying things I had never said before. He pushed me. I fell, hitting my head on the dining-room table. I fell onto a box of my possessions I had taken out of the attic.

'On top of the box was a pair of rice flails, which I grabbed and used to club my father. I remember him falling. My next memory was finding myself sitting on the floor of the hall. I got up and went into the sitting room and saw my father's body. I could feel no pulse. In complete panic I checked the kitchen and the bedroom, where I found my mother's body. It triggered my memory of also attacking her. I could find no pulse. Then I realized I had killed both my parents.

'Sometime later I contacted Mark and told him what had happened and told him the only thing for me to do was to kill myself. He persuaded me not to and said he would meet me at the house. When Mark arrived I was in the sitting room holding the shotgun. Mark eventually calmed me down and talked me out of taking my life. Mark and I then took my parents in the hired van and buried them. We then returned home and tried to remove all traces of what had happened.

'My feelings of guilt and remorse have built up since that night. I find it increasingly hard to live a life. I wanted to help my uncle and aunt end the uncertainty but I was worried about the effect on my grandmother of bringing the murder up again. I was particularly concerned for Mark who had helped me and supported me in coming to terms with what I had done. I felt certain the police would not accept the truth, which was that he was not involved in the killings.

'Soon after my arrival in Gibraltar I instructed my lawyers to offer that I would return to Jersey if Mark was not prosecuted but they made it clear that there would be no discussion along those lines. I have still not understood how I was capable of committing these horrific crimes. I think it was probably caused by the bitter childhood memories awakened by the argument. I feel relieved that this is all out in the open. I am appalled at what I did to my parents. I am very sorry that Mark is suffering when his only involvement was after the killing and to help and protect me.'

Then Fitzgerald read out Mark Newall's statement:

'My brother and parents drank a great deal of alcohol. They drank champagne before dinner and several bottles of wine at dinner. On returning to the house they started on the whisky. They started to argue, not violently, about my brother's career prospects and other matters. It was an argument I had heard before. I was sober and not interested so I went home. Some hours later I was contacted by Roderick and he was crying and incoherent. He stated he had killed my mother and father in a drunken row and was going to kill himself.

'He kept saying he was sorry. I went straight to my parents' home and found my father and mother both dead. They had serious head injuries. My brother had blood on him, he was crying and in a distressed state and holding my father's shotgun.

'I told my brother that the best thing to do was to call the police. There was nobody else in the house. He said he would shoot himself. He felt the police would not understand the circumstances. I argued with him for some time and eventually I agreed to help to conceal the crime.

'It was then and is now my belief that if I had not done this he would have killed himself. I found in the boiler room, garage and garden shed tarpaulins, tools and other equipment to clean the house and dispose of the evidence. There were several pairs of rice flails on the floor. Roderick gathered them up and I didn't see them. Roderick said he had cut them up and disposed of them. I am very sorry I did not call the police. I know I made the wrong decision. I lied to the police – to everyone – to give my brother an alibi. I will always bitterly regret the pain and anguish and trouble that has been caused since that night.'

Superintendent Fitzgerald then told the court that, during a subsequent interview with Roderick Newall in prison just over a month earlier, he had admitted causing the fire at the Grève de Lecq; one of the items he disposed of may have been a rice flail used in the murder.

After both confessions had been read out Sir Cyril Whelan said, 'Under the circumstances I have no difficulty in submitting that a prima facie case is established in the case of both accused.' The Magistrate, David Trott, fixed a date for the court transcripts to be signed – a necessary preliminary stage before sentencing in the Royal Court. The boys were then led out of the courtroom, looking neither left nor right; they climbed into the van and were taken back to the prison. The hearing had lasted just forty-five minutes.

The brothers were now dealing with their confinement in very different ways: Roderick, with the weight of uncertainty about the future removed, seemed much more settled. He was writing letters to his friends and receiving visitors and generally seemed to be coping well. In April he wrote a letter to Amanda Newall: he complained about his impending thirtieth birthday, but said he was now much more settled and realized he was much better off than many people.

His picture had been seen around the world and was the source of some bizarre attention. Adoring fan letters flooded in from dozens of young girls across the country, who had seen pictures of the dashing young former army officer.

Mark, on the other hand, had retreated into a shell, choosing not to write or speak to anyone; he had one visit from his cousin William to discuss his control of shares in the family firm, but he refused to see even his close friends the Ginsburys. Both boys had won the confidence of the prison governors by their polite manner and co-operative ways.

However, the police decision to press on with the investigation against Mark flew in the face of the deal struck in Gibraltar. It was to lead to accusations of bad faith and deceit being slung between the prosecution and defence. It was not over yet.

EPILOGUE

August is the height of the tourist season on 'Sunny Jersey'. The hotels are full to overflowing, the narrow winding roads are clogged with nose-to-tail traffic and the beaches are packed. But on Monday 8 August the streets of St Helier were packed with a rather more ghoulish sightseer than usual – a crowd of a hundred jeering onlookers gathered outside the Royal Court of Jersey to see the brothers, each handcuffed to a policeman and smartly dressed in suits and ties, led into court for the final judgement on their crimes.

Inside the imposing chamber the heat was stifling. Along the bench, resplendent in red robes, sat a dozen officials of the court, including the Attorney General. Dozens of curious summer holidaymakers filled the public benches alongside the many local observers.

After recounting the details of the Newalls' disappearance and the subsequent investigation, the Attorney General Michael Birt pointed out that in his confession to his uncle, Roderick was asked whether there had been any mitigating circumstances for the murders, whether they had been carried out in a moment of 'crazy drunken rage'. Roderick had replied 'no'. This, said Mir Birt, could only mean one thing: 'The Crown says there is strong evidence to suggest the murders did not occur on the spur of the moment, as [Newall] suggests. Whether they did or not, he struck his father repeatedly on the head whilst he was lying stunned or unconscious on the ground. He also struck his mother repeatedly on the head with sufficient force to kill her when she too must have been lying on the ground. For this, he used a different weapon. It was indeed a terrible crime.'

Describing Mark Newall's part in the crime as 'chilling and shameful', the Attorney General dismissed his confession, saying it disguised 'the most callous disregard for his parents' fate and understates the extraordinary efforts and length taken to hide a vicious crime and its perpetrator.'

'As the disappearance ot Elizabeth and Nicholas Newall became a desperate concern for friends and relatives and all the other citizens of Jersey, these two defendants were prepared to perpetuate, week after week, month after month, the myth of their parents' disappearance,' he continued.

Rising to reply, the brothers' advocate David Le Quesne rejected strongly any notion of premeditation. He claimed that many of the items used in the burial were not brought at the builders' merchant, but were lying around the Newall house. If the crime was planned, he said, why was so much blood shed and the bodies buried in an awkward place? He did not wish to indulge in character assassinations, but such crimes did not happen in normal, happy families – the brothers' own uncle, Stephen Newall, had said during the taped conversation in Scotland, 'We watched from the sidelines and saw two very badly treated little boys.'

Mark had known from a very early age that his parents did not like him, said Mr Le Quesne. He had entered banking at the age of eighteen, determined to excel, and had done so. His parents relied on him for the management of their finances and his income had exceeded theirs. At the age of twenty-one Mark had had to make a snap decision when he returned to his parents' house and found his brother about to shoot himself with their father's shotgun. 'Thereafter,' said Mr Le Quesne, 'Mark Newall's life was on the edge of an abyss. He knew he had committed a serious crime and that any moment the storm might break. He lost his job and his position in the world, all because of a wrong decision at the age of twenty-one.'

In his judgement the bailiff, Sir Peter Crill, did not express a view on premeditation, but in the feeding frenzy of press and television crews outside the court the police continued to stress strongly their belief that premeditation was involved and hâtred and greed were the motives.

In their impassioned briefings to the media, the police said that the original £900,000 inherited – including the £400,000 in Kenneth Newall's bequest – may have tripled through Mark Newall's astute investments. Possibly more than £200,000 might have been spent on the Gibralter extradition legal costs, but it is thought sizeable sums have been stashed away in foreign accounts far out of reach of Stephen Newall and Nan Clark who are suing the brothers for the recovery of the Newall estate. The only asset of value that remains is their parents' house, 9 Clos de l'Atlantique.

Standing side by side, both brothers were impassive in the well of the Royal Court as Sir Peter Crill passed sentence. Addressing Roderick Newall, he said: 'Throughout the ages, the crimes of patricide and matricide have particular odium. This court shares that view.' Roderick received two life sentences to run concurrently and bowed slightly as sentence was passed. Mark Newall was sentenced to two concurrent terms of six years and may be free in less than four.

Another wave of jeers rose up as the two brothers emerged from the court and were helped into the van that would take them back to La Moye prison.

AFTERWORD

At a press conference held at the end of the inquiry Assistant Chief Officer Paul Marks, who had been promoted, was asked if there were not serious criticisms to be made of the police. He said it was impossible with an inquiry of this size for everything to have been carried out perfectly and according to plan. 'I would challenge any police officer to say they would get it right first time,' he said. He reminded the press that the inquiry had in effect been completed backwards with the discovery of the bodies coming at the very end rather than the beginning.

On the subject of the deal that had been struck in Gibraltar the most he was prepared to say was, 'There were discussions between defence and prosecution over what steps were necessary to bring matters to a conclusion.'

When asked if the police had got to the truth he said, 'There are only four people who know the truth and two of those are dead.' Asked if he was satisfied that Mark Newall had not been placed on trial for murder of his parents Assistant Chief Officer Marks commented obliquely: 'I am satisfied that we as police officers have presented the lawyers with as much evidence as could be obtained.'

*   *   *

In New Park School in St Andrews in Fife art teacher Gordon McDonald had read of the disappearance of the Newalls and recalled his own days as a pupil at the school more than twenty-five years before.

As a small boy he had lived in mortal terror of his history teacher Nick Newall whom he suspected of never even liking children. When he discovered that the Newalls had gone missing and that people close to them were suspected just one thought went through his mind – that he was not at all surprised.

In a drawer in a tiny cottage on Beaver Island in West Falkland there is an envelope containing the last letter written by Roderick Newall to Jerome and Sally Poncet while free. It was sent from Tangier and in it there is no mistaking his jubilant tone at having overcome all his obstacles. The *Austral Soma* had been fixed up, the fuel and food was aboard. He wrote enthusiastically about how his life was changing and at long last he was coming home and would be with them in weeks. It was posted twenty-four hours before he was arrested.

Just before Christmas 1992 a group of five brothers and sisters sat round a fire in a house in Lymington in Hampshire, signed a Christmas card and handed it to their mother to post.

Mrs Shaw still remembers the thirteen-year-old red-haired schoolboy brought home by her son Charlie during the school holidays and she remembered too the time when it was only the calm, reassuring voice of the seventeen-year-old Roderick Newall down the telephone line that stopped her going out of her mind with worry. Solemnly he had reassured her he would personally fetch her errant son from London and return him to Radley. As far as Mrs Shaw was concerned, Roderick was always Charlie's 'upright' friend. The polite, solid, reliable friend whom she so wished her own son would take after. She has already visited Roderick in prison in Jersey and she is in constant touch on the telephone. She says she will never forsake Roderick Newall.

Today Donna Westend works for the New Zealand Postal Service and lives in a house near Auckland alone except for her two dogs. She is divorced from Tony but he lives nearby and the two remain firm friends. Some months ago she got a late-night phone call. It was Rod Newall calling from prison in Jersey. She had followed the case closely and tearfully he apologized to her for letting her down. She consoled him, told him it was all right, and thanked him for opening her eyes up to the world she had barely known existed. She said she hoped to visit him one day.

A delicately carved miniature Chinese pagoda sits on a cabinet in the headmaster's study of a small Berkshire public school amongst numerous ornaments and trinkets, gifts from various boys over the years.

When he looks at it, Tony Hudson remembers the likable but wilful boy who returned after leaving school and shyly handed it over. When Roderick finally made his confession Mr Hudson wrote to him again and thanked him for doing the right thing and wished him peace of mind for the future.

Mark and Fran Bullock had only intended staying in the Falklands for six months. In the end they were there for eighteen. After leaving they stayed briefly in Sierra Leone but have now moved back to Gloucestershire.

Mark works as a private detective and Fran works for a telephone sales company but most evenings they will get out their extensive collection of photographs of the Falkland Islands and of the strange young man who had come to mean so much to them.

Today Alaster and Nan Clark have retired to their house near Alicante and only venture back to Britain for brief family visits. Nan has always felt that her nephew Roderick would find what he was looking for. He had to grieve and had to confess. About her other nephew she is not so sure and in a letter she received from Mark before Christmas 1993 she could detect not one word of atonement or regret. Just the same arrogance that she knew so well.

In La Moye prison in early 1994 just before he was committed for sentence Roderick Newall received a letter from Helena Pedot. It was apologetic in tone and hinted that her co-operation with the police had been coerced. She thanked him for her trip to Miami and said he should visit her the next time he was in Brazil.

After Roderick's boat the *Chanson du Lecq* had successfully completed rounding Cape Horn, Donna and Roderick had sent Ralph Williams's prized heirloom, the book about Joshua Slocombe's travels, back to him in New Zealand. In the flyleaf it contained a photograph of the young couple standing triumphantly on the Horn after they had rounded it. Today the book is kept by Ralph's Auntie Joy as a souvenir of her charming friendly young visitor as much as anything else.

* * *

Former inspector Graham Nimmo lives quietly now after taking early retirement from the Jersey police in 1991 on health grounds. To this day he blames the strain and pressures of the Newall case for his premature departure. He divides his time between fishing for lobster on his own boat and working in his immaculately kept workshop in the back garden.

The *Chanson du Lecq* continues to sail the world's oceans. After teaching Josephine Hunter to sail it, Rod sold it to her. Jo, always an intrepid traveller, decided to take it back to the South Pacific. The last her friends heard was a postcard describing how she was dotting from island to island much as Roderick had done a few years earlier. The boat still has the sextant from the *Rodmark*, which had set sail from Scotland nearly a quarter of a century before.

Philip Bailhache left the position of Attorney General for Jersey at the end of 1993 and is now a senior judge and deputy bailiff on the island.

In late 1994 the amount of losses incurred by Lloyds underwriters had been calculated at four billion pounds and despite frantic efforts showed no signs of slackening off. If the Newalls had lived it is unlikely their lifestyle could ever have coped with the constant battering of such continual demands. It is possible that they could have had to sell off both their homes and return to Britain where it is unlikely they would have been as happy.

Mark Newall maintains his claim that he had no foreknowledge of the murder of his parents. Before his trial at the beginning of August he was telling former colleagues that he hoped to serve less than six years. On his release he will not resume his City career – instead he hopes to go to university.

Roderick Newall plans to keep a low profile. He has requested that he be allowed to carry out his sentence in the land of his birth, Scotland. He spends most of his time replying to the letters that continue to flood in from the various people he met on his voyages.

Every Sunday in an imposing granite mansion on the seafront in North Berwick an old lady waits for a phone call. When the brothers were small Elizabeth Newall would phone her mother in Scotland and give her the latest news on her grandsons. In tears of laughter or exasperation, Elizabeth would regale her with stories of their latest escapades.

The brothers still telephone their grandmother weekly and each Sunday afternoon when the phone rings and Mrs Nelson stretches out to pick up the receiver her mind travels back to those days when Roderick and Mark were so small and so lovable, and she thinks: those boys – what have they got up to now?